File: RandomWalk_Version 82
(Booksurge Publishing)

Random Walk

Winfried Wilcke

Random Walk

Third Edition

Available via

www.amazon.com

Printing History
February 2008   First Edition (Diggypod)
June   2008   Second Edition (Diggypod)
August   2008   Third Edition (Booksurge Publishing/Amazon)

Content

Story is slightly technical.................................ħ
Story is very technical or scientific.................2ħ

Foreword

The idea for this collection of stories originated just seven weeks ago. I was finding myself crossing the grey winter North Atlantic in the relative comfort of economy class seat 32A of a United 777 flight to Frankfurt, Germany. The jolly good chap in seat 32B turned out to be a pilot, too, and soon we found ourselves swapping tall stories. If you ever had the experience of being a captive audience to a talkative pilot [1], you will know what I mean.
We talked for hours during this United flight, slightly inebriated by the surprisingly generous supply of free drinks, their potency amplified by the thin air at 7000' cabin altitude.
The imminent arrival on another continent always puts me in a good mood. In the eerie dawn of Flight level 390, while listening again and again to "Waltzing Matilda" on my iPhone, I seriously thought about writing some of my stories down.

As we were executing a missed approach in Frankfurt – the widespread undercast covering so much of Europe during the winter months is a real bore - I decided to actually do it and do it right now. Life is short and one never knows what can happen. I wrote the book very quickly – over the Christmas 2007 holidays and a few exhausting weekends.

This book could be seen as an autobiography. However, that was positively *not* my goal. I just wanted to write some funny or perhaps interesting stories based on

---

[1] Q: How do you know if there's a pilot in the party?
A: He will tell you.

Q: How do you know that a date with a pilot is half over?
A: He says: 'That's enough about flying. Now let's talk about me.'

real life experiences – and obviously, I know my own experiences best.

The stories touch on a wide range of subjects – from funny or entertaining stories about sailing, diving with mermaids or scaring myself in airplanes to more serious subjects such as nuclear experiments or cancer. My focus is on events which happened before the year 2000.

Many stories deal with technical topics. These are marked with the symbol 'ħ'. If the subject is more difficult or scientific, the symbol '2ħ' is used.

Exactly one chapter[2] in this collection is fiction; all others are true to life. However, there are certainly errors and omissions in the stories, for which I apologize.

The book is dedicated to my two wonderful wives, Karen Wilcke and Anita Borg, who both have passed away. It is also dedicated to many great friends, who have made life so much fun, my parents, Maria and Berthold and to the brave mothers of Karen and Anita.

I met a lovely lady doctor and fully expect to have a lot more adventures –with her playing a big part- to write up in 15 years. Maybe there will be a second collection, circa 2020. That should be considered timely warning.

I hope that it is as much fun reading this book as I had writing it.

Winfried Wilcke, Silicon Valley, California USA   2008

---

[2] I leave it as a challenge to the reader to figure out which chapter is fictional. The correct answer can be found, as a puzzle, in the book.

The Shipwreck and the Mermaid

- see also page 161 -

The island of Anegada collects shipwrecks. In sailor's lingo, it is a 'low island, only a few feet above the ocean. It is surrounded by an extensive reef system – locally called the Horseshoe Reef. The island is very hard to see from the deck of a boat and the shifting sandbanks of the Horseshoe reef have been the doom of about 300 vessels.

Very few people live on Anegada, since it is so dangerous to take a boat there. GPS does not help much if the bottom shifts with the currents. To the very day, boats get wrecked around Anegada.

The wreck I want to talk about is not your average little boat, though. It is a 245' long Japanese fishing mother ship, called the Chikuzen.

It had served the Japanese well for decades, but eventually it outlived its usefulness. A group of shady investors bought it, apparently with the intend to turn it into a floating casino. That venture never took off, and the big old derelict ship found itself moored in St. Marten. The Dutch harbormaster did not like the rusting hull spoiling his neat and tidy harbor.

Finally, when a hurricane bore down on the island, he had had enough of the Chikuzen's unwanted presence and demanded that the old vessel be towed out to sea. He got his way, but soon the tow cable broke. The captain of the tug declared victory and returned home, while the Chikuzen drifted without a crew, constituting a clear and present danger to the local shipping. When the ship entered the waters of the British Virgin Islands, the local government dispatched another tug to tow it out of BVI waters. However, in heavy seas the tow cable snapped and tore the legs of a tugboat crewmember off. This tug

Shipwreck and Mermaid

returned home, too, and once again the Chikuzen was adrift.

Then the BVI dispatched its Navy, which consisted of one old coastguard cutter donated by the British and shelled the Chikuzen to sink her. They had a hard time, but eventually they succeeded. In a stormy August night in 1981, the Chikuzen finally sank, about halfway between the main BVI island of Tortola and Anegada. It came to rest on a very large sandy plane, 80' deep...

I had always thought that this impressive shipwreck would make a wonderful for filming a beautiful mermaid...

My lovely first wife, Karen, and I were sailing our 41' C&C sloop for most of 1996 in the Caribbean, enjoying the cruising lifestyle and many remarkable dives. Karen was a skilled and experienced diver and owned a custom-made mermaid suit. (More on page 357)

We finally convinced ourselves –slowly and methodically- that it would be possible for just the two of us to dive the Chikuzen – even while she was wearing her mermaid suit. In hindsight, I wonder about the wisdom of doing it – many things could have gone wrong, with fatal consequences. However, we did it and got some spectacular video footage of a beautiful mermaid gracefully swimming along the rugged structures of this big old wreck and playing with the rich undersea life of the Chikuzen.

A plain sandy bottom is not a very desirable habitat for most underwater life forms, except those, which have figured out how to hide in the sand itself. However, drop a big wreck onto this plain bottom and everything changes. This wreck is a 245' long apartment complex sheltering all kinds of fish – from big schools of yellow tails, wrasses, snappers and amberjacks to schooling barracudas and groupers.

Few people dive the Chikuzen, though, and certainly not many yachtsmen from their own boats. Only a couple of local dive shop operators come out here –rarely-

Shipwreck and Mermaid

to show their customers something very special. Our first challenge was to find the Chikuzen. I asked around the local dive shops on the BVI, but invariably got the same curt answer: you cannot dive there by yourself. However, we can take you there. That was out of the question – Karen did not want to be seen by some dive boat crew while dressing up as a mermaid.

However, I love a challenge – particularly when a sexy mermaid is involved. At least I knew roughly, where the Chikuzen was supposed to be, and sure enough, the nautical chart showed the cute little symbol for a shipwreck in that general neighborhood.

Therefore, after considerable preparations in equipment, we set sail for that magical spot north of Tortola. The island slowly disappeared under the horizon, except for its tallest peaks, and we felt tense and lonely.

I had transcribed the coordinates from the chart into a GPS, and we steered by its guidance. Finally, we arrived at the spot – but how did we know we were really over the wreck? The ocean was too deep to spot a wreck from the surface. The last thing I wanted to do was to jump into the deep water without positive proof that the wreck was below us.

However, we had an ace up our sleeves. We knew that the ship was 245 feet long and was lying on its side. Given the typical proportions of a ship, this implied that the water directly over the wreck should only be about 40-50' deep. However, at the spot, the depth gauge showed 80' – ergo no ship there! It was not surprising that the position shown for the wreck was wrong; the map was drawn before GPS was available.

However, if one assumed that the position was not too far off, a methodical search pattern might show us the wreck. I devised a rectangular search pattern, with 2 mile long legs. For over an hour, we motored along these GPS-defined lines, with nary a change in the depth finder. Then, suddenly, it seemed that the ocean below us turned into a lighter shade of green. Could it be?

Sure enough, the depth finder suddenly jumped, climbing to 60', 50', and 45' and then dropping again. We had found it! The position shown on the map was more than a mile off. BVI dive operators may not appreciate this information, but here are the no-longer secret and verified coordinates for the wreck:

Chikuzen: North 18° 37.142',West 64° 30.970' (WGS84)

We had solved the first problem – finding the wreck – and I had proved my navigational prowess to my wife and lovely mermaid. However, the much more important problem was now facing us – how to anchor or moor our boat over the wreck. This was a very difficult challenge. Anchoring was out of the question. Let me explain why...

Have you ever wondered why an anchor holds when it is supposed to and let go when it is supposed to? I had always puzzled about this magic, but it took me learning to sail before I understood the concepts. The secret is the angle of pull. All anchors are designed so that when the anchor line (properly called the anchor rode) pulls horizontally on the anchor; its flukes will dig into the seafloor. A vertical pull will break the anchor free.

Thus, the trick is to use an anchor line, which is *much* longer than the water depth at the desired location. The ratio of the length of the rode to the depth of the water is called scope. A large scope will cause a more horizontal pull and anchoring will be safer.

For a quick lunch stop –with the crew on board- a scope of 3:1 is considered adequate and for an overnight stop or other situation where it is important that the anchor holds, 7:1 is used.

In our situation, it was a matter of life and death that the anchor would hold. It was just the two of us and we

Shipwreck and Mermaid

were many miles from shore. If we surfaced and found no boat – and there was no other boat in sight, either – we would in all likelihood just die.

Recently the movie 'Open Water' –based on a real event - depicted just such a tragic story off the Cancun coast, when a dive boat crew miscounted their divers and left a couple stranded in the water. They were never found.

So, a scope of at least 7:1 would be needed to anchor at the Chikuzen. However, since the water was 80' deep, we would need an anchor rode of 7x80 = 560 feet! We had only a fraction of this length on board, since the common anchoring depth in the British Virgin Islands is between 10' and 20'.

Moreover, even if we had so much rode on board, it would not have worked, either, because a boat hanging from an anchor acts like a flag in the wind – it swings left and right in a wide arc. A boat anchored with a 560' rode would swing for hundreds of feet- not a good target to chase after surfacing from a deep, exhausting dive.

An entirely different solution was needed – we had to tie our boat directly to the wreck [see the sketch on page 161]. We had brought along a 300' spool of 3/8" nylon line. This was much thinner than the 5/8" anchor rode the boat used normally, but had to suffice for this dive.

Our plan was that Karen would hold the boat stationary over the wreck, while I dove down, solo, and fasten the 3/8" line to the wreck. This we did. I cannot say that it was my most relaxed dive ever, but I had full confidence in Karen and, moreover, I was always in physical contact with the boat through that line. The maneuver worked flawlessly. See Sketch #1 for the layout.

We moved the boat up current from the wreck, while I donned my dive gear. Karen shut the engine down and I jumped over-board, with the 3/8" line in hand. It was a scary feeling.

Shipwreck and Mermaid

The wreck was not visible from my vantage point, and I was surrounded by dozens of Barracudas, which were slowly circling. This was quite exciting. I had heard of schooling Barracudas, but never seen so many. They like to hang around boats, since prey fish often congregate in a boat's shadow and Barracudas know that. They paid no attention to me.

I quickly finned towards the suspected direction of the boat, and within a couple of minutes, I could make out a shape in the gloom – the Chikuzen! Soon I could see the thick anchor chain of the wreck, lying uncoiled on the sandy bottom. This was the ideal target to tie our boat to.

We had prepared an eye, through which the 3/8" line would run and I fastened it to the wreck's heavy anchor line. Our life would depend on this knot. It would remain with Chikuzen upon our departure, whereas the precious 3/8" line would looped through it and could be retrieved from the deck of our boat after the dive.

I was elated how smoothly the whole operation went and swam back up to our boat, with the standing (free) end of the nylon line in hand. In other words, our 3/8" line served as a double mooring line, with one part going down to the bottom, looped around the eye connected to the wreck's anchor line and back up to our boat.

We also dropped a very thin third line, weighted with a weight belt, from the stern of our boat. It went straight down and served as an ascent line, which would guide us directly back to the dive platform. There is so much to think about when one does an exploratory dive…

We watched our position carefully on the GPS, and it held rock steady. Everything looked good for the long anticipated dive.

Karen slipped into her mermaid suit. It was a custom wetsuit with a long, graceful tail, tailored from thin neoprene and coated with yellow-golden Lycra. Standard

Shipwreck and Mermaid

Scuba equipment completed her outfit. She did not use a Buoyancy Compensator vest, since the fishtail gave her so much thrust that she could ascend easily from any depth.

I got myself a new air[3] tank, video camera and a strong dive light, powered by a heavy lead-acid battery hanging from my belt. Karen wriggled to the dive ladder and sat down, her fin dangling in the water. I helped her to don the tank and weight belt and then we both jumped into the ocean. A grand adventure, which we had planned for a long time, was finally coming true…

In the excitement, I had forgotten to mention the schooling barracudas to my wife, and I could see from her questioning look that this big school was quite a surprise for her. I nodded reassuringly and pointed downward. Following the vertical line, we quickly descended. Soon the wreck materialized out of the greenish gloom. Karen looked very impressed; her big blue eyes were wide open behind the dive mask. We left the guidance of the descent line and swam to the nearly vertical deck of the big ship.

Karen, swimming like a dolphin, covered the distance to the ship in no time, while I was trying hard to keep up with her. Dual fins are much less efficient than a fish tail.

Very large mast and booms, once used to lift the catch out of the hold of the ship, were protruding from the deck. The masts were now nearly horizontal, as the ship was resting on its side. The visibility was perhaps 50', so only a small part of the entire ship could be seen. This added to mystery and an impression of a huge size.

Karen found an open deck hatch and swam into it. Soon only her tailfin was sticking out of it. However, she carried no light herself and did not dare to penetrate the

---

[3] Divers use **AIR** and occasionally special gas mixtures, but never, ever oxygen except in extraordinary circumstances. For the last 60 years, reporters and other media people just can't get that right. Even at a shallow depth of 20m, pure oxygen is about as deadly as cyanide gas.

wreck any further. The ship was like a crowded city of animals. Schools with hundreds or thousands of big, silvery Amberjacks were hanging around the bottom of the wreck.

Karen entered the swarm, and it closed around her. We had noticed on previous dives that fish are less afraid of a diver in a mermaid suit. This is probably related to the high efficiency of the fishtail, which creates less scary –to fish- turbulence than dual fins. It was an astonishing sight to see the golden mermaid swim among thousands of fish as if she were part of the school – or a queen. It made for great video footage.

We slowly made our way around the big wreck, Karen leading the way, pointing out unusual animals. We encountered a very large, dignified looking grouper. It may have been six feet long. Karen approached it and slowly, unhurriedly the grouper withdrew as she came too close. It disappeared slowly into a gaping hole in the hull. Maybe that is where one of the cannon shells had hit the ship?

Later she found a big, roughly heart shaped outline in the sand. As I watched from a distance, she poked at it and a big stingray lifted itself out of the sand. I wished she were more cautious, but Karen loved all animals and felt very comfortable around them.

As we rounded the stern of the Chikuzen, we immediately saw the single propeller and rudder. Karen undulated over the propeller, dwarfed by the four big blades. I knew with great certainty that the engine would not suddenly start, but still, the view of my beloved Karen touching the monstrous propeller blades gave me the creeps.

We slowly ascended the rounded bottom of the hull, heading into the light of the dim, distant sun. The water was too deep and too turbid to see the sun itself, but there was no question where the light came from. The curvature of the hull, combined with the brightness of the distant sun

Shipwreck and Mermaid

evoked a strong memory of planetary scenes in the movie
2001, A Space Odyssey.

The schools of fish looked like meteorite clusters
streaming by. It was an otherworldly experience, but one
which I could beautifully capture on DV video tape. We
continued our exploration, ascending to the ship's top rail.
As always, Karen was ahead of me. As she rounded the
deck rail, she very excitedly pointed at something. I never
saw what it was, forgot to ask her later and will now never
know what she had seen.

We did not encounter any sharks, in spite of the
enormous number of fish living around the wreck. I was
not surprised – sharks are a rarity in the Caribbean. Karen
discovered a pair of her favorite fish – Queen Angel fish.
The pair was probably a couple, since Angelfish stay with
one partner for their entire lifetime. The mermaid and the
Angelfish couple played along the boom of one of the big
freight lifting masts, chasing each other playfully.

We entered what looked like an auxiliary steering
station and Karen had fun pretending to be a – shall we say
- helmsperson. The crew could never have imagined that
one day a lovely mermaid would float there, holding the –
now coral encrusted - wheel!

Finally, our time in this wonderful but alien world
was up. My tank pressure had dropped to 1000 psi, and it
was time to find our boat again. It was easy, since the
anchor chain of the wreck, lying parallel to the hull, was a
perfect guide.

As we slowly swam along the chain, we suddenly
discovered an old weight belt lying on the sand, right next
to the chain. Someone else must have dropped it here.
Karen picked it up. She had no trouble carrying this
additional weight.

As we swam along the anchor chain, we suddenly
saw a thin white vertical line dancing near it. It was the
descent line, which we had lowered from the stern of our

Shipwreck and Mermaid

boat. A weight belt, attached to the end of the line, was yanked from the sea floor when a wave raised our boat, and gently deposited it on the seafloor when our boat descended in a wave trough. The feeling of relief which washed over me upon seeing this dancing thin white line was one of the most intense I've ever experienced. It meant that the boat was still there and we would live.

Karen swam to our line and fastened the newly found weight belt to our own weight belt. By the time she was done, we both had around 800 psi in our tanks and we started the long, gradual ascent along the thin line.

I felt very happy and relaxed a climactic and wonderful dive with a beautiful mermaid and a fantastic wreck, all of which safely captured on video tape.

Shipwreck and Mermaid

Germany

- see also pages 162 to 164

Long before all this happened, I grew up in postwar Germany. My mother timed the date of my birth very well. It was September of 1949- just when the Deutsche Mark (DM) was introduced. This brand new currency, in combination with the extremely successful and generous Marshall plan, triggered the German economic miracle. It lasted for over twenty years and was admired all over the world.

It was an incredibly exciting time. The vast damage done during World War II opened up big economic opportunities in Germany and Japan. Many fortunes were made, there was plenty of work for everyone, and the future looked very bright – especially compared with the nightmarish first half of the 20th century. After the Sputnik shock of 1957, science and technology were held in high esteem. It was a great time to grow up.

The only downside – and it was a very big one- was the constant fear of nuclear annihilation, which could strike humankind at any moment. I was only 13 years old when the Cuban missile crisis of October 1962 happened, but I have never been more scared, because there was absolutely nothing one could do.

It helped a lot to grow up in a supportive family, where I was the only, but definitely not spoiled child. My parents strongly encouraged studying and working hard, which meant endless hours of school homework.

My mother lives in the world of business, whereas my father's avocation is the arts. I include black and white reproductions of two of his many beautiful paintings at the end of the book. Both parents are very healthy and will be rather amused to read this collection of stories.

Germany

We lived in Frankfurt, where I went to school. Frankfurt is a center of business, not known for its art and culture. However, is a great and politically very liberal city. In fact, the first attempt to form a democracy in Germany – in 1848 – occurred in the free city (*Freie Reichstadt*) of Frankfurt.

In 1965, my parents purchased a new house in a romantic little town about 25 km outside Frankfurt. The town is famous for its acidic hard cider and half-timbered houses. My parents did not make me change schools, which meant a lot of tough commuting by bicycle, train and walking. However, this challenge provided me with a sense of independence, which was very good for a teenager.

My high school (Helmholtz Gymnasium) in Frankfurt was a practical, no-nonsense public school with excellent teachers. The next story is a tribute to the best teacher I ever had.

Germany

A Robot Mouse on TV (ħ)

- see also page 164

Back in high school, in 1968, I built an artificial mouse. This was eleven years after the Russian Sputnik launch had shaken the West's belief in its superiority. Now science and technology were hot. The space race was the big topic, as was the American War in South East Asia. That is what the Vietnamese call it – makes sense, no? Student unrest, civil liberties and assassinations shaped much of the mood of this transitional decade. Times of great changes may be unsettling, but in hindsight they are often golden ages of progress.

The term *high school* refers to the German school system of that time. High school lasted nine years and ended with an extensive, multi-day testing marathon called the *Abitur*. Passing the Abitur was the prerequisite to attend any German university.

Fundamentally, I disliked high school. Our teachers loaded us up with so much homework that it averaged 5 hours a day. This was in addition to 6 hours of actual school attendance and a long commute. You do the math. As a card-carrying nerd, I took homework far too seriously – at the detriment of developing social skills as a teenager.

Our class had an outstanding mathematics and physics teacher, Herr (Mr.) Heinz Vierengel. He was incredibly skilled in explaining complex subjects and encouraged those of us who showed special interest in science and math to spend time in the well equipped physics laboratory and equipment collection of the school. He allowed us to do our own unsupervised experiments.

Among other not entirely noteworthy achievements, I demonstrated conclusively that it is tricky to pipe steam from a metal boiler into a beaker filled with cold water. Our assignment was to determine the latent heat of steam. We took the measurements without problem, but then I turned the Bunsen burner off and left the steam hose in the beaker. As the boiler cooled down, a low pressure developed inside, which sucked cool water back into the boiler. Thus its pressure got even lower, which sucked back more water and so on. The upshot of all this was a very loud bang and a suddenly flattened boiler in the shape of a pancake! The bang came as quite a surprise. I should stay away from steam – that was not my only bad encounter with the third phase of water.

We had a very fancy gadget in the physics lab – a Field Emission Microscope or FEM. This device allows the user to see individual atoms. However, the FEM was easily destroyed and had not been used before we got our hands on it. However, I can proudly report that the experiments done by a friend of mine, Robert Holzer and me were successful and the microscope even survived them.

A FEM is surprisingly small. It has the approximate shape of a big light bulb, with a number of stumps protruding from its neck. Its operating principle is based on the fact that the electric field surrounding a sharp metal tip is very high, as it is inversely proportional to the local radius of the tip. When a sufficiently high voltage (a few thousand Volts) is applied between this tip and a positively charged electrode (the anode), electrons get pulled out of the metal and are accelerated towards the anode. If the tip has edges – like a crystal – then the very highest field is at these edges and they emit most of the electrons.

The FEM bulb contained a sharp, single crystal Tungsten tip. This was the negative electrode. The inside of the bulb acted as the anode. It was coated with a conducting and luminescent material, forming a hemispherical white screen, similar to a TV monitor. The voltage was applied between the tungsten electrode (-) and the screen (+).

Robot Mouse on TV

When the high voltage was turned on, a ghostly white pattern appeared on the screen. This was the image of the crystal structure of the Tungsten tip.

One of the stumps near the neck of the 'bulb' contained a little amount of barium metal and a filament heater. When the barium was heated up, some of it evaporated and a few barium atoms landed on the tungsten electrode. The arrival of these atoms could be clearly seen. It looked as if a snow shower had arrived, with each 'snow flake' being one atom!

It was also possible to heat the tungsten tip with a second filament. When we turned up its temperature, the barium atoms started to vibrate noticeable. The thermal motion of the atoms could be seen directly. It was truly amazing. If one increased the tip temperature even further, the barium atoms started to disappear from the tip. It was like watching a snow shower in reverse, with more and more of the white dots disappearing.

For a couple of high school students interested in physics, seeing individual atoms with their own eyes was a defining moment. It truly conveyed the magic of science to us and forever cemented Robert's and my career decisions.

A couple of years later, Herr Vierengel handed me a thin textbook, written in 1953 by a British Neuroscientist. It was called the "The Living Brain" by Dr. William Grey Walter.

The book contained a chapter in which the author described an artificial electronic mouse, which he had built. It could autonomously navigate in a room, search for light, and home in on it. Herr Vierengel suggested that I could build a more modern version of such a mouse and participate in a science contest called "Jugend Forscht." It was sponsored by the German magazine "STERN." This sounded like fun and I spent most of my last year in high school – instead of preparing for the big Abitur test – to build my mouse.

Robot Mouse on TV

My grandfather, an experienced blacksmith, helped me with many of the mechanical aspects, since it was quite a complex undertaking. In 1968 integrated circuits were not yet available to youthful experimenters, only to IBM and NASA-class institutions. Thus I had to design all my electronics with expensive discrete transistors and relays.

When it was completed, the mouse was quite a cool robot. It was about 30 cm long and had the approximate shape of a real mouse. Two steel whiskers sprouted from its nose, and two photoelectric cells took the place of its eyes. It also had a microphone and could detect if something touched it, or if it touched an obstacle.

The normal operating mode of the mouse was to explore its environment by randomly moving about. The mouse sensed bumping into an object (or being hit) by a sensor which was part of its shell. When it touched an obstacle, such as a wall or the leg of a table, it reversed its course for a few seconds, turned by a random angle and tried again. Thus it was very successfully maneuvering around an ordinary room.

Today one can buy the Roomba vacuum cleaner robots, which operate on very similar principles, except their navigation is a lot smarter because of the availability of microprocessors. These were not even invented yet in 1968.

The mouse was strongly attracted to light. When it spotted a light, as from an incandescent bulb, it maneuvered toward it. It was fun to put a light on the head of the mouse and set a large mirror on the floor. Soon the mouse began to perform a complex dance in front of the mirror. It looked as if it were trying to mate with its mirror image.

There is a well-known experiment in psychology called the Pavlov effect[4]. It is also called a conditioned reflex and was first observed with dogs. They were trained

---

[4] Pavlov effect – does it ring a bell?

Robot Mouse on TV

that the sound of a bell meant food. Soon they started to salivate upon hearing the sound, even if no food was presented yet.

I built a similar conditioned reflex into the mouse. Normally the mouse ignored sound. However, it could be trained that a whistle meant a warning. During training, I blew a whistle and then lightly kicked the mouse. Soon the electronic critter would try to avoid being hit by moving backwards as soon as it heard the whistle.

This conditioning worked very realistically. If it heard the whistle a number of times without actually being hit again, it would 'forget' that a whistle meant danger and ignore the sound. However, it I started another training session, the mouse would now learn more quickly that a whistle was a warning signal.

It is very remarkable that the implementation of this rather complex and realistic conditioned reflex behavior with analog circuitry was so simple. In my design, the charge state of a big capacitor corresponded to the degree with which the mouse associated a whistle with danger. Simple transistor circuits added or removed charge from the capacitor, depending on the relative timing of whistle and hit.

There were several more features I built into the mouse. My parent's house has a stairway leading to the basement. It would have been bad if the mouse tumbled down the stairs. Like a Roomba robot, the mouse had an optical sensors looking downward and detected the presence of a void in front of it.

Its attraction to light provided a convenient way to feed it. I built a feeding station, which looked like a little doghouse. It had metal sidewalls and a 25 W lamp on top of it. The mouse would be attracted by the light and enter the station. When its metal whiskers touched the walls, it would stop and recharge its battery. When feeling fully

Robot Mouse on TV

charged, the mouse would leave its feeding station and resume its tireless exploration of the house.

Once a neighbor brought his dog – a midsized terrier – to my parent's house while the mouse was buzzing around. The dog was beside himself. He ran around the mouse, barking his head off. I have not seen a dog that upset ever since. We had to drag him out of the house before he calmed down again. I have to try the same with a Roomba some time!

As can be imagined, designing, building and debugging the mouse took a lot of effort – about ¾ of a year. However, it was ready in time for the statewide competition, which was held in Frankfurt.

Unfortunately, man and mouse won only the third price, even though it performed flawlessly for the judges. I was terribly upset. Part of the reason may have been that I spent all my time getting the mouse to work properly and prepare, in the background, for the annoying Abitur. I had no time to do a lot of literature searches for similar projects. Thus, when the judges asked me extensively about comparative work, I had no good answers to their questions. This was clearly perceived as a big negative. I learned from this experience early in life that it is always good to know the competition...

However, it was most gratifying that the STERN magazine published a large, double spread photo of the mouse, its feeding station and me as the introduction to its big article about the 1968 *Jugend Forscht* competition. We had put a small light on the head of the mouse, and the STERN photographer did a great job with a time exposure. It showed the mouse moving about in its search pattern for light and obstacles. What an experience – male centerfold exposure at age 18 ;-)

Robot Mouse on TV

This article attracted the attention of one of the two German TV channels and I got invited for a live demonstration of the mouse on TV.

The test runs went fine, and then came the big moment. It didn't start out well, because the light operator turned on additional stage lights as we went on the air, which confused the mouse. I yelled at the operator[5] and when he –after some confusion and delay – turned them off, everything went well, at least for some time. The reporter asked me questions and the mouse did its act. Then something happened, live on TV, which never had happened before and never afterwards. The ends of the two steel whiskers were soldered to two small steel balls, so that no one would get hurt by the sharp points. As I was being interviewed, the mouse played around my feet and the ball at the end of one of its whiskers got caught in my shoelace!

The mouse could not handle this situation, since its whiskers were not protected by the touch sensing mechanism of the shell. I knew that and was hopping around on one foot, trying to prevent damage to the mouse while untangling the shoelace and the whisker. How ridiculous this must have looked live on national TV.

The mouse still exists. Come to think, next time I am in Europe I will replace the rechargeable batteries and see if it still works.

---

[5] I had completely forgotten about this initial mishap when first writing the book. My parents had to remind me about it.

Robot Mouse on TV

Holy Mountain – *Die Wasserkuppe*

- see also pages 165,166

An ancient volcano looms over the peaceful rolling hills of central Germany. It is the highest mountain in the State of Hessen; about 150km east of Frankfurt, right next to what was once the iron curtain. It is called the Wasserkuppe.

Since the mountain last erupted, 20 Million years ago, time and weather have taken its toll. The Wasserkuppe is no longer a pointy cone, but has become a rounded mountain – a "Kuppe." Still, as you drive up to it from the old town and Bishop's seat of Fulda, you will soon see it. At 950 m, it is a lot higher than the neighboring mountains.

This is not tall by alpine standards, but it is still an impressive mountain – particularly when clouds hang around its summit or a dense fog creeps up its vast slopes. Mysterious highland peat bogs surround the Wasserkuppe and frequent storms howl over the highlands of the *Hohe Rhön*. When this happens, you surely want to be in front of a fireplace, drink hot Glühwein and listen to the old farmers telling stories about ghosts and goblins haunting the bogs.

Wasserkuppe means Water Mountain, and the name is very appropriate. The river Fulda originates near its summit. The Fulda is one of the two rivers forming the mighty Elbe River, which is central Europe's second largest river and the lifeblood for the important harbor city of Hamburg.

However, there is a fun side to this sometimes foreboding mountain. For the glider pilots of the world, this is where it all started, right after World War 1. The sport was brought to a first climax in the years before World War 2 and now has spread all over the globe.

Holy Mountain

The Wasserkuppe holds a very special place in my heart. It is here where I first stepped into an airplane and first soloed a glider ten years later. To the very day I try to visit the Wasserkuppe each time I am in Germany.

However, let us start from the beginning. Right after World War 1, the French and British had had more than enough of dealing with the Red Baron and its fellow fliers. Thus the Treaty of Versailles, signed after World War 1, explicitly forbade Germans to fly.

However, there was a loophole. The treaty discussed only powered flight. The Frankfurt engineering professor Oskar Ursinus and a band of aviation-minded students at the Technische Hochschule in Darmstadt decided that this was their chance to continue flying.

They built primitive wooden gliders, which consisted of nothing more than a strong wooden keel, an open seat with a control stick, a fat wing and a tail (empennage). They launched these barely flying contraptions with strong rubber bungee cords.

The town of Darmstadt is located in the flat Rhine River valley and the flights lasted only seconds. Thus Oskar Ursinus – later called the "Rhönvater" or Rhön-Father – searched for a better place to fly gliders. He eventually found the Wasserkuppe. Except for its often awful weather, this mountain is an ideal place for soaring. The wide, round summit is devoid of trees and other obstacles (Not entirely free, though, as I only know too well.) The slopes drop of for miles in all directions – the perfect place to launch a glider.

Imagine the scenario of a 1920 glider launch. The intrepid pilot sits on his small wooden seat on the open keel boom. Two long rubber bungee cords stretch out in front of the flying machine in the form of a big V. Three groups of men – sorry ladies, they were all guys – were involved in the launch. Two of these, like in a tug-of-war, manned the two bungee cords and the third was holding on to the tail of

Holy Mountain

the glider. On command, the two bungee teams out front would run hard, stretching the rubber cords. On the release command, the third group would let go of the glider's tail, hurtling it into the air. The acceleration snapped back the head of the fearless pilot (yeah, right), which hit a wooden board mounted behind his seat. An old Army helmet was essential to protect his skull. When he regained consciousness, he found himself a few dozen meters above the descending slopes of the Wasserkuppe – enough for a flight of a few hundred meters and perhaps one or two minutes duration.

From these primitive beginnings, the gliders evolved with amazing rapidity to graceful sailplanes. By 1930, they looked very similar to the sleek fiberglass gliders of today. The pilots discovered the various ways by which nature provides lift. Within a few years, they stayed aloft for hours, gained kilometers of altitude and flew engine-less cross-country flights for hundreds of kilometers.

These stories kindled my interest in experiencing soaring for myself. As a teenager, I had built balsa wood planes with and without engines. They were equipped with a remote radio control, which I had built myself from scratch. I have many fond memories of walking the slopes of the Wasserkuppe with glider in hand, looking for that perfect launch spot and wind condition. Quite a few of these short flights ended in crashes, but there was always this special UHU-Hart glue, with which one could repair even the worst damage to a balsa wood model.

In 1974 I signed up for a 2-week course to fly gliders. It was expected to culminate in a few solo flights and we might receive the first soaring badge – the *A* wings. The price was right – only 800 Deutsche Mark. This included not only all the flying, but also lodging and food.

Holy Mountain

Best of all, it was to be held at the historic soaring school on the summit of the holy mountain itself.

I arrived in the middle of a pea soup of fog – the infamous Wasserkuppe fog can compete well with a London fog. It was barely possible to see the white line of the glistening wet road as I was inching my way up the mountain. A strong wind buffeted my yellow Volkswagen Passat – it seemed hard to believe that it was the middle of summer. After a tense drive, which seemed to last forever, the ghostly outline of the school appeared in the fog. I found my way to the check-in and was assigned a bunk.

The room reminded me very much of Luftwaffe barracks. That was not surprising – in the thirties the Nazis had supported the young and enthusiastic soaring movement in Germany for their own nefarious reasons. They saw the soaring enthusiasts as future Luftwaffe pilot material. Unfortunately, that is exactly what was in store for the young men, who had come to the Wasserkuppe for completely innocent reasons.

A few years later, they found themselves flying Messerschmitts 109 fighters and Heinkel 111 bombers against England and the allied air forces. Few survived, as they had to fly missions until they were shot down.

However, these thoughts quickly disappeared, as the remainder of my class comrades trickled in one by one. Most were younger than I was. Quite a few were sons of US Air force personnel stationed here at the big radar station on the summit of the Wasserkuppe. This gave our small band an interesting, international flavor. A couple of young women were in the group, too. I tried, mostly in vain, to get friendly with one of them, Tina, during the two weeks up there.

Our senior instructor was a grizzled Luftwaffe pilot, who, over dinner, kept us spellbound with his war stories.

Holy Mountain

A number of younger and some part time instructors rounded out the instructor team.

Since my English was better than that of most of the instructors and the German language skills of the US kids were non-existent, I volunteered to translate the instructor's lectures into English. Overall, that worked quite well. But I could never quite figure out why all the US kids grinned when I talked about the angle of attack – which is an important concept in flying. Only later one of the chaps confided that I consistently pronounced 'angle of attack' as 'angel of attack'. No wonder they found this so funny.

Our school gliders were old Schleicher Ka4 tube and rag wing gliders. Their fuselage was made from welded steel tubes, covered with fabric, as were the wings. They had wooden spars and ribs. This is an ancient, but trustworthy design. I would soon learn how strong it is!

The Ka4 instrument panel was very simple. The four basic instruments were airspeed, vertical speed, altitude and compass. A stick, two rudder pedals, a towrope release and a speed-brake lever completed the cockpit equipment. There was no radio. The Ka4 is a low performance trainer, with a glide ratio of 19:1. That means that from an altitude of 1 mile it could glide 19 miles, assuming no helping lift from thermals or wind. Today's extreme soaring planes have huge glide ratios, up to 60:1.

The Alexander Schleicher factory is located just a few miles down the Wasserkuppe mountain, in the quaint little town of Poppenhausen. They had named the Ka4 the Rhönlerche, which means Rhön Lark. We mostly called it the Rhön Leiche, which means Rhön Corpse, since its glide ratio was so poor.

Nevertheless, the Ka4 was a perfectly good plane to learn the basics of flying and gliding. However, do not think about soaring with eagles in this plane. More like soaring with the vultures. It had two seats, with the instructor in the back and the student in the front seat. The

Holy Mountain

stick and rudder pedals were duplicated, so the instructor could take control if yelling into your ear was not having the desired effect. The old Luftwaffe – or Air Force – tradition of hitting a student over the head with a rolled-up map seemed to have gone by the wayside. Gliders are quiet enough that one can actually hear what the instructor is saying. Many are not silent, though, as the roar of the wind at 65 mph can be quite substantial.

Over 30 years have passed since these first flights, but I can still remember my heart pounding before that first takeoff. The old rubber bungee method had long since been abandoned in favor of a motorized winch, which launches the sailplanes into the air.

A brawny 350 HP winch, mounted on a truck, was positioned about one km in front of the glider to be launched. The end of the winch cable was hooked into the bottom of the plane. The idea was that the winch would rapidly reel in the cable, thus yanking the plane into the air. It was the same concept as a kid launching a kite by running into the wind. The maximum obtainable altitude was about 300m/1000'. Then the glider was directly above the winch, and the pilot would release the cable, which fell back to the ground, to be used for the next launch. More on this later...

I still remember getting the first time into the pilot's seat after all these years. The instructor – his name was Walter - admonished me to step on the sturdy wooden running board at the bottom of the cockpit but not on the thin fabric, lest I ended up with a tear in the fabric and one foot outside the plane. Then he helped me to strap in with a sturdy four-point harness. The four straps – two over the shoulders, two over the thighs - converged on the chest, held together by an aluminum rod and a spring. In an emergency, one could simply pull on the rod and all four straps would be released in an instant. A very simple, but ingenious solution. The heft of this industrial-strength

Holy Mountain

harness impressed me, forever, with the undeniable fact that piloting any aircraft is serious business – even an old glider. Gravity doesn't care how you got up there…

Walter climbed into the backseat and strapped himself in. Then the canopy was lowered over us. This simple act conveyed a certain sense of grim finality. What am I doing here? A helper lifted the wing of our glider off the ground and looked expectantly at us. "Ready?" Walter asked.

I must have said yes, because before I knew it the cable stretched towards that winch in the far distance and we were rolling on the single wheel. But that impression lasted only for an instant, as the 350 HP of the winch accelerated the light glider faster than a Formula 1 race car. Within a second or two we were high in the air.

The plane pitched up steeply. Only blue sky showed in the windscreen. It looked like we were going straight up, even though the actual launch angle was closer to 40 degrees. "Always keep the stick against your tummy" Walter explained. I barely heard him. The acceleration pressed us hard in our seats, as we climbed out steeply. That is how it must feel to take off in a rocket, I thought.

As we gained altitude, the climb angle decreased and we could again see the Rhön below us. The view was magnificent - 50km away I could even make out the town of Fulda and beyond that, a gleaming apparition in the shape of a huge white cone. We reached our maximum altitude in less than a minute. The climb rate decreased to near zero. Walter pushed the nose forward and told me to pull the big wooden release knob. With a bang the cable released – what would happen if it ever did not?

We were free, soaring. "Watch the horizon. That is how it should look when we are in a normal glide. Got it?" Yeah, I kind of got the idea and nodded.

"Take the controls," Walter told me. Gingerly I took the stick. Its wooden handle was smooth, polished

Holy Mountain

from the sweaty iron grip of countless flight students before
me. But I will never forget the exhilaration of making this
big winged beast obey my every move. I pushed the stick a
bit forward. The horizon rose up, the rush of the wind
increased and the controls felt stiffer. I pulled back and the
opposite happened.

"Take it easy – we do not want to get too slow and
stall the glider," Walter warned me. As with any new
vehicle, it takes some time to get used to the proper control
inputs and avoid over-steering and pilot induced
oscillations.

"Try a turn. Bank the plane and step simultaneously
on the rudder," the wise man in the back said. I moved the
stick to the left – for some reason left turns always came
easier to me – and the glider banked left. But it turned
right!

"More left rudder- much more left rudder. You need
to overcome adverse yaw. Push on the left rudder until the
yaw string is straight," Walter said. What the heck did go
on here and what was this adverse yaw thing? Later did I
learn that banking a plane slows down the raised wing
because of the increased drag of the downward aileron, thus
making the plane turn *away* from the desired direction.

A main purpose of an airplane rudder is to
overcome this increased drag of an raised wing. The rudder
– a vertical control surface- is reminiscent of a boat's
rudder, but its purpose in flight is not to steer the plane,
only to overcome the adverse yaw.

Plane controls are very counter-intuitive, as I soon
learned. Controls have to be neutralized when the plane is
established in a turn. If you want to go around in a circle in
a car, you do *not* neutralize the steering wheel while
turning. But that's exactly what you must do in a plane.
Otherwise the turn will tighten ever more and the plane will
quickly enter into a steepening spiral dive.

Holy Mountain

If you want to spark a heated discussion among power pilots, just ask them if the elevator controls altitude or airspeed, then sit back and watch the fun. I wonder if it ever came to fistfights over that question!

Since we had only 1000' feet altitude to play with, we soon had to think about landing. One traditionally flies a left-handed rectangular pattern around an airstrip. The part of the rectangle where one flies in the opposite direction of the take-off run is called downwind (Gegenanflug), since that is exactly what it is. The next turn, perpendicular to the runway, is called base leg and the last leg is called – not surprisingly – final (Endanflug).

When we were on downwind and with the "runway" – which was only a 15' patch of asphalt- visible on our left side, Walter allowed me to make a full circle, as we still had sufficient altitude. When we saw the runway again over our left shoulders, Walter took the controls and banked the glider hard into the base leg (Queranflug). I sure was glad that there was an entire mountain below us where we could land. The idea of bringing a plane down on a narrow stretch of asphalt looked insanely difficult from my current vantage point!

As we turned onto final, we seemed far too high. "No worries mate," Walter said. Or at least the equivalent in German. Suddenly I felt the plane lurch, pitch down and vibrate.

"This are the speed brakes," Walter explained. Since one gets only one chance to land a glider –unlike a power plane, which can go around if the approach looks doubtful – most gliders are equipped with powerful dive brakes, which allow to control the glide path over a wide range of steepness. The handle acts like a throttle in reverse. Initially you may pop out the brakes to -say- 30% of their maximum extension. If the plane is getting too low, you can retract the brakes. If you are too high you can extend them more. The brakes make it actually quite easy to land a sailplane precisely.

That view of the intended landing spot growing in the windshield remains one of my favorite sights today, decades and about 4500 landings later. Walter deftly controlled the glide path, and just a second before touchdown he held off the glider in a graceful flare. It sat down on its single wheel and bounced along the grassy surface. He held the wings off the ground until we were nearly at a standstill. Then it was no longer possible to keep the wing horizontal and it dropped gently to the ground.

"Das war toll" I said and sat for a few seconds, savoring this experience. Walter opened the canopy and we got out. With the help of a few fellow students we pushed the Ka4 back towards the short asphalt launch pad.

Crash

When a glider releases the winch cable, it is more or less directly over the winch. The cable falls down and therefore its business end is about one km away from the take-off pad. To maintain a rapid succession of launches, an ingenious trick is used on the Wasserkuppe. A second, much thinner 'retriever cable' is connected to the end of the launch cable. A small winch is located at the takeoff pad. As the glider is launched, the retrieve cable rapidly unwinds from the drum of its small winch. When the glider has dropped the main cable, the thin retrieve cable is used to pull the big cable back to the take-off pad.

I had volunteered to operate this return winch. It was a much more enjoyable job than running around and pushing sailplanes back to the take-off pad! Seniority has its privileges. At 24, I was one of the older students in the class. I will never forget the sound when the metal triangle - which connects the launch cable, the retrieve cable and the hook assembly – bounced over the asphalt of the take-

Holy Mountain

off pad. Together with the smell of the cut grass near the take-off site, this will always remind me of the Wasserkuppe.

Sometimes the thin retrieve cable would break. I actually looked forward to this, since this meant that we could launch the old Diesel tractor, which was stationed near the take-off pad and hunt for the broken end of the retrieve cable. This was my first exposure to off-road driving, and I loved it. It was fun to drive this old beast. The starter motor was kaput, so it was mandatory to park the old tractor at a spot where it could coast downhill to crank the Diesel. Wow betides the hapless soul who forgets this iron rule of flying on the Wasserkuppe!

I took my position at the controls of the retrieve winch and worked for a few hours, waiting for my next flight. While doing so, the wind shifted. Flying from the summit of a grassy mountain has the advantage that one can simply rotate the whole setup to align it with any wind direction. This new wind direction was uncommon, and Walter, who was not a full-time instructor on the Wasserkuppe, was not very familiar with it...

Finally the time for my second flight had come. We strapped in, launched, did some maneuvers on downwind and Walter turned the glider onto base leg and final. As the Wasserkuppe is an old volcano, a few little mounds of basaltic rock were sticking out of the grassy slopes. On short final, it seemed to me that we were heading towards one of these mounds, but I was not sure. Walter certainly knew what he was doing, or so I thought.

As we got lower and lower, I started to say something, but it was too late. With a sickening crash the wooden keel of our glider hit the rock. My glasses flew off my nose, hit the canopy and, fortunately, fell right back into my lap. All the dirt at the bottom of the glider shook loose and for a moment we were engulfed in a cloud of

Holy Mountain

smelly dirt. The glider bounced back into the air, but only for an instant. A second later we hit the grass and the glider came to rest.

We got out quickly, while the crew was running towards us. The plane did not look good. The bottom of the glider was badly damaged. Its wooden keel was splintered, the steel tubing buckled and the fabric around the cockpit was torn and ripped. With the rush of adrenalin flowing, both Walter and I felt physically fine. However, that did not last. We both experienced back pain for days.

Walter shook his head and I felt guilty for not saying something faster or perhaps even pulling on the stick. But it all had happened so fast. I also know now that trying to grab the stick might have caused a much worse accident, such as a stall.

Well, the glider was out of action. Later it was repaired in the Schleicher factory down the mountain and put back into service. But Walter had had enough. He left his summer instructor position, or got fired – I do not know the details. Professionally, it did not matter to him, since in his daytime job he was an engineer. Nevertheless, the view of him filling out reams of paperwork for the Bundes- luftfahrtamt (German FAA) is something I will not forget.

The time went by fast. We flew during the days and partied during the nights. Somehow, we got by with 5 hours sleep. The exercise in the crisp mountain air helped to keep us awake. The weather was benign. We all took off many times, as each flight lasted only about 5-10 minutes. Gradually I was taking on more and more of the flying responsibilities, and eventually the solo looked plausible.

However, before that happened, I paid extra for a long – one hour – flight in the Schleicher motor glider, which the flight school owned. This was a cross between a power plane and a sailplane. It had a modified Volkswagen 2 liter Limbach engine and a feathering propeller, but the long wings of a real sailplane.

Holy Mountain

The school owned serial number *one* of this motor glider. The Schleicher factory had donated it to the school, since it could not be sold to a regular customer. As an engineering test plane, it was rough around the edges. The fuel tank was still mounted right behind the heads of the pilots, who were sitting side by side. The smell of gasoline and the sloshing sound of the fuel inches away from one's ears were a bit disconcerting.

Also, the feathering gear did not work very well. If one shuts down the engine of a propeller plane in flight, the propeller will *not* stop. Rather, the wind rushing over it will keep it wind-milling at about 1300 RPM. This takes energy, which greatly increases drag (wind resistance) - not something acceptable for a sailplane.

Thus the propeller was feathering. This means that the blades could be –manually- rotated 90 degreed from their normal position, aligning them with the airflow. However, that could only be done if the propeller was stopped completely. This had to be accomplished by raising the nose of the plane so steeply, that it nearly stalled. At such slow speed, there was not enough airflow over the propeller to keep it turning.

However, it was a cumbersome maneuver, and it was difficult to slow the plane just enough to stop the propeller from wind milling, but not having it fall out of the sky due to a wing stall. For a young, inexperienced student it was a pretty disconcerting maneuver.

However, it was a pleasure to cruise over the mountains and towns of the Rhön, and this flight greatly contributed to my desire to learn to fly a power plane. My new instructor, who had also been an experienced Luftwaffe pilot, appeared very casual about this whole flying thing. While we flew the motor sailor, he discovered a rattle in the dash he did not like. Thus he proceeded, using his Swiss army knife, to dismantle the dashboard while I was flying. I wish he had not done that. But he got

Holy Mountain

it back together in time for landing. Flying Messerschmitts while being shot at by squadrons of B17 Flying Fortresses gives one a different risk tolerance for flying, I guess.

Finally, with about 50 dual flights under my belt, I was ready for my first solo flight. Tradition dictates that the flight instructor will never pre-announce it – the student probably would not sleep the night before. Rather, the day begins with a few more dual flights. If the wind is gentle and the student did well, he is sent up aloft alone, with no prior warning. However, one can sense when solo time has come. The instructor keeps his hands mostly off the controls – which is always hard to tell in tandem seating arrangement, though – and keeps asking these funny 'What would you do if…?" questions.

Strangely, I do not remember the actual first solo – only that the other students hit my butt after landing. That is an old tradition, supposedly to make an important organ for flying (the butt) more sensitive. In politically correct America, this old tradition has been mostly abolished in favor of cutting off a piece of the student's shirt, writing his or her name on it and posting it in the flight school lounge.

I had done pretty well, hour-wise, as I soloed as the second member of the class. I soon soloed a few more times and thus earned the 'A' wings, which is the first level of soaring accomplishments. Since there were a couple of days left, my instructor declared that I would have time to earn the B wings.

While doing the required flights for the B wings, I had what amounted to an actual 'rope break' situation. One of the more feared soaring scenarios is that during a takeoff the towrope breaks and leaves the plane in a dangerous position. Its nose will be high, speed is rapidly deteriorating and the pilot must make a quick, unscheduled landing.

Exactly that happened to me at my sixth solo flight. I had barely left the ground when there was a big bang, the

Holy Mountain

plane lurched and I knew immediately that I was in trouble. But fortunately the correct reaction was also the intuitive one – if you see nothing but sky in the window the natural reaction is to push the stick forward with all you've got. I did that, the plane picked up speed without stalling, and since the terrain was dropping away from me I had a few seconds to select a landing site.

The landing was uneventful and I felt kind of proud at handling a potentially very dangerous situation well. The rope actually had not broken. We suspected that the cable had not been hooked up quite right. It was done by a young lady, who was not exactly at the top of the class when it came to mechanical aptitude. But maybe I am not fair – we never will know exactly why the cable ripped out of the hook mechanism.

Now, 34 years later, a good friend, Dr. Wolf Weber, talked me into partnering with him in a high performance Rollwagen-Schneider LS4 sailplane. Once again I am learning how to fly sailplanes. In aviation, learning never stops. That's what makes it so fascinating.

Here in America, the common launch method is different. Rather than being yanked unceremoniously into the air by a big winch, we employ a power plane to tow the glider into the air. It has the big advantage that one can climb much higher and seek out lift. This greatly increases the changes for a good, long soaring flight, but is also much more expensive and it requires more skill than the 'stick to the tummy and do not worry about a thing' winch launch still widely employed in Europe.

Holy Mountain

Luftwaffe (German Air Force)

- see also page 167

At the age of 18, I got drafted into the German Air force –
the dreaded Luftwaffe of World War II movies. I really,
really did not want to go into military service, but it was
unavoidable. When the draft letter told me to expect
Luftwaffe rather than the Armee (Army) service, I was
greatly relieved.

The year was 1968, the year the Russians invaded
Czechoslovakia and things got a bit tense around Europe
just then. Some of the professional soldiers in the Luftwaffe
were practically drooling at the prospect of war. Idiots!
Still, being drafted into the Luftwaffe in 1968 was a lot
better than being drafted in America and sent to Vietnam.

The medical examination found me healthy, except
for needing glasses. For some reason, the docs determined
that I was unfit for two types of duty: working with
electronics and flying planes. Of course, I do both today.
The prohibition against (military) flying might have to do
something with me wearing glasses, so this part is
understandable. However, the prohibition against working
on electronics will always be a mystery.

For obvious reasons, there is often strong animosity
between pilots and medical doctors, who are gatekeepers to
the cockpit. This is wonderfully depicted in the great movie
'The Right Stuff'.

I was sent to boot camp in the old Donau (Danube)
river city of Ulm. It has the tallest cathedral in Europe,
which is a breathtaking piece of architecture – especially
breath taking when one climbs a tower. The upper parts of
the towers are light, airy stone structures. I never felt my
fear of heights more than near the top of this cathedral. By

Luftwaffe

the way, about 85% of all pilots admit to a fear of heights, but it generally does not show up in airplanes, even open ones.

Fortunately I escaped the drudgery of boot camp soon by volunteering to work in the telephone exchange of the barracks. However, at least I got the chance to learn how to shoot small arms. This was fun.

The *Bundeswehr* (German armed service) used the Heckler&Koch G3 automatic rifle, the Walther P1 9mm pistol and the Israeli UZI 9mm machine gun. The G3 is a hefty weapon, using the standard NATO caliber 7.62(mm) ammunition. I am still not sure whether this is the same as the Winchester 308 cartridge. I liked the G3 – it was a very reliable weapon, easy to clean and easy to shoot precisely.

The pistol was another matter. It was a re-issued World War II Walther P38, which held eight 9 mm cartridges. Today, the 9 mm caliber is the most used pistol ammunition in the world [6]. Many American police departments have discarded their trusty 0.38 caliber revolvers for fancier 9mm automatic pistols. They are more complicated to use, but have more firepower. I was terrible at using the pistol – never hit anything. It would have been more dangerous to an assailant if I had thrown the pistol at him!

After boot camp I was sent to barren fields near Augsburg in Bavaria to attend the Bundeswehr language school. The idea was to learn enough Russian to listen to Russian pilots patrolling their side of the iron curtain. I had forgone learning French for learning Russian in high

---

[6] As an aside, James Bond's weapon is the Walther PPK, which stands for Polizei Pistole Kurz (Police Pistol Short) and fires the feeble 7.65 mm pistol cartridge. This caliber – known as 0.32 in America- can barely stop an angry Wiener dog, unless fired by Sean Connery or Roger Moore.

Luftwaffe

school, so this assignment even made sense. The commander of the school was a Colonel, very intellectual and master of seven languages. But even so, it was very tough for him to learn Chinese. Ever since, I have a lot of respect for all the Asians who managed to learn English so well.

While attending this school, I became good friends with two other students. Our time in Augsburg did not feel like military service anymore, more like being in a small university dorm. In hindsight, the time in the Luftwaffe was not at all bad. After graduation, we all got sent to our areas of deployment. The three of us stayed together and we were sent to the small town of Wunsiedel, near the iron curtain in the Fichtelgebirge.

The single product made in this town is now quite well known in America. It is a sweet herbal liquor called *Jägermeister* and can be found in most liquor stores in the USA. Even in Arizona.

Deployment

A tall, futuristic looking tower dominates the summit of the highest mountain of the Fichtelgebirge. The mountain is called Schneeberg – or Snow Mountain. That was where we worked after deployment. We used fancy Rhode&Schwartz VHF radios, which had an integrated frequency scanner. The output of the scanner was displayed on an oscilloscope. We did not know in advance which frequency the Russians would be using on a given day. But as soon as they transmitted, a spike on the scope indicated the frequency of their transmission. We quickly tuned our radios and by the second or third transmission we had a lock on him.

Most of the time it was boring duty. The pilots were cruising in fuel-saving slow flight up and down the eastern side of the border and nothing ever seemed to happen.

Luftwaffe

However, one day an air show was held on the other side of the border and suddenly all hell broke loose. We draftees couldn't follow the fast and furious transmissions. Fortunately, we had a native Russian speaker on our shift. He understood what had happened. A bleacher, which had been built for the air show, had just collapsed. Probably too much brass.

While in Wunsiedel I came close to firing my P1 in anger. The mountain tower and its auxiliary buildings were considered a highly classified area and were surrounded by a very tall fence. Civilian guards with fearsome German shepherd dogs patrolled inside the fenced-in area. Late one night I came down the tower, planning to raid the vending machines in the cafeteria.

Suddenly, a big watchdog charged around the corner and confronted me. The handler of the dog was nowhere in sight. The guards were usually old men, and he must have decided to let his dog run free. The moment I moved, the dog snarled, jumped and put his big jaws loosely around my shin. However, he did not close his jaws – yet! I talked to him calmly, but he would not relax his grip. Rather, he tightened it more.

Ever so slowly I moved my arm towards the P1 gun, which I carried in a holster. As I moved, the dog tightened his grip more. I knew that there was no chance to shoot the dog before he would crush my leg. However, he would not get any second chance, I hoped. Fortunately the standoff ended when the guard ran around the corner, huffing and puffing. I had some rather angry words with him. The whole encounter drew some blood from my leg and I have a somewhat tense relation with aggressive dogs ever since.

During my entire Luftwaffe time, I never got to fly. But at least I sat once in an Lockheed F104 Starfighter. This deadly plane (mainly to the pilot) is often described as a

Luftwaffe

missile with a man on it. The stubby wings were only about as wide as a desk and their leading edges were as sharp as a knife. In the hangar, the edges were covered with a plastic protector to avoid injuries to staff. The top speed of the Starfighter was Mach 2.5, or over two times the speed of sound.

The Luftwaffe ordered 800 of these planes for use as fighters and fighter-bombers. This was a dumb decision. The F104 was designed as a very fast interceptor for the blue skies of California, not for the grey and rainy weather of middle Europe. To make up for this shortcoming, the German version of the F104 was stuffed with vacuum tube avionics. The Luftwaffe lost about 130 of its 800 Starfighters due to peacetime crashes. A joke was going around that it was easy to obtain a Starfighter:
Just buy a field and wait.

SCUBA Diving

- see also page 189

I was about 20 before I ever saw an ocean and will never forget that early evening in Yugoslavia, as my parent's baby blue 1963 VW Beetle crossed a ridge and there it was. Hazy in the distance beckoned the first ocean I ever saw – the landlocked, salty Mediterranean, cradle of Western civilization. Perhaps my fascination with diving, sailing and islands is related to this late start with getting to know the ocean.

The coastal road of Yugoslavia is one of the most beautiful roads in the world. It is comparable to fabled Highway 1 in California, which winds it way along the long California coast. Both coasts are fabulous meetings of land and sea. Big mountains tower over a blue sea, cliffs and canyons tumble into the sea. But the details of the landscapes are different. The coast of Yugoslavia is dotted with romantic Mediterranean fishing villages, where colorful boats are pulled up on the strand and grizzled fishermen sit on their boats and mend their nets. I will never understand how they manage these unruly heaps of netting and cork.

The mountains above the California coast are lush and green because they are often shrouded in fog. By the way, that's why many lighthouses along Highway 1 are so small and built low. If they were taller, the light would be inside the fog layer, rather than beneath it.

There are no fog problems along the Adriatic coast, although it is often hazy. The Adriatic is the finger of the Mediterranean sea, which separates Italy and Yugoslavia. On the Italian (western) side, the coast is a wasteland of cheap tourist hotels and crowded beaches. It has been nicknamed Teutonen Grill, i.e. a place where German tourists are getting sunburned. However, the Yugoslavian side of the coast is spectacular. Compared to the coast of California, it is rugged and dry, except for occasional stands of fragrant pines and olive trees.

      I had talked my father into taking an introductory SCUBA class with me, in a Yugoslavian dive school south of Rijeka. My mother, sensible as most women are, decided to stay on dry land. It was during this trip that I first saw the ocean. We arrived at our hotel late in the evening and early next morning we showed up at the dive school. They even had our pre-paid reservation in hand and we were mightily impressed. This was 1969, when in communist Yugoslavia tourism was still an experiment.

      At the entrance of the school was the remnant of an exploded Scuba tank. Maybe the Yugoslavians still had something to learn about this marketing thing! Only the bottom of the steel tank remained. It looked like the rusty petal of a flower. Except, the 'flower' consisted of nearly one-inch thick steel, split and twisted by the force of the blowout. This sight left me with a deep, livelong impression and respect for the forces lurking inside a compressed gas tank. Oh yes, it was used as an ashtray – after all, in the Mediterranean most everyone smokes.

      My dad and I got issued our dive gear. It was the old-fashioned, traditional Jacques-Cousteau equipment. We carried two heavy steel tanks directly on our backs and used an old-fashioned two-hose regulator. These are the big regulators made famous by old TV shows like Sea-Hunt. Today, everyone uses a much sleeker single-hose regulator and a Buoyancy Compensator (BC).

      The BC is the centerpiece of Scuba dive equipment. It combines an inflatable vest, tank harness and lead weights into one piece of equipment. Back then, the BC

SCUBA Diving

had not even been invented yet, and we took care of our buoyancy by adjusting our weight belts for the dive ahead.

Many of today's divers outright refuse to believe that one can dive without a BC at all, but little do they know. When the BC first entered the German market, they were laughed at as 'Rentner Lift' (or senior citizens elevator). Real men dove with out them. Mermaids still dive without them.

Capt. Jaques Cousteau and Emile Gagnan are the inventors of SCUBA. Their key insight was that a human who is breathing air under *exactly* the same pressure as felt by his lungs could freely breathe under water. This was the aqualung or, in the English speaking world, the 'self-contained-underwater-breathing-apparatus or SCUBA.

They designed a simple gadget, consisting of a rubber membrane and a needle valve, which reduces the very high pressure inside a Scuba tank to just the right level needed by the diver to breath. The pressures and forces a diver deals with are impressive.

At sea level, the atmosphere will squeeze each square cm of your body with a force of 1 kp. If you are British or American, it will do so with a force of 14.4 pounds per square inch. However, if you are 50m (160') underwater, the surrounding pressure is 6 kp/cm^2 (or 86.4 psi). That's a lot, comparable to the pressure of life steam in an old locomotive. Still, that's nothing compared to the 300 kp/cm^2 of a fully filled European tank.

The regulator better gets this right. If it were only a bit off from the target pressure – which is the surrounding water pressure – than either the diver's lungs will get squashed or blown to pieces. However, regulators are very simple, reliable devices and accidents due to faulty regulators are nearly unheard of.

This said, in our dive club we sometimes practiced breathing – very, very carefully – directly from the air tanks, without using any regulators. We just cracked the high-pressure tank valve a tiny bit and cupped our mouths over the tank valve. It is indeed possible to breathe this way without blowing up one's lungs. However, it is not exactly a recognized procedure.

The old two-hose regulator we used in this class sent pressure-regulated air from the tanks through a fat rubber hose to the mouthpiece. The exhaled air went through a second big hose back to the regulator, where it was expelled into the surrounding water. This system has the advantage that there are no bubbles near your face, scaring fish, but that is its only advantage, compared to a modern single-hose system.

The fat old rubber hoses were leaking constantly. We were always swimming on our left sides, trying to purge the water by squeezing the other side and blowing air into the hose. If the hose flooded for some reason, it was very hard to collect enough air in your lungs to purge it. Modern single hose regulators solved all these problems. With these, if water gets into the system or your mouth, you just push a button and a big rush of air gets rid of all water.

Still, it was magical to dive, even with this old, leaky system. The Mediterranean was already pretty devoid of fish by then, but the water was still of impeccable clarity and the remaining fish were fascinating to watch.

My favorite citizens of the deep are the Octopi. These are very smart invertebrates. They communicate and signal their emotions using color patterns moving constantly over their bodies. If they turn dark red, beware. Such an Octopus is mad as hell and can bite badly with its parrot-like beak.

An Octopus is a very curious critter. You can attract them easily and they like to feel with their eight arms all over your mask and face, play tug-of-war with your fingers and wrap themselves around the hose(s) of your regulator.

SCUBA Diving

It is difficult to convince them to let go. An animal with eight arms and hundreds of suction cups always has an upper hand, if one may say so. It is easy to remove one or two arms of an Octopus from your body, but he has six (or eight) more. Incidentally, the muscles of all cold-blooded animals (per square centimeter of cross section) are much weaker than ours.

There is a big shortage of 'apartments' for Octopi. They look for caves where they hide during the day, safe from their many predators. At night, they go themselves on a prowl. The Mediterranean fishermen like to exploit this shortage of Octopus apartments. They tie little amphorae-shaped clay bottles in a row on a long string and drop the assembly on a sandy ocean floor.

After a day or so, virtually all of the bottles are taken over by apartment-seeking Octopi. Then the fisherman hauls them up to the surface. The Octopus knows that something funny is going on, but it is so desperate to cling to the precious 'apartment' bottle that it will hang on even as the bottle breaks through the surface. Then it is too late for an escape. The fisherman quickly bites into the Octopus' neck, killing them in an instant. What a way to make a living.

My father and I had a few fun days, exploring the coastal waters of the Adriatic sea. Diving was easy in the good old days. Once you figured out how to purge the old regulators and how to clear your ears on descent there seemed to be nothing else to learn. The ear clearing skill is easy to learn, at least for most people. Just grasp your nose through the mask, hold it shut and blow. Then a clicking sound in your ears will indicate that the pressure has been equilibrated. At the same time, the dull pain on your eardrums will go away.

There is nothing to do on ascend; the design of the human ear takes care of excess pressure in the ear upon returning to the surface. That is most fortunate, of course, as diving would be impossible otherwise.

A simple, relaxed Scuba dive in shallow clear warm water without currents is very peaceful – like a stroll through a park. Shallow means less than about 20m/60' of depth. Propulsion is easy with swim fins and one can descend or ascend effortlessly. Only the ears and sinus cavities need some attention upon descending. But the deeper you already are, the less clearing is needed. Most problems with buoyancy variation and ear clearing occur close to the surface, where the relative pressure changes are biggest.

Different species of fish react very differently to a diver's presence. Octopi are happy to play, parrotfish do not care and the feisty damsel fish defend their territory viciously with mock attacks. These are mostly directed against the glass plate of the diver's mask.

Yellow tail fish accustomed to humans love to crowd divers, demanding a hand out. A spray can of softened cheese is ideal for this. The little strings of cheese are like pale yellow worm wriggling through the water and are irresistible to most fish. Once, at the popular wreck of the RHONE, I was mugged by a school of dozens of yellow tails, because I carried a can of cheese. The cheese can was mostly empty and had now positive buoyancy. When I accidentally let go of it, it quickly rose out of my reach. The yellow tails now completely ignored me and rushed after the can tumbling to the surface. It was a hilarious sight - a cheese can acting like a pied piper. I was laughing so hard that I lost my regulator mouthpiece.

Scuba Club (Mis)adventures

After returning from this vacation, I was hooked on diving and joined the dive club of the city of Hanau east of Frankfurt in 1970. Soon I bought my own equipment. It consisted of a thin, 4mm thick neoprene wetsuit, a Spanish-made single hose regulator which still works (2008), a tank, weight belt, depth and pressure gauge and mask, snorkel and fins.

The club met weekly in the pool run by the city and we practiced free diving without tanks, trading regulators for out-of-air situations and other training procedures. Afterwards we ate Jäger Schnitzel and drank a lot of Pilsner beer. Slowly I became an accepted member of the club and was exposed to its politics and intrigues. Fin swimming racing competition was a major part of the club's activities. I did not care about participating, but couldn't help noticing how all winners were using big, homemade monofins. A monofin is simply a big, triangular shaped piece of epoxy glass fiber with two rubber foot pockets attached. I was very impressed by the speed advantage of these big monofins, a lesson that led directly to the mermaid experiments decades later.

Hanau, a city with about 100,000 inhabitants, was too small to have its own professional diving team for its fire brigade and police. Thus, whenever an underwater task was required, our club was called upon. As one of the junior, but very active members I frequently participated in these activities.

Once there was a search for military rockets. The US Armed Forces had a heavy presence in Hanau at the time, and one day we were called upon to search for some rockets, which had been stolen and supposedly thrown into the Kinzig. This is a small, shallow river converging with the Main river near Frankfurt.

We were asked to find the rockets, each about 1.2 m long. It was the midst of winter, and it was very cold. Ice formed on our dive suits whenever we surfaced. I wore only my thin, 4mm suit, designed for Mediterranean diving, and was terribly cold. The Kinzig had a strong current and we stretched a heavy rope across the river. We divers were hanging onto the rope, feeling for rockets in the inky blackness of the muddy river. Team members ashore moved the rope a few feet and we repeated the search. We never found the rockets, though.

Another time we were looking for a body of a driver. His car had crashed into the river. Divers are only called in for search, never for rescue. It's always too late by the time divers can show up.

The chap had been underwater for a few weeks. I happened to find the body and dragged him ashore. It wasn't a nice sight. The fish had eaten his eyes, cheeks and other soft parts. On top of all this, when we dragged him up the steep Kinzig shore, I slipped and fell flat on him. Yikes! I had to suffer jokes about this incident for months.

Another memorable dive was the search for a safe, which had been stolen from a nightclub. The perpetrators were quickly caught and they admitted that they had thrown the safe into the Main river. They did this at a spot nearly 100 km east of Frankfurt, where the Autobahn crosses the river on a very tall bridge. There they claimed to have stopped and thrown the safe over the bridge, after they were unsuccessful in opening it.

The nightclub owner rode with us in a police cruiser. He was a rather unpleasant fellow and I was very tempted to refuse getting into the muddy, dangerous river waters for this character. But in the end, I did go. Ego never fails men. There was no chance of finding the safe in the dark, turbulent waters by a random search. We got the two burglars – young kids, actually quite nice fellows – to walk with us the length of the Autobahn bridge, while the fast Autobahn traffic was rushing past us. Then they said: "It was about here." We looked 110 m down, into the brown floods of the swollen Main river. That wasn't enough location information.

Then I had an idea. When the perpetrators lifted the heavy steel safe over the bridge's banister, they probably

SCUBA Diving

left significant scratch marks. Sure enough, soon we found such marks, very fresh looking! We got a very long line, weighted it with a lot of lead and lowered it directly from the scratch marks on the banister, down into the river. Then we drove down to the riverbank, put on our dive gear and swam with the current to the point where the long vertical line entered the rushing water.

We followed the line down through the inky darkness and very soon we hit the bottom. We had prepared a short second line, which could swivel around the master line dangling from the bridge. We used it as a guidance to swim in an ever-increasing circle around the vertical line. Sure enough, within minutes, we came across something hard and boxy lying half buried in the mud of the river.

We tied the radial line to what felt like a handle and surfaced. Divers practice a lot to tie nautical knots with their eyes closed! We quickly pulled the object on land and it was the safe. The water still poured out of it as the nightclub owner opened it. I did not like the guy, but at least he donated a couple of hundred DM to the club.

It is amazing how seriously people in Europe take their club activities! Their politicking puts professional politics to shame, it seems. However, I became good friends with another member of this club, Lothar Fichtel, and he soon convinced a few other divers, including myself, to found another club in the nearby town of Bruchköbel.

Lothar became a very good friend and mentor. We wrote a thin textbook about snorkel diving, called "Schnorcheltauchen, leicht gemacht." Its first edition was sold out quickly. Its cover featured a very pretty picture of one of Lothar's daughters.

This is when we learned that a book's cover picture is very important. For the second edition, the editor

(Kosmos, Franckh'sche Verlagshandlung, Stuttgart) noted that there were some strands of hair caught under the lip of the girl's mask. Theoretically, this is a no-no because it can cause leaks. I know from experience as a heavily bearded diver that such a leak does not pose a hairy problem.

Lothar and I laughed off the concerns of the editor. Never laugh at an editor! He absolutely insisted that we replace the cover page with another one. Finally, we gave in. The new picture was far less cute than the one used for the first edition. The second edition – with exactly the same text- sold only at 6% of the rate of the first edition and was soon relegated to the overstock bins. This hurt...

That same editor oversaw the translation and publication of our book in Norway. That would have been fine – except, he snuck in a chapter about spear fishing! We were aghast. Neither Lothar nor I condone spear fishing and we had been very public about condemning it. It was extremely embarrassing to us that we were suddenly seen as the authors of a book condoning and even advising on spear fishing. We had not even known that this chapter had been added until after we got a copy of the Norwegian edition.

Let me say a few words about the problems of deep diving. There are several unrelated dangers as one dives below 10m (30') depth. During the first few meters from the surface, the building pressure makes it necessary to equilibrate pressure in the middle ear; otherwise the eardrum would rupture. That is normally an easy task, accomplished by blowing air into one's nose, while one holds it shut. A cold prevents clearing of the ears and disables even the most experienced diver and will ruin any dive vacation.

If one were to breathe pure oxygen – which is not done anymore – oxygen poisoning would become dangerous at about -12 m and deadly around -20 m. When

SCUBA Diving

breathing air, oxygen poisoning becomes a problem around -70 m. Nitrogen narcosis is another effect. I used to feel its onset around -40m in my twenties, but now I have gotten less sensitive to it. The symptoms vary very much from person to person. Around -60m to -70m, the dense air makes it surprisingly hard to breathe. Beyond -100m, one needs to reduce the level of both oxygen and nitrogen in the breathing gas. The best gas for very deep diving is a mixture of helium and a few percent of oxygen. This whole complex field is called technical diving. Technical divers look like an entire hardware store on the move.

Lothar went for his "Gold" level CMAS certification. CMAS is the world's topmost SCUBA federation, founded in southern France. This is a tough test. It calls for very scary things like finding a Scuba tank deposited in -35 m (113') depth by free diving! If you find it, you can breathe from it. If not, you are in real trouble.

That task is hard enough in the clear waters of the Mediterranean, where you can see the tank soon after submerging. However, in the dark, dirty waters of northern Europe, that is positively risking your life. I myself completed only the Silver level, which calls for a -30m (97') free dive. Today I think that the CMAS requirements were simply asinine. Another prerequisite for the Gold level was a SCUBA dive (on ordinary air) to -60m depth. That is 200' deep! Again, this is tough enough in clear waters, but very dangerous in the muddy waters of Germany. However, I agreed to go diving with Lothar to fulfill this requirement.

We drove to the mountains of the Eiffel, southeast of Cologne. Numerous former volcanic craters dot the area, some filled with deep lakes. We picked the Pulvermaar for this dive. It is the deepest lake in northern Germany. I was quite nervous, particularly since my first trip to America, critical for my PhD thesis, was scheduled for later in that week. In addition, we knew that several divers had already died in this crater, doing just such stupid dives as we planned.

We got into the cold, dark water and descended. The 20,000 year-old crater is very deep and its walls are descending at an angle of over 30 degrees. Fortunately the water was clear enough so that there was still some dim light down there.

At about 45m depth, I started to experience the first symptoms of nitrogen narcosis. It is thought that the high nitrogen partial pressure affects the operation of the neuron synapses, with all kinds of interesting effects possible. In my case, nitrogen narcosis manifests itself as tunnel vision. It was like looking through a role of toilet paper. Other divers get giddy or offer their regulators to fish.

A little bit deeper, around -55m, I lost consciousness but kept on moving. Lothar, initially, did not notice that something was wrong with me. I just seemed to continue the dive, except I was now crawling on hands and knees down the crater wall. At first, he wasn't particularly concerned. He knew that I tend to experiment.

When we reached -60m, he grabbed me by my shoulders and turned me around so that I would crawl back up. I have absolutely no recollection of all this. He only got concerned when I turned around again and continued down the crater wall. Down here, in the dim twilight of a deep lake, there was hardly enough light to see what was happening. He knew that something was very wrong and kept steering me towards the distant surface.

Slowly we made our way back up the crater. My own recollection is that I was asleep in my bed. An alarm clock with red, glowing hands was sitting above my bed. Then I looked at it closer and saw that it showed the number 45. That's not a time! Slowly I came to and realized that I wasn't in bed, but deep underwater.

SCUBA Diving

Fortunately, I did not panic and we concluded the dive uneventfully. However, I had the biggest headache of my life. In hindsight, we think that my tank was contaminated with a trace of carbon monoxide gas. That can happen quite easily if the compressor is driven by a small gasoline engine and exhaust gases enter the air intake. My symptoms were consistent with this hypothesis. We wrote up the whole story and it was published in the German dive magazine 'Tauchen' in 1974.

Another time we drove to Isle d'Hyere in southern France. That was around 1972. Years later, I saw a film clip by Captain Cousteau himself, taken there in 1949. The richness of fish life in '49 was startling. By 1972, the area was already pretty dead. We had driven in a convoy of 3 cars from Frankfurt, throughout a long night, to arrive on Easter Sunday. We went diving right after our arrival. It was a delightful dive, very peaceful. I was lying on my back at a comfortable depth, watching the silvery bubbles of my exhaled air tumbling to the surface far above.

The next thing I remember was one of my buddies shaking me to wake up. That was the first and only time I fell asleep underwater. It was fortunate that I did not loose the mouthpiece of my regulator. It would have been a rude awakening to find myself under water with no air to breath!

Another memorable dive in these early days was in the shallow waters of the Ostsee (Baltic sea). We camped on the sandy shore of this shallow inland ocean, which borders the countries of Denmark, Germany, Sweden and Finland. It was a boring dive, except for the fact that huge numbers of jellyfish formed a dense layer about a meter above the sea floor. We had to push the jellyfish aside to reach the bottom. Fortunately, this species didn't sting.

What made this trip interesting was an encounter with some fellow who had lost the outboard engine of his boat. That happens quite frequently. If they aren't secured properly, they can easily vibrate loose. He had done well, though, to take good bearings of the spot where the engine went overboard. He asked if we could help. Sure, we could.

We motored to the spot and in surprisingly short time we found the engine under the jellyfish layer. This was plain luck, since the jelly fish layer prevented us to see the bottom. However, we did not have a line to retrieve the motor.

So I ended up to act as a human buoy by staying over the outboard while he and the rest of the crew returned to the shore to find a line. That doesn't sound so hard – and it wasn't – but the sun was sinking quickly and we were about a km from shore.

If you have ever seen the movie 'Open Water', you know the feeling. Except, I wasn't with my fiancée, I was alone, just treading water, getting very cold and was hoping they would get back before sunset. They did, but just barely. I dove back down, wrapped the rope around the outboard, we retrieved it and went back to shore for a serious northern Schnapps and Herring dinner!

There were many other stories on the topic of semi-professional diving, such as experiencing a simulated very deep dive in the pressure (hyperbaric) chamber of the German Kriegsmarine (Navy), setting moorings in the Hudson river and several other search missions. But this came to an end for a very good reason...

After I had moved to NY and met my lovely first wife, Karen, I convinced her to learn to dive. She did so, in the dark, cold, and muddy waters of Lake Mahopac. After she got her Scuba Certification Card, she told me in no uncertain terms: "I've had enough from cold, dark waters. All our future dives will be in the tropics!"

Women are always right. Especially in this case.

SCUBA Diving

Nuclear Experiments (2ħ)

See also pages 168,169

To many people, the idea of nuclear experiments may sound mysterious, perhaps dangerous or shrouded in secrecy. Thanks to Hollywood, visions of mad scientists with fuzzy white hair and big machines throwing lightning bolts come to mind. Actually, the part about big machines and lightning (when things go awry) is quite correct.

There are four distinct classes of nuclear experiments.

The oldest and simplest involves a usually lone scientist doing experiments with some kind of radioactive material on a **bench top**, using photographic plates, ionization chambers and similar simple radiation detection devices. This was the typical setup around the beginning of the 20th century, when the phenomenon of radioactivity and soon thereafter the atomic nucleus was discovered.

It was astonishing how much about the structure of the nucleus was discovered with these simple experiments. The famous names of this age were Madame Curie and Ernest Rutherford. Madame Curie discovered radium by slaving for years over big vats of Pitchblende ore. Over years, she carefully distilled the ore into about a gram of pure radium (and also discovered polonium). Rarely was a Nobel price more deserved than hers. She died of cancer contracted from working so long with radium. Her husband, Prof. Pierre Curie, was an important scientist in his own right. He was the discoverer of the piezo electric effect, which is used today as the tuning element in all radios, TV's and computers.

The second class of nuclear experiments is very visible, but has fallen out of favor. It involves the growing of *large mushrooms*. I won't go there, even though the physics of nuclear weapons - in particular of hydrogen bombs - is absolutely fascinating. It was always very interesting to listen to the stories of the old-timers who were involved in this kind of gardening. As Robert Oppenheimer put it – it was 'technically sweet'.

By the way, nuclear guys involved in this line of work avoid the word bomb like the plague. The thing in question is addressed as device or gadget – but never with the B-word.

The third class uses *nuclear reactors* as a source of neutron radiation. That class is today pretty empty, at least as using reactors as tools for nuclear physics research, which is the science that cares about the atomic nucleus itself. Chemists, solid-state physicists, biologists, materials scientist and other practical types use reactors like an expensive light bulb with which they illuminate their experiments – except they don't use light, but the copious neutron flux coming from the reactor core.

The fourth class is completely dominating experimental nuclear and high-energy physics, and it is the one I know best. These are *accelerator-based* experiments. The precision, flexibility and safety against accidental radioactive contamination of accelerators is so overwhelming that nearly all experimental nuclear physics is done with the aid of these great machines.
Seen from a distance, all accelerator experiments pretty much look alike. A big machine – the accelerator – produces some sharply focused beam of nuclear radiation. This beam hits some target, which hopefully is *not* destroyed. Sometimes it is, to the consternation of the

Nuclear Experiments

experimenters and the frustration of the graduate student responsible for mounting a new target at oh-dark hundred.

As the beam hits the target, nuclear reactions are initiated. This is not a self-sustaining (or run-away) chain reaction as in a nuclear reactor or nuclear (ahem) gadget, but it occurs at a slow, steady rate. When the accelerator is turned off, the reaction will stop.

Most of the time, the reaction rate is frustratingly low, and the experimenters will gang up on the poor operators of the accelerator to tune it up and give them more 'beam current'. It is rumored that the promise of a bottle of Jack Daniels (after the operator's shift is over) is the best beam-tuning device known in nuclear physics. I would not know.

Most of the beam passes through the target without doing anything interesting and gets eventually stopped in a beam dump. A story about an interesting failure of a very big beam dump is told later in this book.

A few beam particles hit the very widely spaced target nuclei – an atom is mostly empty space - and initiate nuclear reactions. These may create new particles, which speed away from the reaction zone and are discovered in radiation detectors set around the target.

As these reaction products hit the detectors, they create tiny but very characteristic electric pulses. These get piped through long shielded coax cables to the counting 'hut'. This is usually an air-conditioned room somewhere near the business end of the accelerator, jam-packed with specialized nuclear electronics to pick-up, amplify, compare, decode time-sequence and generally mess with the incoming pulses.

The now thoroughly mangled pulses get written on heaps of reels of computer tape, to be analyzed later by the experimenters and their graduate students. This typically

Nuclear Experiments

takes a few years, and the final result are a few papers and PhD theses and perhaps a Nobel price. Such is the progress of science.

The data rates of modern accelerator experiments are unbelievably high – the Large Hadron Collider (LHC) coming now on line in CERN will create raw data at a rate of about one Petabyte (a Million Gigabytes) every two seconds!

From this level of description the curious reader may wonder if after 80 years of doing accelerator experiments nuclear physicists have run out of variations on the same theme. The short answer is no. Please realize that my description is about on the same level as describing a surgeon's activity as cutting and sewing tissue. The devil is in the details – like which organ the surgeon attacks with his sharp instruments.

Similarly in nuclear physics – by changing beam type and energy, targets, detector types and other variables there are billions of different experiments possible. On a higher level, however, the skeptical question has a strong element of truth to it. There have been few new deep physics insights gained by doing nuclear experiments during the last generation of physicists.

This may have something to do with the fact that the brightest young students no longer gravitate to nuclear or high-energy physics field – as in days past - but to the more practical and potentially more financially rewarding areas of life- and computer science.

Let me illuminate these abstract descriptions with a few stories of my own experiences doing accelerator experiments. For now, let me focus on the very simple experiment, which got me a Diplom Physiker degree. This was the pre-requisite condition for entering the graduate program at the Johann Wolfgang Goethe Universität in

Nuclear Experiments

Frankfurt am Main. This Universität was a good place to learn the basics of nuclear physics research.

It has an excellent reputation in Nuclear Physics, based on the work by Prof. Walter Greiner and his team and the proximity to the bleeding edge GSI Heavy-ion accelerator laboratory halfway between Heidelberg and Frankfurt.

On an aside, Prof. Greiner is a colorful character, with many stories circulating about him. Some may even be true. One of the stories claims that he once was in the hospital, scheduled to have liver surgery. While he was there, he read a few textbooks on liver surgery. Then, he ordered his surgical team to a bedside audience. He lectured them how he wanted the surgery to be performed, speaking from the unshakable belief that physicists can understand anything and physics is the queen of science (true). I just can envision the scene and the clash of very big egos. But I am really proud of Professor Greiner, holding up the reputation of physicists anywhere.

I never worked for him, though. He did invite me to become a graduate student in his institute, but I was afraid to become too specialized as a theoretical nuclear physicist. It was probably a good decision to decline the offer. Otherwise I might have ended up writing papers with abstracts sounding like this:

"We formulate a group-theoretical projection technique for the quantum-statistical description of systems with exactly conserved charges corresponding to local non-Abelian gauge symmetries. The formalism is specified for $SU(N)$ internal symmetry and a partition function related to a mixed canonical–grand-canonical ensemble is defined. Its perturbation expansion is derived, and we point out potential applications. We also study single-particle Green's functions for the calculation of mixed ensemble averages with the help of a generalized Wick's theorem and find that a connected-graphs expansion is impossible."
H.T.Elze and W.Greiner, Phys.Rev.A 33 (1986).

Nuclear Experiments

To be honest, I have only a faint idea what this abstract means. So I went on to do graduate work in experimental – not theoretical- nuclear physics under a young experimental physicist. His name is Prof. Thomas W. Elze. Studying experimental physics would train me in many more things than just nuclear physics, I reckoned.

Prof. Elze had just returned from a multi-year stay in the USA. This and the fact that he was a very nice chap with a lot of practical horse sense played a major role in my decision in becoming his first graduate student. It paid off – he subscribed to the American attitude of getting a student through the PhD program quickly, rather than forcing him to make a career out of it. (Sorry to say, the chances are 98% that a physics student is a he). The latter was and is the tradition in many German university departments.

I received a PhD in only 2.5 years, which, to my knowledge, set a record for that physics department at this time. I will be forever grateful to Prof. Elze to relentlessly pushing me to get this degree done quickly.

A simple Experiment

Now let me finally get to the experiment itself. The Institut for Kernforschung owned a small Van-de Graff accelerator. It was about the size and shape of a fat V2 rocket. It wasn't pointy nosed, though.

Inside the thick-walled steel tank was a conveyor belt for electricity. I mean that quite literally. A long, continuous rubber belt was spinning between two rollers mounted at the opposite ends of the tank. Electrons were sprayed onto the belt at one end, transported to the other end and 'scraped' off there. The receiving end was inside a hollow metal sphere, and the electrons couldn't escape from the sphere, thus building up a charge of up to 3 Million Volts. That was on a good day.

Nuclear Experiments

The steel tank surrounding the entire contraption was filled with a special gas –SF_6– under high pressure. This allows much higher voltages to build up before the electricity finds a way to escape from the metal sphere. If this happens, it will be in the form of a big, thunderous lightning bolt. We dreaded when that happened – it interrupted the experiments and the discharge weakened the gas by ionizing it. This made it harder to build up very high voltages again. The bang was hard on the nerves, too.

A source of ions was located inside the metal sphere. Ions of light elements, like hydrogen (protons) or deuterium were formed in the source and accelerated by the 3 Million voltage difference. They formed an ion beam inside a acceleration tube located next to the electron conveyor belt, then left the accelerator through its bottom and entered the basement. There the ion beam was bent by a strong magnet by 90° and – now moving horizontally – was piped through more beam tubes to the various experiments.

The basement setup looked like a railway switching station; except the rails were beam pipes and the trains were nuclear particle beams. The beam pipes entered various chambers, which contained the target and nuclear detectors set up by the experimenters. By modern accelerator standards, this was a tiny machine, just good enough to train students and do some modest 'clean-up' physics experiments.

Still, I was thrilled. It was an impressive environment – the low hum of magnets, the whirring of fans and chucking of pumps, the yellow and red RADIATION warning signs all over, mazes of coax cables – it was heady stuff. It looked like a cross between a computer room and a ship's engine room.

The experiments I performed under the guidance of Professor Elze in Frankfurt were simple. Their objective was to determine the shape of the nuclei in various rare

Nuclear Experiments

earth metals, such as Samarium, Erbium, Gadolinium and Dysprosium. These materials are now, 30 years later, extensively used in super strong magnets, crucial in the building of electric and hybrid cars. The nuclei of these metals aren't round, but were already known to be elongated. We wanted to explore if the shapes were even more complex, like having a waist or a bulge around the equator. The result was successful – yes, these nuclei have such complex shapes. The actual experiment involved shooting Helium ions (also called alpha particles) onto a very thin target layer of these rare earth elements.

Part of my job was to make my own targets. That is not a trivial task. It involves similar techniques as are used, in much greater refinement, for the making of integrated circuits today. Both involve the precise deposition of very thin films of various materials on a substrate. My good friend, Hans Juergen Wollersheim, worked on a similar experiment and we could help each other.

The first step involved making a thin layer of Carbon, which acted as carrier material or substrate for the actual target material. Carbon is light, strong and doesn't interfere with the nuclear experiment we planned.

We mounted several clean microscope slides in a vacuum chamber and ignited a carbon arc next to the slides. As the arc burned in the vacuum – no oxygen was needed, as it was a purely electrical arc – it deposited a thin layer of carbon film onto the microscope glass slides. When they were nicely black looking, we let the air back into the chamber and took the slides out. The chamber always stank horribly after such a deposit burn.

Then came the tricky part of floating the carbon films off the glass slides. This was done in a bowl of water. It was a slow and frustrating process. Often the carbon film would not float off, or rip to pieces. When a nice film was floating serenely on the water's surface, I tried to capture it onto a metal frame. The frame was a thin strip of

Nuclear Experiments

aluminum, with a round hole of about 7 mm diameter punched into it. I submerged it fully and then slowly raised it from underneath a floating carbon film. The goal was to catch the film so that it would cover the hole. If it did, it would stick to the metal and we would end up with a nice target carrier. After working for a few days on this, we had made a batch of these carriers.

Now came the next step – depositing the actual rare earth target material on the carbon carrier. Rare earths are metals with very high melting and boiling temperatures. The idea was to evaporate them by focusing an extremely intense electron beam onto a sample of the rare earth material and evaporate enough of it to deposit a thin layer of the sample onto the carbon film.

The electron gun was a simple, but frightful device. It operated at over ten thousand volts, used high currents and produced extremely bright light. The visual impression was similar to that of arc welding. But the task at hand was much more subtle. At first, nothing worked right - the pure power and heat of the electron beam's presence in the chamber broke the painstakingly prepared carbon targets and flung the expensive isotope samples all over the vacuum chamber. We solved this by careful grounding the source and positioning the targets better, but still many films broke. But after a couple of weeks of holding the nose against the grindstone – or electron gun – Hans Jürgen and I finally had a batch of acceptable targets for our experiments.

The actual experiments were not as hard as making the targets. We – very carefully – mounted the targets we had created with so much effort in the center of a large vacuum chamber.

A simple, solid-state Silicon charged-particle detector pointed at the target from about 10 cm away, under an angle of 45° to the beam direction. The detector – a little cylinder the size of a short stack of quarters – was cooled

Nuclear Experiments

with liquid alcohol to a temperature of about -50° Celsius. This improved the detector's energy resolution. We sealed the chamber, connected the detector to an amplifier system and a PDP-8 data collecting mini-computer and then the experiment could begin.

Soon the invisible helium ion beam from the accelerator hit the target. Some of the projectiles were 'elastically' scattered from the e.g. Dysprosium nuclei in the target. These all had the same energy when they entered the detector. We immediately saw a rapidly growing peak of these uninteresting events on the computer's monitor screen.

After a while, we saw a much smaller peak growing to the left of the main peak. These were projectiles, which had managed to set the target nuclei spinning, but at the lowest possible speed. Since this was a quantum mechanical system, only certain rotation speeds of the target nucleus are allowed. The projectiles gave up some of their kinetic motion by spinning the nucleus and therefore entered our detector at a slightly reduced energy. That's why they showed up to the left (lower energy side) of the main peak.

After waiting a day, we could see a third, tiny peak grow even further to the left. This peak corresponded to collisions where a projectile had managed to spin the target nucleus faster, exciting it to a second rotational state. The relative sizes of the three peaks would eventually reveal to us the shape of the nucleus. We spent several weeks collecting data like this.

The small accelerator wasn't heavily subscribed, so it was pretty relaxing work. I ate many cans of Chef Boyardee ravioli during this data collection run. When the ravioli were too hot, I poured liquid air over it, of which we had plenty, because the lab had its own air-liquefying machine. It was always good for a laugh for bystanders to see the thick fog billow from my plate. Stale liquid air is

Nuclear Experiments

dangerous, though, because nitrogen boils off first and therefore the liquid slowly turns into liquid oxygen. But my dinner never exploded.
We had more funny moments. Once I came back from a short trip down into the beam hall and found the operator and the accelerator's chief engineer broadly grinning at me. I asked what the matter was. Well, when I was down there, alone, I had heartily picked my nose. Unfortunately I had forgotten about the video cameras in the hall.
The lab had a small swimming pool of very clear cooling water associated with it, deep in the basement. One night I took my Scuba diving gear (the water wasn't radioactive) and swam around in the nice, warm clear water. Nothing much to see, though. I did a few other – shall we say private- experiments. Unfortunately, one of them set off radiation alarms in the whole accelerator building, but no damage was done. This nuclear physics student had just learned the hard way that bombarding Aluminum with 3 MeV Deuterium beams produces very intense gamma radiation.

The trusty old Van de Graff held up well and soon we had our data. The next few months involved analyzing the results with the aid of a fancy quantum mechanical scattering model running on the computer center's Univac 1108. The probability of a projectile flying past a nucleus without affecting it or setting it into some spinning motion depends strongly on the shape of the nucleus. For example, a round target nucleus can't be induced to rotate at all. By comparing our data with the computer simulations, we could unambiguously determine the shape components of our targets. Hans Juergen and I split our data and we wrote our master's thesis on the quadrupole moments of rare earth nuclei, respectively.

Nuclear Experiments

My PhD thesis work involved similar type of work, except I performed it at the much larger and more powerful Tandem van-de Graff of the University of Rochester, NY. This accelerator was the size of a small submarine, lying horizontally and could create voltages up to 13 Million Volts DC, rather than the 3 Million Volts of the Frankfurt machine. 13 MV DC is a serious voltage by any measure. If the insulating gas broke down and it sparked, the building rang with the shock from the discharge. At least we weren't in California, so there was no confusion with earthquakes.

For the thesis, I studied the transfer of particles between projectile and target, rather than looking at the shape of nuclei. Not surprisingly, it was more complex than my master's work and involved building my own position sensitive detector, using a large magnetic spectrometer and preparing mildly radioactive Uranium and Thorium targets. But I'm not going to discuss it in detail. It was just a vehicle to get the scientist's union card – the PhD.

Nuclear Experiments

Hurricanes

See also page 171

Over the years, my first wife, Karen, and I had to deal with a few hurricanes.

My first encounter was with a weak hurricane, which was making its way up the Atlantic seaboard. It was expected to hit New York City on the same day I was scheduled to return from an IBM business trip to Burlington, Vermont. The small airline flying a turboprop – which looked far too ugly to be able to fly, but fly it did - between the Burlington, Poughkeepsie and Westchester County airports had cancelled all flights. This made sense, since the Poughkeepsie airport had no radar coverage at the time. Delays were unpredictable and fuel planning tricky, to say the least.

These overpriced flights between the three cities were used mostly by IBM engineers and executives, and I always thought the cabin should be labeled IBM confidential and open, rather than smoking and non-smoking. This was in the dark ages when smoking was allowed on public flights.

Anyhow, I wasn't going to miss my first hurricane. I rented a Hertz car, and with a colleague, also a hurricane newbie, drove the long way form northern Vermont to New York's Westchester county. We could have saved ourselves the effort. The hurricane was not exciting – it was just bad weather with gusty winds, lots of rain and flooded roadways.

This was my first lesson – whatever else you can say about Hurricanes – first and foremost, they are very inconvenient. Over the years I had hurricane encounters in the Caribbean and Bermuda, but never in the Pacific. Most of them were rather harmless. But two – Dean and Bertha- were interesting and are etched into memory.

Hurricanes

Green Skipper meets Dean

The first one was hurricane Dean, which hit the eastern Caribbean in 1989. This was the very first time when Karen and I had chartered a (crewless) bare boat and we explored the British Virgin Islands by ourselves. This went smoothly, especially after we had had guidance from a professional skipper on the first two days.

On an aside: That in itself was a surprise. I had hired a skipper through the charter boat company and they arranged for him to show up on the appointed day. We expected some suntanned, young man, with a gold chain dangling from his neck. Instead, a little gray-haired old lady with a small bag walked down the dock, introduced herself as Margaret and announced that she was our skipper!

It turned out that she was a California grandmother with seven kids. When she turned sixty, she had enough of being always busy for others, left (on good terms) her family and became a skipper in the Caribbean. Well, that's one of the great things about California - here, such a surprising action is respected, even admired. Margaret turned out to be a great instructor, and she became good friends with Karen. They kept in touch for years, and we visited her nice apartment in later years, overlooking the entrance of Tortola Yacht Harbor.

But back to hurricane stories. Margarete had left a week ago and we were finally sailing on our own. I knew that one *should* listen to the weather forecast every day, but this advice was hard to take seriously. It seemed to be the same day after day: "Winds from the southeast to the northeast at 12 – 20 knots, wave height 3' to 6', daytime temperatures 25-30 Celsius, and occasional showers." We knew it by heart. What made it even more tempting to skip the forecasts was the poor radio reception among the high islands of the Caribbean. Hurricanes weren't on my mind at all, which was dumb, given that it was the season.

Then one day, towards the end of our cruise, we had an unusually beautiful day. Normally, the skies in the Caribbean are dotted with scattered clouds, which have bases around 2500'. This is particularly true for mountain islands, where cloud formation is triggered by the lifting action of the terrain. These clouds often disgorge short, but intense tropical rain showers.

On that particular day, there was not one cloud in sight! We had planned a romantic, relaxed day on the beach and in the clear blue water of our favorite hidden cove, doing what adults do on a very empty beach. We remarked on the complete absence of boats. That was rather unusual. Normally, in this part of the Caribbean, one can always see a few sails on the horizon. Naturally, the absence of boats was most welcome to us. We idly wondered about it, but did not worry. Why ask questions when you are having a real good time? After a splendid day, many rum punches and a good dinner we went to our bunks.

The boat was anchored with two anchors. As a green, cautious skipper I liked to put two anchors out, which are arranged like a big V splayed out in front of the boat. An outlying rock and the main island form a notch through which the trade wind howls day and night – particularly at night. Anchoring in a windy spot is good, though. The strong wind keeps mosquitoes away, it dries laundry well and there was no danger of the wind slacking and the boat drifting onto rocks. Thus I felt very safe at this anchoring spot and slept well, as I nearly always do. Karen was a light sleeper, though. (Notice to all aspiring Captains – it is good to have a first mate who is a light sleeper!)

Karen woke me up at 04:00. It was pitch black as there was no moon and this was an uninhabited island without man-made lights.

Hurricanes

"Listen, Honey – no wind! What is going on?" Karen asked. I staggered on deck, flashlight in hand and made my way to the foredeck. I was still quite groggy from all the rum we drank the night before. Karen was right, it was completely calm. That is not what you expect in the Caribbean trade wind zone.

The bow of the boat was a mess. Instead of two anchor rodes pointing away from the boat in the usual orderly V, they were just hanging limp in the water. What was worse, they were twisted around each other several times. I looked at the ship's compass. We were pointing to the West – opposite from the trade wind direction! Something was seriously wrong, but I still did not catch on. There was nothing I could do in the darkness. Untangling this mess without daylight would have been very difficult.

So I went back to my bunk and slept again. But at the first gray light of day I got up and went on deck. The view of the sky was scary. It was completely covered by low, racing clouds, clearly the signs of an impending storm. Around the same time the regular weather report was due, and I tried my best to decipher the weak voice over the hissing of the background noise.

The message was unmistakable. "Hurricane Dean is expected to arrive at the central Virgin Islands around 10:00 this morning." Oh-oh – that was not good. Worse - it could be deadly. A green skipper on a boat with tangled anchor lines and a hurricane to arrive in a few hours is a bad situation. What a mess had I gotten us into! No wonder there were no boats to be seen yesterday. What a dumbo not to listen to the forecast for days on end in the middle of hurricane season!

But I calmed down soon enough and figured out a strategy to disentangle the twisted anchor rodes. It was easier than I had feared. The other good news was that we were only about 2 hours' sail away from the boat's home base in Fat Hog's bay on the main island of the group. We

Hurricanes

should be able to make it to the base before the arrival of the hurricane. How sudden is the storm onset, anyhow? By 07:00, we were free and clear, ready to sail, with the anchors neatly stowed and the Diesel humming smoothly.

The sky turned even more frightful. Low hanging, dark roll clouds dominated the view, portending the imminent arrival of a hurricane. But the wind was still very weak, and the wave height was normal for the sheltered Sir Francis Drake channel.

By 08:00, I started to relax – I knew we would make it in time to the base and then it would be someone else's problem to deal with the boat. That is one of the undeniable advantages of renting a bare boat – if the going gets tough and you make it to the base, you can hand over the keys to the charter company and your boat worries are over.

At 09:00 the radio brought surprising news: "During the last hour, Hurricane Dean has been making a sharp turn to the north and the brunt of the storm will bypass the Virgin Islands." No kidding – that was too good to be true. But a look at the sky confirmed the good news – it was definitely looking lighter towards the east and darker towards the north. The radio report was clearly correct. There were no major islands located to the north, for hundreds of miles and this hurricane did minimal damage to anyone on land.

By the way, the cloudless day was not a coincidence. First, I read some old accounts of hurricanes – including the history of the sinking of the RHONE in these waters in1867. They invariably start with a description of a beautiful, cloudless day and a barometer which is falling very quickly.
If you watch a satellite photo of any hurricane, you will see a ring of cloud free sky surrounding the hurricane itself. It looks as if the hurricane sucks in moisture, which normally condenses into the low hanging clouds. Ever since, I have

Hurricanes

always greeted a day with clouds in the sky with some relief (in the tropics).

Big Bertha

Our second major hurricane encounter while sailing was with Bertha, which hit the Virgin Islands on the sixth of July, 1996. It was a strong category III early season hurricane, with peak wind speeds of 135 mph. That's not enough to do major damage to an island, but it rips the leaves off most trees, leaving the islands dark and foreboding. But that lasts only a few days. Tropical plants regrow leaves very quickly, and soon the hills are covered with a delightful spring-green cover. Overall Bertha did about $270 Million damage, mostly in the US. But we are getting ahead of ourselves.

After the close encounter of the dumb and scary kind with hurricane Dean in 1989, I made it a habit to keep a keen weather eye out for hurricanes. An invaluable tool is a tiny shortwave radio made in Germany by Grundig. It is much smaller than a pack of cigarettes, but receives the six major short wave bands in addition to FM and AM. Two AA batteries power it forever. With its shortwave bands, it is always possible to receive stations such as the BBC, Voice of America, and Deutsche Welle. Many nights, lying alone in a tent on a mountain or sailing on the ocean, the presence of this tiny short wave radio gave me great comfort. The human world was still there, something easy to forget out when dealing with nature in the rough.

Thus, Hurricane Bertha did not sneak up on Karen and me. We were in the Leeward Islands, not far from St. Marten, and Bertha was spotted early. It went through the usual cycles – tropical wave, tropical depression, tropical storm and finally, with sustained winds exceeding 64 knots – it became a hurricane, category I.

Hurricanes

I watched it very suspiciously, because the first couple of eye position plots seemed to put it right on track to intercept our position. There were two choices now. One was to raise all sails and head south as quickly as possible. Hurricanes never go south of $12°$ northern latitude – they can't live near the equator. (There is a corresponding rule on the southern hemisphere). But I did not feel like embarking on a long voyage, which would span nearly the entire length of the arc of the eastern Caribbean islands. The boat was low on provisions and water at the time, and it interfered with the Scuba and video plans we had. In addition, the severe storm warning center in Miami kept assuring its listeners that Bertha would take a sharp turn to the north. Having been saved by just such a sharp turn of hurricane Dean seven years before, that possibility sounded credible.

But I wasn't going to bet our lives on it. The boat's original homeport was Nanny Cay in Tortola. While Nanny Cay is not a great hurricane hole – it is protected by high mountains from the north, but completely open to the south, it had good facilities to secure a boat. I knew the North/South base crew there well and trusted their advice. So we sailed quickly towards Nanny Cay.

In the meantime, the dots representing the hurricane positions kept accumulating – and they clustered on a perfectly straight line, pointing directly to our island group. This was in direct contradiction to the forecast from Miami. We kept heading for Nanny Cay and arrived a day before the hurricane. By now it was a borderline category III hurricane. We rounded the familiar breakwater of Nanny Cay and entered a zoo of boats.

We temporarily docked the boat and I rushed on shore to find the fleet manager for North South, Walt. He was busy supervising work, but advised us that the best strategy would be to create 'cradles' of boats. In a cradle, adjacent boats are connected with heavy nylon lines – 5/8" to 1" thick. The outermost boats in the cradle were tied to iron cleats mounted on the piers.

The pier system consisted of a long concrete walkway along the water line and numerous wooden finger piers jutting out perpendicular to the concrete pier. Cleats were mounted on both the concrete and the wooden piers. We joined a cradle of about eight boats between a pair of finger piers. The idea was that the whole mesh of boats would move more or less as one unit. Lines connecting the outer boats with the cleats were taking up the storm force and preventing the boats from colliding with the piers.

The marina staff and we skippers and crew worked furiously. All sails had to be taken down and the booms were tied to the deck. Bimini tops and anything else, which wasn't bolted down, had to be removed from the decks. We collected water, charged batteries and tried to secure more food and water – the marina was a beehive of activity. Walt offered Karen the option to ride out the storm in his apartment, while he was busy running around in the boat yard. He was very grateful when she accepted, because he knew that she was very dependable and would take good care of his apartment in the storm. Karen, having lived in Florida, St. Croix and New Jersey had lots of hurricane experience.

Finally there wasn't much left to do except to wait. It was still dark, around 06:00 when the hurricane arrived. The NOAA computers in Miami had been wrong, the straight edge ruler had been right. For someone who has been building supercomputers, but isn't very fond of any computer, I had rather mixed emotions about this.

The first bands of rain appeared just as daylight broke. Again, low hanging roll clouds covered the sky, looking grey and menacing. It would be a very long day. As the wind picked up, it became quickly apparent which lines did not carry their fair share of load and we all were running around again, jumping from boat to boat to help

Hurricanes

each other to redistribute the wind loads. It was a cold experience. Drenched by the driving rain and exposed to the strong winds, hypothermia was a real possibility. One can get very cold in a tropical storm! Many of us put on yellow rain slickers, but I had none. The palm trees were now bending so that their trunks were nearly horizontal. But they did not break – evolution had seen to that.

The hurricane was moving slowly – agonizingly slowly. During the entire morning the storm grew stronger. We heard over Tortola radio that the eye was aiming directly for us. The message was right. After an eternity, around noon, the wind and rain stopped suddenly. We had entered the eye. But there was no sunshine, just a high, light gray overcast. It was very quiet. Contrary to what I had heard, no birds were singing. It got very muggy – we were after all standing in a chimney, which funneled hot air into the upper atmosphere. Hurricanes are the heat engines, which power our global weather systems. We were all happy to get warm again, though.

It took an entire hour before the eye had passed over us. It was a big eye and the hurricane was moving at a moderate speed of 13 knots. We were worried about the backside of the hurricane, which is often worse than the front side. Actually, this is not a matter of chance, but mainly caused by the vector addition of the rotational wind speed to the forward motion of the storm. In any case, the backside WAS stronger – a lot stronger.

We had been worried about dry rot in the wood of the pier – and that worry was only too justified. Suddenly, with a sound like a canon firing, one of the cleats on a finger pier let go. It could not stand the tremendous load of several big boats tearing on it. Since the docking lines were all made from nylon, which stretches easily, they act like powerful springs. The cleat shot in the air like a cannon ball. Fortunately, it did not hit anything and couldn't fly very far, as it was still restrained by multiple lines tied to it.

Hurricanes

It just shot between two boats and ended up dangling in the water.

This was bad news – very bad news. Now the remaining cleats had to carry even more load and more might let go. This could trigger a chain reaction, where in the end more cleats might depart. This could lead to the loss of all the boats in our cradle. There was no choice but to brave the intense storm again – and the chance to be hit by a cleat turned into a cannon ball.

But we all knew that this was a job, which had to be done. In the howling wind and driving rain we tugged with all our strength on lines, re-cleated dock lines and did whatever we could to balance the loads. Obviously, it is impossible to tighten a line under heavy load, but we could release less tense lines and add more lines. In the meantime, we could hear the unmistakable sound of a few more cleats letting go, fortunately none in our local cradle. We lost only one more cleat, when the brittle old concrete of the main pier couldn't handle the load.

As it got dark, the worst of the storm was over. I borrowed a 4x4 Suzuki Samurai and made my way up to Walt's apartment to see how Karen had fared. The apartment was in good shape, except for water leaking under the windows. By about 20:00 the wind had died down, and we were ready to have a stiff drink, while waiting for Walt to come home. It turned out he did not come – too much cleanup work in the marina was waiting for him.

Overall, it had been a very successful fight. None of the boats in the water was lost or severely damaged. The only boat casualties were two yachts stored on dry land. They were knocked over. In both instances, the furling jib had not been removed and the wind had gotten under them, partially unrolling the sails. There was no way that a boat with an unfurled jib could stay upright in hurricane winds, sitting high on stilts.

Hurricanes

This interesting day had a rather weird ending. I still do not know what to make of it…

Walt's apartment was located high on a rocky knoll, overlooking the very shallow Seacow Bay west of Tortola. I happened to lean out the window and look down into the dark night. A large car drove slowly along the coastal road and stopped right below Walt's place. The coastal road was about 70' below us.

A lady in a flowing white dress left the car. She was ghostly visible in the pale moonlight now filtering through the thinning overcast. She appeared to be in some kind of distress, staggering noticeably. The door on the other side of the car opened and a man got out, also apparently well dressed. Maybe they had attended some kind of hurricane party? While I was still looking down, some argument ensued. It was impossible to make out details, but the lady turned away from the man and walked right into the ocean bay! It seemed that she was wearing high heeled shoes – not exactly the right kind of foot wear for walking on a reef.

The bay was extremely shallow here and so she walked some distance and still was only up to her knees in the water. At this point it was clear that something very serious and very strange was going on. I grabbed our boat's powerful 4D cell flashlight, which I had brought up to the house and directed the beam onto the lady. Her white dress reflected the light well.

The man, still on the shore, looked up and yelled at me: "Keep the light on her, keep the light on her!" Then he entered the water, too. I did my best to focus the beam, but she was making astonishingly good progress for someone who, by now, must have been walking barefoot. The man – and I could see now that he was indeed wearing a dark suit, was stumbling after her through the shallow bay. But he was not much faster than she was. I carefully

Hurricanes

optimized the focus of my flashlight and steadied it on the windowsill, using books which Karen had brought me.

We were dumb founded about what was going on below. "Try to call the police," I asked Karen. She tried, but there was no dial tone – not surprising right after a category III hurricane. "Walt must have a VHF marine radio here in his house," Karen said. She found one, and its battery was in good shape. We expected that the BVI police would listen to marine channel 16 – the distress and initial maritime call-up channel, and indeed, they did. I could not hear the actual conversation, which Karen carried on with the police department as I was too busy to still focus the light onto the ghostly outline of the lady below.

Her progress had stopped. She was now well over 300' from shore, and the water had gotten too deep to walk. If she was thinking about committing suicide, she seemed to have second thoughts now. Slowly the man caught up with her. They were too far away for us to see what was happening, but eventually they both returned together. As they were approaching the water's edge, the man yelled up at us, "Thank you, thank you, thank you!"

They both got into the car and drove away. But the strange experience was *still* not over. Tortola Radio AM was back on the air on 780 kHz, and we were tuned to it. An announcer with a smooth Caribbean accent was chatting, giving local news and playing cheerful steel drum tunes. He was rambling on about all kinds of things.

Suddenly he went off into a direction, which made us perk up. He was berating his listeners to behave decently and 'not embarrass the guests on our beautiful island and take it easy after a hurricane'. The longer he rambled on, the clearer it became that he was talking about the incidence, which Karen had reported to the BVI police. He appeared very upset that this couple did behave inappropriately in the aftermath of the hurricane experience.

Hurricanes

Well, we never heard anything more about it. We hypothesized that it was a lover's quarrel, amplified by the stress of this long lasting hurricane encounter. But we never found out anything more. But it had a happy ending – she lived another day. We were now quite sure that she had had suicide on her mind when she headed for the dark water in her evening gown.

I felt as if we had just experienced one of the Italian stories straight out of Guareschi's *Don Camillo and Peppone,* where young women walk into the river Po for matters of the heart as a matter of course.

Los Alamos (2ħ)

See also pages 170, 172,173,174

Los Alamos is world famous as the birthplace of the atomic bomb. Today it is the site of one of the premier research laboratories of the US Department of Energy. It is located 25 miles northwest of the beautiful old town of Santa Fe, New Mexico and perched at 7000' altitude on the side of an extinct volcano called *Jemez* mountain.

New Mexico is truly a state of enchantment, just as the state license plates claim. The crystal clear desert mountain air allows one to see forever, clear across the Rio Grande valley to the lonely Sangre de Christo (Blood of Christ) mountain range and south to the tall Sandia Crest of Albuquerque. The Spanish word Sandia means melon, and whoever observed a sunset in Albuquerque, with the sun painting the Sandia crest crimson red, will understand why the Spaniards picked this name.

The volcano on whose slope Los Alamos is located was estimated to be 30% higher than Mount Everest today. It blew up in an explosion – which completely outclassed Mt. St. Helen's explosion in 1980 – and left a caldera at an altitude of about 11,000 feet. The caldera is so large (180 square miles) that it doesn't look very impressive, rather more like a common mountain valley. Whenever I am flying to Los Alamos from Santa Fe, I'm trying to visualize the sight as it once was, 14 Million years ago.. It is befitting that Los Alamos should be located on the site of an ancient explosion of immense scale.

I had a scary winter driving experience along the rim of that caldera. I had just arrived, alone, by rental car from Santa Fe and decided to take a spin along the road circling the crater before checking into the Hilltop House hotel. It was early winter and there was no snow on the

Los Alamos

ground. Thus I had no concerns driving this high altitude road with a rental car – a crappy Ford Pinto- which had no snow chains or M&S tires. But mountain weather can change very quickly, even in benign New Mexico.

While I was driving along the rim, with the road winding up and down the various clefts in the caldera, the sky suddenly darkened and snow began to fall in massive quantities. Soon the road was completely covered with deep fresh snow. It seemed like a prudent move to turn around while there was still time – but it was already too late.

The rim road was steeply descending along a long, straight line on the outside of the caldera. The car, equipped with summer tires, could not be stopped. It just kept sliding downhill, and my best efforts in steering and braking only achieved that the car did not pick up more speed and stayed on the road. The Pinto moved slowly, at 5-10 mph and I was seriously considering abandoning the car by opening a door and jumping out. This seemed quite preferable to the alternative of tumbling down the steep side of the mountain - if I lost lateral control- and getting killed in a pile of cold, hard steel.

What kept me from taking the plunge was my fancy new Ricoh SLR camera lying on the passenger seat. Well, I kept the car on the road. Eventually the road made a gentle left turn and started climbing again. The car came to a stop at the lowest point between the two grades. There I was stuck. No attempt in getting the car up either side succeeded.

The situation wasn't too good. It was getting dark, nobody knew where I was and I had not seen another car for hours - and the snow was falling heavily. This was long before everyone carried cell phones. They tend to be useless in emergencies far away from civilization in any case. Visions of carbon monoxide poisoning and slowly dying of hypothermia danced in my head.

Los Alamos

But fortunately, a heavy General Motors 4WD SUV happened to pass by within an hour. It was equipped with studded M&S tires and the driver was more than happy to tow me up the grade, back towards Los Alamos. We successfully got the little Ford Pinto up to the road's highest point and I had no more difficulties to make it back to Los Alamos.

It was my first experience with a phenomenon, which repeated itself in years to come: dangerous experiences often occur on harmless little outings. One doesn't take little trips seriously, and bad things can happen when one least expects them. The surprise ending of the great old movie "Wages of Fear" makes a case in point.

The recent (2007) disappearances of both Steve Fossett and Dr. Jim Gray also demonstrate the truth of this observation. Steve Fossett, a world-renowned adventurer, disappeared on an apparently harmless little flight while looking over local Nevada salt lakes for racing purposes.

Jim Gray, an experienced sailor and world famous computer scientist –whom I knew well- disappeared on an easy solo Sunday sail from the Golden Gate bridge of San Francisco to the Farallon Islands[7]. These are only 27 miles off-shore from the Golden Gate. So far, no trace of either man has been found. I participated in the search for Jim Gray by flying along the shores north and south of the Golden Gate, looking for his distinctive red-hulled 40' C&C sailboat, but without seeing anything. His many friends in Silicon Valley and Microsoft helped in this big search effort, but to no avail. We may never know what happened to him, because the undersea topology between the Golden Gate and the Farallons is very rough, whereas I am sure that Steve Fossett's plane will be found eventually, probably by some hikers.

---

[7] 'Devil's Teeth' by Susan Casey is a fascinating book about the Farallons and their resident white sharks.

Los Alamos

Back to Los Alamos and the Jemez mountain. Plentiful water from snow melt supports a rich Western mountain forest with coniferous trees and green mountain meadows. It also carved deep canyons into the soft tuft stone making up the mountain slopes, thus cleaving the area of the town of Los Alamos into several distinct mesas.

This natural isolation was very convenient when Los Alamos was converted by Dr. Robert Oppenheimer at the beginning of World War II from a school for boys into a nuclear lab. One mesa is dedicated to downtown and civilian affairs, whereas others host the various LANL lab divisions.

One mesa is dedicated to the Clinton P. Anderson Meson Physics Facility (LAMPF) – a very large accelerator specializing in producing intense and exotic beams, such as muons. Today it is mostly used as a powerful neutron source in the nuclear weapons stewardship program and for other applications.

When I worked there, only 45% percent of the Lab's budget was atomic weapons related. There was ample opportunity to do pure research in Los Alamos, for which no special security clearance was required. The times spent at LAMPF, as a visiting scientist from Rochester, was among the most enjoyable of this period of my life.

Just arriving in the old airport of Albuquerque was a treat. Unlike the hectic airports on either coast, there is a peaceful, nearly serene atmosphere at ABQ. Indian artwork decorates the walls, and the floor was beautifully tiled. This was before the time when everyone used wheeled luggage and tiles were not a problem. A Twin Otter turboprop plane operated for the Los Alamos National Lab whisked lab visitors to the mountain airstrip of Los Alamos.

As it flew along the Rio Grande valley, the top of the Sandia Crest was about level to your right, the beautiful city of Santa Fe ahead and soon – too soon – the Twin

Los Alamos

Otter descended into the airport of Los Alamos. That is like landing on an aircraft carrier. The runway is built on a mesa, and is authorized only for one-way use. One must land towards the Jemez mountain, and take off in the opposite direction. It would be impossible to launch towards the mountain, as it rises too steeply for most civilian airplanes. They cannot out-climb the raising terrain. The Canadian Twin Otter is the ideal plane for this kind of mountain flying.

Research

Wolf-Udo and I often stayed at the Hill Top House hotel. For years, while Los Alamos was still a forbidden city, it had been its only hotel. It was old and carried a fascinating aura of the early history of the atomic age in the forms of pictures, worn out easy chairs, legends ('this was Dr. Oppenheimer's favorite stuffed chair') and old newspapers.

We did our experiments at the LAMPF Meson facility, located on the adjacent mesa. LAMPF already was an impressive machine, nearly 1 km long, capable of accelerating 1 mA[8] of protons to an energy of 800 Million electron Volts and consuming Megawatts of electrical energy in the process. One mA doesn't sound like much – a small flashlight bulb uses about 300 mA. But power is the product of current and voltage.

This was serious business – a far cry from the relatively feeble accelerators of the Frankfurt or Rochester Universities. The LAMPF beam carried 0.8 Megawatts of energy along, an incredibly intense bundle of focused proton radiation. It could melt anything in seconds. LAMPF's intense beam wasn't used directly. Rather, it hit

---

[8] 1 mA = 0.001 Ampere (unit of electrical current)

Los Alamos

several auxiliary 'production targets', where it created big quantities of exotic particles, like pions and muons. These were collected and formed into secondary beams. The actual experiments were using these secondary beams. Only a couple of facilities in the world (our main competitor was Dubna, USSR) had comparable facilities.

Since nothing can stand up to this beam for any length of time, the production targets were rapidly rotating spinning disks of graphite, which has an extremely high melting point. Since the beam had a diameter of only 1-2 mm, the quick rotation of the target disks did not give the beam enough time to melt a hole into it. Still, the disks were glowing red hot, with a fiery circular trail marking the beam impact. This could only be seen via radiation-hardened video cameras, since the vicinity of each production target was a hellhole of intense radiation. Any work there was done by a huge rolling robot, built around the landing gear of a B52 bomber. LAMPF is a case where turning the accelerator off does not stop radiation.

There were several production targets along the beam line, each producing two secondary beams. After the primary beam had penetrated the last production target, it still carried a lot of its energy. The spent beam was directed into a steel walled and water-filled pool. This was the beam dump. Since nearly 800 kW of power (0.8 MW) were dumped into this pool, the water heated up rapidly and had to be cooled continuously. And therein lies a story…

It was in the wee hours of the morning – as always. Our experiment was going well, all our electronics and detectors worked smoothly and the data were trickling in fine. Udo and our graduate student Bill Johnson had gone to sleep. I was alone in the counting hut, half asleep myself, just barely enough awake to notice if anything blew up.

At some point I went to the men's room, where I noticed some water on the floor. That is not unusual in a

Los Alamos

restroom, and I did not think much about it. A couple of hours later I went again. Now there was a lot more water on the floor. Well, maybe I should notify facilities of the leak. So I called the control room of the big accelerator, which was nearly half a mile upstream, told them about the water puddle and hung up. About 15 minutes later, back in the counting hut, the phone rang.

"You are the guy who reported the water in the men's room at experimental area E?"

"Yes, what's up?"

"Did you step into the water?" asked the voice at the other end of the line, quite concerned. I did not like the tone of the question.

"No, why?"

"Good. The water is rather radioactive. We have a leak in the beam dump, and the water is from the pool!"

Oh no, I thought. That's all we need. Now they need to shut down the accelerator, just when our experiment is going so well.

What else should I have been concerned about?

It did not take long before the sleepy lab turned into a beehive. In no time the experimental area was surrounded with official looking grey government Chrysler cars and trucks. Excited health physicists and security types were milling about. A lot of people had gotten an early wake-up call, but I must say I was impressed with the speed and scope of action. Slowly it got bright enough to see the parking lot outside.

An entire network of little rivulets of water had spread out over the parking lot. Fortunately, our car was parked in a dry spot. There was a lot more (radioactive) water there than I thought initially. The accelerator had been shut down, of course, and at least no new radioactive water was being produced. We secured our experiment,

Los Alamos

turned off pumps and high voltage power supplies, watched, and waited.

A couple of hours later, the health physics team had concluded to do nothing. The radioactive water was contaminated only with short half-life activity, and the decision was to let the water run down into the next (uninhabited) canyon. The activity would die out over the next couple of days and do no harm whatsoever. When it was established that our car could leave the parking lot without crossing any of the hot rivulets, we were free to go and get a good day's sleep. That's truly a treasured rarity during an experiment…

This is a good point to clarify the relationship between half-life and activity. Most people think that radioactive stuff with long half-life is very dangerous. The opposite is true for the person actually handling the material. Long half-life means that in any second only a small number of nuclei decay, leading to a *low* rate of radiation activity. Conversely, short half-lives mean high radioactivity. I hate working with Tritium, the super-heavy version of hydrogen. Its half-life is 14 years, it is a gas and it decays with a very soft kind of beta radiation. Soft means that the beta radiation is not energetic; it cannot even penetrate the thin membrane of a normal Geiger counter tube. Thus it goes easily undetected. But its radiation is very intense because of the short half-life and it is energetic enough to destroy lung tissue – and as a gas, it can easily get there. I'd work with Plutonium any day, compared to Tritium. Fortunately, it can be easily alloyed with metals and is mostly used in this form, for example for hydrogen 'gadgets' and future fusion reactors.

The theme of our experiments in Los Alamos was the interaction of muons with very heavy, radioactive elements, such as uranium, plutonium and even heavier elements. Muons are the heavy cousins of ordinary electrons. They are 207 times heavier, but have otherwise identical properties. Thus they 'orbit' a nucleus just like an electron will, but their orbital radius is 1/207 of the equivalent electronic orbit.

Atoms obey strict quantum mechanical rules, which govern how many electrons are allowed in a given orbit. It's a bit as if there were railroad tracks around a nucleus and only a certain number of trains (electrons) are allowed on each track. Many electrons can share a track way out in the large diameter orbits, far away from the nucleus, but only a couple on the tight orbits close to the nucleus. (Chemistry is the science of the details of these orbital rules and their complex consequences).

A muon doesn't compete with the electrons for available orbits. It has its own tracks, 207 times tighter than the corresponding electron tracks. Any electron or muon 'desires' to settle in the lowest, most stable orbit. A muon, which is the only one of its kind in a man-made muonic atom, has the complete freedom to do so.

A muon injected into an atom is like a comet entering the solar system from interstellar space. It will quickly drop from orbit to orbit until it finally settles into the tightest orbit possible. Since plutonium nuclei are very heavy and therefore of large diameter[9] (in terms of the subatomic world), and muon orbits are of small diameter, this most desirable orbit is actually *inside* a plutonium nucleus. See Sketch on page 172.

I'm using here a very classical, non-quantum mechanical language. Actually, the muon's position is described by a probability cloud around the nucleus, which peaks at the radius of the classical orbit.

But in any case, the muon spends a lot of time inside the nucleus. This is a weird concept, which can only

---

[9] The radius of a Plutonium nucleus is about 8 fm or 8×10^{-15} m, which is about ten-thousand times smaller than that of the Plutonium atom.

Los Alamos

make real sense in a quantum world. A classical analogy is a group of elephants, which are mutually attracted and stay close together, nearly touching. The elephants correspond to the protons and neutrons forming a nucleus. The muon is like a mouse running around among the elephants.

Eventually, the muon and its host nucleus will take notice of each other, and the results are not good for either – the muon will be destroyed and the nucleus will break apart.

We used this amazing richness of muon/nucleus interactions to do the very first measurement of the speed (or duration) of nuclear fission. Since fission was discovered in 1938 by Otto Hahn and Lisa Meitner in Berlin, people envisioned it to be similar to the breaking apart of a water drop into two smaller droplets. This model, refined quantitatively as the 'nuclear liquid drop' model has been very successful to explain some aspects of the fission process.

But still, in the early eighties, over 40 years after the discovery of nuclear fission, nobody knew how long it actually took a nucleus to fission. We set ourselves the goal to measure this time by using the injection of a muon into a very heavy atom, such as plutonium 239, as the trigger to fission the nucleus.

The concepts behind this experiment are a bit complicated, but let me try to explain.

When a muon descends through the succession of orbits after its capture by the atom (not the nucleus), these successive jumps release energy. It is like a stone rolling into a crater, releasing energy as it descends. This is the same process which causes ordinary light emission, but muons, being so heavy, release 207 more energy for each jump than an electron. The first jumps are small, releasing little energy, but the jumps get larger and larger. It is like descending a latter where the top rungs are millimeters apart, and the lowest ones are meters apart.

The last jump, leading to the final muonic ground state, is huge and releases an energy packet of approximately 6 MeV. In most cases, these 6 MeV escape harmlessly –for the nucleus- as a gamma ray photon into free space and the muon settles peacefully into its final orbit inside the nucleus. It will spend a nuclear eternity there -about 100 nano-seconds- before it interacts with the plutonium nucleus and blows it up. We do not care about this case. But sometimes the nucleus happens to absorb the powerful 6 MeV photon. That is just enough of an impact to kick the nucleus over the 'fission barrier' and it will break into two pieces – i.e. fission – right away.

In this case, what is the fate of the muon? It could get kicked out of the fissioning system – after creating all this havoc that would be its well-deserved fate – or it may be captured by one of the two smaller nuclei (called fission fragments) created by the breakup of the plutonium nucleus. The fission fragments are not created equal. One contains about 90-100 nucleons[10] and the other about 130-140 nucleons. This adds up to the 239 nucleons of the original plutonium nucleus, except for a few neutrons which escape in the fission.

The muon's probability to be captured by either the heavier or the lighter fission fragment depends on the ratio of the 'speed' of the orbiting nucleus and the speed at which the fission process proceeds. Let me make up an analogy to make this plausible.

Imagine a hobo is waiting to jump upon a freight train. One train heads for sunny California, and he would like to travel there. The other one heads for snowy Chicago, and he'd rather not board that one. Both trains are passing

---

[10] Nucleon is the common term for both protons and neutrons, which constitute nuclei. Protons are positively charged, neutrons have no charge and act as glue, keeping the nucleus from disintegrating.

him at the same time on two equally accessible tracks. But the California train is moving much faster! His choice clearly will depend how fast he can run, relative to the trains. If he can run as fast as the California train travels, he will pick that one. If not, he has to use the Chicago bound train.

If is known how fast hobos can run, we can deduce the speed of the trains. If many hobos would do this, then, by counting how many end up in Chicago and how many in California, one can quite precisely determine the speed of the trains. Well, equate the hobo with the muon and the freight trains with the two fission fragments, and then you have the basic idea of the experiment.

The actual analysis involves some very highbrow mathematics, since it requires solving the relativistic Dirac equation for the muon in a time-dependent field. The latter is the electric potential well created by the separating nuclei. Fortunately we had a theoretical physicist as collaborator, who delighted in solving this kind of heavy-duty mathematics. Another collaborator was Dr. John Browne, who became the director of Los Alamos in 1997. He was a great guy to work with - knowledgeable, humorous and completely unflappable.

To do the experiment, we had to build a fission chamber. This was a stack of isolated titanium foils, coated with plutonium 239 and mounted inside a gas cell. Alternating foils were connected to a high voltage source. Fission products would ionize the gas and this could be detected as external pulses.

We exposed this fission chamber to one of the secondary muon beams. The muons had to be slowed down to the speed of an airplane to give them a good chance of being captured in the plutonium. A group of gamma ray counters and other detectors allowed us to observe the chain of events – from muon capture to the fission event to

Los Alamos

the eventual demise of the muon bound to one of the fission fragments. The lifetime of the muon is much longer when bound to the lighter fission fragment than for the other case. This allowed us to determine which fission fragment it rode along with. As you can see, this experiment relied on an entire chains of nuclear events.

The results were very clear. It takes about 10^{-16} seconds for a plutonium nucleus to fission. Compare this 'long' time with the later story (starting on page 123) about strongly damped reactions. These take only 10^{-21} to 10^{-23} seconds to complete. In other words, nuclear fission is slow as molasses – about a million times slower – compared to the fastest nuclear reactions we know. Yet it is a million times faster than the clock period of a computer we may be able to build in 2015. Nuclear computers, anyone?

Dealing with weapons-grade[11] plutonium 239 was interesting. Our biggest plutonium target weighted much less than the critical mass of a nuclear device, which is a few kilograms. Yet so many plutonium nuclei were decaying in this chunk of heavy metal that it was very hot to the touch. Any Geiger counter in its vicinity went berserk, and it was wise to not dawdle while inserting the hot thing into the experiment. Still, like many other nuclear physicists, I seem to be healthy as a horse, except from some radiation damage of my corneas. That goes with the territory.

---

[11] Weapons-grade plutonium-239 may contain at most 7% plutonium-240. The latter is undesirable in a nuclear gadgets as it leads to premature ignition or a 'fizzle'.

Los Alamos

HAL Computer Systems (ℏ)

See also page 175

In the summer of 1990, I was managing a 55 person organization at IBM Research, which was working on the creation of scalable supercomputers based on the "message-passing" model. Later on, this research would lead to the creation of the very profitable line of IBM SP supercomputers. But that is not the point of this story.

Most of the staff worked in Yorktown, NY, but some lived in other states. One of them was an old friend, Dr. Bob Montoye, who had moved to Austin,TX.

Bob is one of the brightest guys I know. He is responsible for the innovative Multiply-Add floating-point unit, which was the key for achieving the outstanding performance of the IBM RS 6000 processor. When it came on the market, it was much faster than its competition, such as the workstations sold by SUN, MIPS and Intel.

But like many computer geniuses, Bob wasn't fond of paperwork. He traveled a lot, but he hated to fill out his travel expense accounts. Then, one day, Bob came to visit me in Yorktown. I thought it was just a routine trip, to discuss his work, but he walked into my office with a stack of completed expense account forms under his arm. He stated that he would submit all 26 missing expense reports now! I looked at him, I looked at the stack he carried and looked at him again.

"So, Bob, you are quitting IBM?" Bob's face got pale.
"Who told you?" he asked.
"Nobody did. But remember, we have known each other for quite some time."

That was true; we had shared a messy office when we both joined IBM. We both contributed to the mess, although not quite equally.

HAL Computer

"There is just no way you'd fill out all these forms without a terribly good reason, such as you are about to leave and do not want to loose all this money. Now close the door, sit down and tell me. It won't go beyond these four walls."

Bob calmed down quickly and told me the story. My hunch was correct. A young IBM Fellow – Andy Heller – who had been the father and driver behind the RS 6000 – had decided to leave IBM and start his own company. We'll not discuss the reasons behind it.

Bob knew Andy well, whereas I knew him mostly from hearsay. Andy was very bright, the youngest IBM Fellow ever. That was a big deal. He had started in IBM as a machine operator and quickly worked his way up to the point where he was now heading the RS 6000 development.

I was stunned and intrigued. The new company was called HAL. Everyone thought that the name was a play on the computer HAL in *2001 - A Space Odyssey*, but the real story behind the name was different and is still a bit secretive. It was also the reason that the proper spelling was HaL rather than HAL, but few people ever used it.

I soon thought about going to HaL, too. First, it was finally a chance to move to California. Second, I always thought about participating in a startup and thirdly, there were some upcoming organizational changes in IBM, which I did not care for. Last but not least, I smelled big trouble for IBM in the years ahead. That turned out to be very true – in 1993, IBM nearly collapsed.

The SP supercomputer project was well on its way and it seemed like a good time to move on. Karen and I discussed it over a long lunch in an airport café. At this lunch, we decided to give it a go. She was very nervous about moving away from the East Coast, to what she perceived to be a crowded Silicon Valley. But Karen also knew how much it meant to me to move to California and she agreed. A few days later I called Bob and Andy, and they invited me to visit HAL in Campbell, near San Jose.

HAL Computer

The company had already acquired a 55,000 sqft lease in one of the non-descript light industrial buildings, which dot Silicon Valley. Since there were hardly any people there yet, nearly all the space was empty. Andy – in his rather grandiose style – described a vision for a company, which would build UNIX-based commercial enterprise systems. It had nothing to do with neural networks as the name HAL might imply. This was rather disappointing to me, but I decided to go for it anyhow. But I always had some misgivings how good Andy's vision was.

In the next few years, we did not announce what we were doing and thus a lot of speculation ensued that we were building a completely new, brain-like computer. When the truth was finally known, Silicon Valley yawned.

But I was very impressed with the caliber of the small group of people already there. Other than Andy and Bob, I was particularly impressed with Fred Buelow, VP of Engineering. Fred had a very long, distinguished career in the valley. He had originally worked for IBM, then joined Amdahl in its very early days and contributed greatly to its success. Later he founded or participated in a succession of startups. He lived in the town of Los Altos Hills, which is one of the most prestigious towns in America, populated with Silicon Valley executives. Fred and I became friends, leading to a friendship, which lasts to the very day. When I have difficult decisions to make, I still ask Fred for advice.

Other great people who joined were Stephen Goldstein, who headed the performance group, Myke Smith, a tower of strength, Dr. Wolf Weber, fresh from Stanford and Pat Helland, now a very senior guru at Microsoft. The important concept of Service Oriented Architecture (SOA) was largely Pat's brainchild. Wolf is now at Google and partner in our sailplane. Both were key architects for major parts of the new HAL machines.

HAL Computer

I flew back to NY and, after a discussion with Karen, called Andy back, and said that I'd like to join as Director of Architecture. We quickly agreed on the details and I moved out to California.

For the move, I had bought a brand-new, fire-engine red Ford Ranger. It turned out to have a bad roof leak, which was eventually repaired on warranty, but made for a wet trip to California. We loaded my stuff on the truck, while Karen stayed behind with the mission to sell our NY house. Another old friend, Gary Hoffman, offered to accompany me on the trip. Thus the two of us set out, with cooking pot and rifle, to head west. The picks and shovels were missing, but we felt a very strong kinship to the prospectors of old.

It was a great trip – the only time I've driven across the entire USA. Gary eventually went on to found his own company, Skipstone, in Austin. Today he lives in Silicon Valley, too, and we often meet.

Bob Montoye and his girlfriend had rented a fancy house in the expensive town of Los Gatos south of San Jose. It was up on a knoll, overlooking the southern end of the valley. I sublet a one-room guesthouse, next to a nice swimming pool. One might say that I jumped into the California lifestyle with both feet.

Karen soon visited and started house hunting. She had been worried about finding something suitable, but soon came up with a wonderful place. It was a relatively affordable town house in the nice San Jose suburb of Almaden, 550' above sea level. The house had a great view north over the valley and, best of all, it bordered a county park, which was crowded with animals.

Among these was a healthy population of wild pigs. One of these caused both of us to climb into a tree during one evening walk. This leads to another story (page 243). Karen was in heaven, as she had not expected to be so close to nature in Silicon Valley. A very cocky cockatiel, JoJo

HAL Computer

adopted us at an airport and became our pet. Actually, it was the other way around. He certainly thought so. Jojo is around in 2008, with Wolf and Veronique and still crazy.

ISA

I was only a few weeks in HAL, when a huge issue came to a head. What would be the instruction set architecture (ISA) of the computer we were going to build? The ISA is the logical face of the machine. It defines what the programmers see and it is the true soul of a machine.

Famous examples of ISA are the IBM 360/370, the Intel 86, the IBM PowerPC, MIPS and the SUN SPARC. We all agreed that HAL would build a 64-bit machine. All the architectures listed above are 32-bit architectures and we knew that in a few years the world would need the power to deal with very large data sets. For this, 64-bit addressing would be needed. More bits do not make a computer run faster per-se, but it allows it to handle vastly larger sets of data.

The big question was – which architecture should we use as the basis of our machine? Hal's founder, Andy, was pushing for creating an entirely new architecture, consistent with his aggressive style. As head of architecture, I had the nominal responsibility for the decision, but it was also clear that this was a decision of such fundamental importance to the future of the company that everyone would feel entitled to his vocal opinions.

The final decision would be made by Andy. This was not so much a technical decision – even though it masqueraded as such – but more driven by business issues, techno-religion, ego, marketing, alliances etc. A computer architect needs to be as much a diplomat as a technologist, because architecture is at the intersection of many –usually conflicting- interests within a computer company. Science is about knowing. Engineering is all about compromise.

HAL Computer

A wrong choice of the ISA would be deadly. Today, 17 years later, the ISA question is not so critical anymore because Intel's x86 (in its 32 and 64-bit variants) has won the battle for the most widely used general purpose ISA. But in 1991, people screamed at each other about this subject. It is noteworthy that of all the major architectures, the x86 is the most convoluted and ugly one. Hardly anyone - least of all the engineers in Intel who have to implement it - would disagree with this statement. I once cynically observed speaking on a conference panel that *the commercial success of an architecture is inversely proportional to its elegance.* All the architectures listed above follow my rule.

At this time it was becoming increasingly clear that Fujitsu would be our main funding source and partner. Fujitsu already worked with SUN, and therefore SPARC would be a natural choice for HAL. It had some clear business advantages – IBM couldn't well sue HAL for appropriating RS 6000 architectural ideas if we based the company on SPARC. Fujitsu would be happy and there would be a large installed user and software base. On the other hand, Andy and some other people in the company really, really wanted us to do our own ISA.

The more I looked into the subject, the more I thought that the right answer was to base it on SPARC, but modify it so that it became a 64-bit architecture. Moreover, we would have to do it in such a way that existing 32-bit programs could run on the new machines. Seasoned veterans like Fred Buelow and the president of HAL, Phil Dauber, shared this view.

But there was the counter argument that SPARC was a rather ugly version of the RISC family of architectures and therefore all SPARC machines would be slow. In particular, SPARC had a construct called register window. I do not want to explain the details, but it had to do with a clever way to transfer 'arguments' between

HAL Computer

programs. It was one of these inventions, which were too clever for their own good. They work great for a PhD thesis, but not so well in real life. But SPARC was stuck with register windows.

I launched a cross-company taskforce, with representatives from Fujitsu, SUN (Dave Ditzel), ICL, LSI Logic, Ross, Amdahl and HAL participating. Our task was to determine once and for all how much performance loss a 64-bit SPARC-based machine would incur, compared to a clean 64-bit design. We worked day and night for a week. By the end we had the result and it surprised quite a few people. There was less than a 7% performance loss!

With this result, the debate was over. We would create a 64-bit version of the SPARC architecture. The taskforce morphed into an architecture working group, now headed by Dave Ditzel from SUN. Over a period of about two years we hammered out the myriad details, which are required to define an entire architecture. It was a sometimes contentious, but overall very productive collaboration between several companies.

The main work, split about equally, was done by the HAL and SUN team members. Our work was published as the SPARC V9 Architecture Manual[12], with David Weaver and Tom Germond as editors. Within HAL, Joel Boney quietly did the lion share of the technical architecture work. My personal contribution to this work was more as a diplomat than as a technologist. Creating a new architecture is a very contentious process. Billions of dollars were at stake - as well as egos of the architects. The latter is the much bigger problem.

The many systems based on the SPARC V9 architecture were a huge success. By the late nineties, all machines sold by SUN and Fujitsu/HAL used V9. The total revenue of all SPARC V9 based systems sold to date is in the order of

---

[12] **ISBN:** 9780130992277

HAL Computer

100 Billion dollars. In hindsight, it seemed incredible that this project could lead to this level of revenue. It seemed often like an abstract exercise among squabbling architects, even though I knew intellectually that the stakes were huge.

In retrospect, the endless and heated sessions with SUN, Amdahl, Fujitsu etc. were important. They assured that nothing fell between the cracks, and we created a stable, well-balanced architecture. The famous slogan by SUN – *we are the dot in dot-com* – was based on the SPARC V9 systems.

Dave Ditzel later left SUN to found Transmeta Inc, but switched into the x86 camp. We are now neighbors, which is a coincidence. Silicon Valley is a small world.
I don't want to create the impression that the architecture is everything. There is a huge step from having an architecture – which is basically a book and perhaps a software simulator – to building a real machine. This takes the hard work of countless engineers and a lot of investment. The ISA architecture defines an interface – the interface that software sees. How this architecture is implemented in silicon is called micro-architecture. Micro-architecture is not directly visible to software, but it determines the speed of the machine, its cost, energy consumption and other parameters, which are big factors in the commercial success of a computer.

The right ISA will get you into the door. The micro architecture will decide if you make a sale. Two machines with the same architecture, but different micro architectures will run, by definition, the same software. If they do not, something got screwed up. It happens sometimes.
While HAL and SUN were partners in creating the SPARC V9 architecture, we parted our ways when it came to creating the micro architecture and building the actual machines. Now we would be competitors. In the end, SUN did a better job, I think. Their *Ultrasparc* machines were slightly slower, but more elegant.

HAL Computer

Building a machine with a new architecture from
scratch means creating highly complex integrated circuits.
This is similar to what Intel does and it takes many
hundreds of millions of dollars to do so. This was too much
money to raise from venture capitalists. Given the initial
positive contacts with Fujitsu, it was natural to turn to them
for funding and partnership.

I remember very well that first meeting with the
president of Fujitsu, Sekizawa-san.[13] It was not the first
meeting between HAL and Fujitsu, but it was the first one I
participated in. I vividly remember a few highlights.

Sekizawa-san said literally: "We are good at getting
the details right, but we need you American cowboys for
truly new ideas."
Over the years, I worked closely with Japanese engineers
and made many friends in Japan. The stereotypes are not
untrue. The Japanese engineers are very good in making
sure that things really work, and countless times they came
to members of the architecture team with an apparently
innocent question, which invariably started with
"Wilcke-san (or whoever was on the hot seat) – can you
please explain…."
You could bet that there was something, which we had
overlooked! On the other hand, our Japanese friends were
far less willing to stick their necks out and propose
something crazy. That's the area where Californians
excelled. I think that a good collaboration between
American and Japanese engineering teams is a very
powerful partnership and wish it were more common.

There was another funny moment in this meeting,
which I remember very fondly. My German accent is
strong – think Dr. Strangelove - and it hasn't diminished
over the years. Hence my American friends were very
skeptical that Sekizawa-san and the other Japanese would

---

[13] The suffix –san attached to a name expresses respect.

HAL Computer

be able to understand me at all. However, in the middle of an intense discussion, Sekizawa-san suddenly turned to me and said

"Wilcke-san, I can understand you well, but have a difficult time with many of your colleagues!"

My colleagues were stunned, but I wasn't. The way Japanese and Germans pronounce syllables – except the ones, which contain an R – seems to be quite similar.

However, in spite of a promising start, things were not going smoothly for HAL. We had a rough culture, which was an expression of the founder's cowboy attitude. We had many jokes, which played on the phonetic similarity between HAL and HELL, and declared that the company colors were blue and black.

Nevertheless, in spite of his rough language and frequent outbursts, Andy deeply cared about his people. His real problem was that he was given to extreme micro-management, and that got us into deep trouble quickly. He saw himself as the real decision maker in all but the most trivial technical decisions. This delayed progress and, given his and mine and Pat's natural tendencies to make things architecturally *clever*, we introduced needless complexity and delay into the design process. Now I know that complexity is the ultimate enemy which the IT industry has to fear. I see little progress there, but maybe there is hope. I just (2008) came from an IBM Research strategy meeting, and at least the problem was acknowledged.

Because of complexity, the delivery of the multiple chips, which constituted the central processing unit of the HAL machines, got delayed. Andy had set the goal to build our machine in two years. It took five. In hindsight, five years is about as good as it gets when one creates a new company and architecture, designs several complex chips and builds software and systems for it. But it did not feel this way when we were living it.

HAL Computer

One year, we gave, as a joke, a coffee mug to each HAL employee. It said 'Tapeout 1992' on the outside. Tapeout is a key milestone in building a chip. But when you filled the mug with hot coffee or tea, the 1992 changed into 1993 and then 1994! It was good for a great laugh each time someone saw this gag.

The delays and frictions within the team made for rough going around 1993. It was clear that we had to forgo our dreams of an IPO and we had to discuss with our sugar daddy Fujitsu an acquisition. Fujitsu, as always, was good to deal with. In the sales agreement a very fair valuation for HAL was reached. I can't say enough good things about Fujitsu, based on my experience in HAL. They have been patient, honest, straightforward and generous to a sometimes arrogant and cantankerous partner (us).

Part of the condition for the sale of HAL was that we had to agree to golden handcuffs. The team had to stay on for two years to reap the full financial benefits of the buyout. I eventually became CTO, but still decided to leave in 1996 and go sailing in the Caribbean, very soon after the golden cuffs were off.

Production

HAL delivered the first systems to Fujitsu for sale in Japan in 1995. For a long time I treasured owning one of the first HAL workstations. Even in the year 2000, it was a quite fast machine. We had done many things well. But Fujitsu never had the gumption to sell HAL machines in the USA and therefore compete with SUN on their home turf. Rather, they sold them only in Asia, under the HAL/Fujitsu label. This was very disappointing for the US team. It feels a lot better when the product you are working on is well-known among your peers, rather than appearing only as an abstract set of sales in Asia. To be honest, I never saw the actual sales numbers, since I was sailing the Caribbean by then.

Eventually, during the rough times of the internet bubble bursting in the year 2000, Fujitsu decided to dissolve HAL as an independent company and integrate it into the parent company. Many HAL engineers became Fujitsu employees. Later in the decade (in 2006), when SUN's fortunes had turned for the worse, SUN licensed the Fujitsu/HAL machines – now in their fifth iteration and is now selling these as their top end machines! That surely is an ironic twist of fate, made even more amusing by the fact that the SUN VP who initiated this deal was applying for a job as CEO of the IBM IceCube spinout which I had launched in 2006. But that spinout makes for another story (in Random Walk Volume 2, if I ever write it).

Nowadays I'm watching this all from a distance. Yet I am still quite fond of Andy, the great team in HAL and his crazy band of American cowboys.

What have I learned from this experience?

First, startups can be exhilarating and fun. They can be financially rewarding even if they do not become household names, at least for the early participants.

Second, complexity is the ultimate enemy of computer design. Any semi-idiot can design a complex computer, but it takes real brilliance to design something simple, which still does the job.

Third, treat a startup as a marathon, not a sprint. Engineering always take much longer than planned, and it is important that the team will not burn out.

Fourth, do not fight yesterday's battle. HAL was patterned too much like an old-fashioned big IBM systems project. In IBM, this project would have required many thousands of employees. I think we pulled it off surprisingly well with only 400+ employees, but a focus on something simpler would have produced a better return on investment.

HAL Computer

Computer Design (2ℏ)

See also page 176

If you took any kind of science class, you may have learned about the three basic computer logic functions – AND, OR and NOT. They are usually explained with switches and light bulbs. For example, one can put two switches *in sequence*, so that switch 1 AND switch 2 have to be turned on before the light bulb will light up. Alternatively, the switches could be wired *in parallel*, so that switch 1 OR switch 2 can turn on the light.

    Then, with a hand waving gesture, the teacher may have stated that this is how computers are built and went on to something else. One was left with the distinct impression that he ignored just a few minor details about how to get from a few AND switches to an IBM mainframe. Something along the lines of 'the miracle occurs here'.

    When I worked in physics, I felt unsatisfied with this big hole in my understanding of an important piece of 20th century technology. But it was not until I joined IBM Research and read a great textbook[14] written by an IBM engineer, that the veil of this mystery lifted.

    This chapter is a slightly ambitious undertaking. I will try to explain in five pages how the CPU (central processing unit) of a computer works. The core of any computer is the CPU and its attached memory system. There is more to a computer, such as various I/O devices like disks, display etc., but the CPU/memory complex is its heart.

    All information in a digital computer is stored as chunks of bits. Today, a typical chunk size is 64 bits and is

---

[14] COMPUTER DESIGN by Glen G. Langdon, Jr.
Computeach Press, 1982 ISBN 0-9607864-0-6

called a computer WORD. Words can contain either data
(i.e. your social security number) or instructions to the
CPU. Just by looking at a word you can't tell if it is an
instruction or data word – you need the context.

A CPU has some similarity to the irrigation system
of a farmer's field. Imagine a field crisscrossed with canals,
which are controlled by valves. A farmer may open and
close the valves and let water flow where it is needed. The
data are like the water, flowing here or there in the CPU.
The valves are controlled by bits in the instruction words.
Each bit is responsible for a valve. If the bit is set to one
(on), the valve gets opened, if it is zero (off), it gets closed.
A sequence of instruction words operates the valves in a
certain temporal sequence. Such a sequence is called a
program.

Let's illustrate this a bit more by writing a tiny program. Its
task is to load two 64-bit data words – **a** and **b** - from
memory, add them, forming the sum **c**. Then it stores **c**
back into memory.

This mini program looks as follows:

```
/*Comment: this program adds two
numbers  a + b = c  */
1) Load data word from memory
   location 1200 and store it in
   register a
2) Load data word from memory
   location 1201 and store it in
   register b
3) Add register a and register b,
   store sum in register c
4) Store register c into memory
   location 1300
```

Computer Design

A register is nothing more than a fast storage device within the CPU itself. It can hold one single data word. Each CPU has a few registers. Our toy CPU has eight and the little program above uses three registers.

The logic needed to add two (binary) numbers[15] is not complicated. It is done with a network of AND, OR and NOT gates. A collection of gates which takes two binary numbers and produces their sum is called an ALU (Arithmetic/Logic/Unit).

The ALU has no notion of time or clock ticks. As long as it is powered on, it will take whatever binary values it finds on its two 64 input wires and produce the sum on its 64 output wires. Let's illustrate this concept with a one-bit ALU. The logic which needs to be implemented is given in the columns below, labeled *input1, input2, sum* and *overflow*. The latter has the same meaning as for long addition. 9+9=8, reminder 1. That reminder 1 is the overflow. Binary adders need that, too. A logic table defines it all:

Input1	+ Input2	= Sum	Overflow	NOT Overflow	Result = Sum
0	0	0	0	1	0
1	0	1	0	1	1
0	1	1	0	1	1
1	1	0	1	0	0

The overflow function is simply the AND of the two *input* bits.

---

[15] The conversion between the decimal numbers which humans use to binary numbers is done by the computer itself. It is a dedicated little program itself, using the same CPU and memory as all other programs.

Computer Design

If it were just for the first three cases, the *sum* bit would simply be the OR of the *input* bits. The fourth case (1+1) makes it a bit harder. But if you AND the inverse (NOT) of the *overflow* with the OR of the *input* bits, you get the *result* shown in the last column of the table. Compare this *result* column with the desired *sum* column and you'll find that they are exactly the same! Voila – we got ourselves a (single bit) binary adder.

Two logic equations can replace all the above words:

overflow = *input1* AND *input2*
result = NOT(*overflow*) AND (*input1* OR *input2*)

Two AND gates, one OR gate and one NOT gate, connected as described above, will build this single-bit binary adder. It is pretty straightforward to extend this kind of reasoning to a 64-bit binary number ALU.

Now let's run out little program. Each line corresponds to one tick of the computer's central clock. Like in a watering system, valves open and close with each tick of the clock and let the data flow forth and back between memory, registers and ALU.

1) `Load data word from memory location 1200 and store it in register` **a**
The switches in the CPU are set such that the 64 bits stored in location 1200 of the main memory flow into the 64 bits of register **a**. (Clock tick 1)

2) `Load data word from memory location 1201 and store it in register` **b**
Ditto for location 1201 and register **b**. (Clock tick 2)

Computer Design

3) `Add register `**`a`**` and register `**`b;`**` store sum in register `**`c`**

Now the outputs of the registers a and b are connected to the ALU. The ALU produces the output in the same clock tick. Register **c** captures the output of the ALU. (Clock tick 3)

4) `Store register `**`c`**` into memory location 1300`

Now the output of register **c** is connected to memory location 1300 and the result data flow from **c** into the memory location 1300.

This simple program demonstrates how 'functional elements' – such as the binary adder – are connected by switches to storage elements (registers and memory locations) so that the data are modified and sent to wherever the program would like them to be. That's about all what is going on in a CPU.

What our little CPU can do doesn't sound impressive, but one doesn't need a lot more to build a simple, but useful computer. Our CPU can even multiply by repeated additions, subtract by cleverly changing the data words (I skipped this step) and even divide by repeated subtractions.

A whole new realm of uses opens up by making the switch settings (the flow of the program) dependent on the actual value found in data words. Does the person have an income and must pay taxes? Depending on the value in the data word 'income', different sequences of actions are taken.

Modern computers have more functional elements, such as entire multipliers or specialized ALU's for doing mathematics on numbers with decimal points. They interleave various operations so that multiple things can go on in parallel etc. This is all done to improve the speed of

Computer Design

the computer, but the basic design principles of a CPU are as simple as described here.

By the way, the storage registers can be implemented by cross connecting two identical AND gates. In a way the teacher was right when he said that the three gates is all you needed to build a computer. Still, he missed the whole point of the actual makings of a computer if he stopped there.

Computer Design

Mr. Murphy takes a Vacation (2ℏ)
- a nuclear Fish story

See also pages 176,177

What can go wrong will go wrong. We all have heard this. There are many variations to this theme, but the idea is always the same – mother nature is not kind[16]. At best, she doesn't care. If you ever spent time on the ocean in a storm, you will hold this to be a self-evident truth. People who have built things have all stories to share which bear out this seemingly universal principle.

My story is the exact opposite. Once in my lifetime, nature showed kindness. It is the story of building a device and finding it could to a lot more than it was designed for.

In the early eighties, I designed and built two nuclear detectors[17] for an experiment involving heavy ions bombarding other heavy nuclei. The purpose of this detector was to detect and measure alpha particles, which were emitted from the ultra-hot reaction products in the aftermath of the nuclear reaction.

Ultra-hot is a terrible understatement. We are talking temperatures of hundreds of billions of degrees Celsius. The central core of the sun is icy in comparison to the violence and temperatures measured in these 'strongly damped' reactions. Our team was exploring these reactions with experiments in Berkeley, Berlin and GSI Darmstadt.

This detector was to be placed near a nuclear target, within a vacuum chamber, which was bombarded with a beam of nuclear particles from the stalwart HILAC

---

[16] Physicist's version: Mother nature is a bitch.
[17] 'A two-dimensional position-sensitive DE-E counter for energetic light charged particles', W.Wilcke et.al., Nucl.Instr. Methods, 188(1981) pp 293.

accelerator in Berkeley, California. We wanted the detector to do several things: detect protons and alpha particles, differentiate them by type, measure the energy of the particles and their entrance location along the x-axis. This means that the detector was supposed to detect particles in a left/right, but not in an up/down sense.

Well, it turned out that the detector, as built, could also differentiate up/down, not just left/right – even though I had given the up/down dimension absolutely no thought when creating it.

This is absolutely astounding. It is like designing a car, and then, while testing it, finding out, by the way, it can also fly! I have never again experienced such a nice surprise while working in science and engineering.

The surprise

Here is what happened. The detector consisted of a thin gas-filled chamber, backed by several scintillation counters. An alpha particle (for example) would enter the gas and loose a little bit of its kinetic energy in it. It would also release some electrons from the chamber's gas as a by-product of slowing down. These electrons can be easily detected externally. The alpha particle then exited the back of the chamber and entered the big scintillation counters behind the chamber. There it lost all of its remaining energy, creating a big light pulse detected by sensitive photo multipliers.

By adding up the two sequential pulses seen by the two detectors one could determine the total energy carried by the alpha particle (or proton). By comparing the magnitude of the pulses, one could even determine the type of particle. An alpha particle left a bigger fraction of its total energy in the gas-filled chamber than a lighter proton.

The left/right position was determined by a clever, but well-known trick. The gas-filled chamber contained, in

Mr. Murphy's vacation

its center, a very thin anode wire made from a very resistive metal. This wire was put at several thousand Volts relative to the metal body of the chamber. As a nuclear particle passes through the gas, it produces free electrons. These drift toward the central wire and are captured there. Some of the electric charge travels left and some travels right along the wire. These two charge components are detected by sensitive amplifiers connected to the left and right ends of the wire.

Because of the resistance of the wire, the charges seen by the two amplifiers are unequal. A comparison of the pulse heights can be used to determine the left/right impact point. For example, if a particle hits close to the left side of the chamber, most of the charge takes the easy path to the left amplifier. Less charge winds up in the right amplifier. A little calculation (divide left pulse size by sum of the pulses) would give us the left/right or x-coordinate of the particle's impact point.

So far so good. All this was basically known stuff and it worked nicely. The big surprise came when we realized that this detector could also detect the up/down or y-coordinate of the impact point. This we demonstrated by bending a wire in the shape of a fish and mounted it in front of the detector. Then we irradiated the whole setup with alpha particles. Within a few minutes, the shape of the fish appeared on a screen in the form of a clearly visible shadow.

The next section describes how this came about. It may be tough reading, though...

As we were looking with an oscilloscope at the pulse outputs of the amplifiers on the ends of the wire, we found that the pulses had very different shapes, even though they all originated from the same source – alpha particles passing through the chamber. This puzzled us for a while. Then we realized what was going on. The pulse shapes have to do with speed differences of the clouds of electrons and ions, which are both released as an alpha particle passes through the gas. The electrons drifted quickly to the anode wire, while the big, lumbering ions leisurely drifted to the chamber walls.

As long as these charges *moved*, a pulse was induced in the wire and detected by the amplifiers. An alpha particle passing far away from the anode wire produced a very different electron/ion travel time scenario than one which passed close to the wire. The integrated pulse was *not* dependent on the y-coordinate, only on the total energy deposited in the gas, since all released charges were eventually collected. But the *rate* at which the charge was collected was very dependent on the vertical distance of the alpha particle track (the y-coordinate) from the wire.

It was relatively easy, using fancy, but off-the-shelf nuclear electronics, to measure the shape of each pulse and correlate it with the y-coordinate. The combination of the resistive division gave us the x-coordinate, and the travel time measurement the y-coordinate. And thus we caught us a fish.

I am happy to say that the detector performed nicely in the experiments in Berkeley. It allowed us to measure not only the billions of degrees $^{\circ}C$ produced in these violent nuclear reactions, but also to determine quite unambiguously that it was a statistically driven evaporative process. That's a fancy way of saying that the cooling of the nuclear reaction products was actually a pretty boring process without real surprises. The ultra-hot nuclear reaction products cool by first emitting alpha particles, then neutrons and finally gamma rays.

Our measurements were totally consistent with this straightforward thermal cooling model. The results disappointed quite a few colleagues, who had speculated

Mr. Murphy's vacation

about the existence of exotic mechanism in the aftermath of these ultra-violent reactions.

But good old statistical mechanics, albeit applied at billions of degrees, explained the experimental results quite nicely. In some sense, this is sad. When one finds exotic results, most likely this is because the experiment is flawed. If one does an experiment correctly, it is more likely that there are *no* surprises. Thus it is always good to be very skeptical about sensational new results.

The entire cold fusion fiasco –wonderfully chronicled in Prof. Huizenga's book[18] on the subject - is an excellent case in point to not believe surprises until they are independently and triple checked.

---

[18] *Cold Fusion – the Scientific Fiasco of the Century;* Prof. John R. Huizenga, 1993, ISBN-13: 9781878822079

Mr. Murphy's vacation

What's in a second? (2ħ)

See also pages 177,178

Real science began when people started to *measure* stuff. Measuring distances led to maps, measuring weights helped to establish commerce. For this story, I want to talk about measuring time, which has been a recurring theme in my physics work. While there are many aficionados of fancy old clocks and the like, I'm not one of them. Some of my interest in this subject stems from the fact that *accurate* measurement of time has made many technologies possible, which have greatly influenced our lives.

Take TV, for example. The fanciful pictures you see on a TV screen are painted by a *single* point of light, flitting about the screen in a carefully controlled way, creating the lively illusion of a moving picture. Without accurate mastery of times shorter than a microsecond [19], TV would be impossible. Today most people in the developed world own several devices, which operate on timescales one-thousand times shorter than a microsecond. That is called a *nano-second* and is one billionth of a second. Examples are cell phones, computers, GPS and DVD players.

I participated in determining the shortest times ever measured, roughly on the scale of *one-ten-thousand* of *one-billionth of one nano-second*, or 10^{-22} seconds. Such short times are not relevant in daily life. They matter only at the very beginning of the universe and during very violent nuclear reactions, involving heavy and super heavy nuclei.

---

[19] A microsecond is 10^{-6} or 1/1,000,000 of a second. The little number 6 counts the number of zeroes in the usual notation, which is getting cumbersome when numbers are very small or very big.
A Megasecond would be 10^{+6} or 1,000,000 seconds, or about ten days. Nobody uses that term, though.

What's in a second?

Human imagination boggles at these scales. If you would equate this time interval, 10^{-22} seconds, to one second, then a single clock cycle of a computer which we might be able to build by 2015 (say 10 GHz) –corresponds to 3 Million years. One second would be yet another ten billion times longer, a million times longer than the age of the universe itself.

Yet, the basic idea behind this measurement was surprisingly simple. It was the brilliant concept by Prof. John R. Huizenga and his team. The team, of which I became a member in 1976, was based at the University of Rochester, NY, but we were doing our experiments in Berkeley, Los Alamos and a couple of European labs, such as GSI Darmstadt and the Hahn-Meitner institute in Berlin.

In 1976 I had received a doctorate in nuclear physics and immediately went to Rochester, to join Prof. Huizenga's team. He was the co-author of the definitive textbook on nuclear fission and a great mentor. John originated many groundbreaking research directions in nuclear physics and chemistry. The beginning of his career dated back to the end of the Manhattan project, and I'm happy to report that he is most alive and well today. We recently celebrated his 85th birthday. Is there something about physics which keeps its practitioners young?

The measurements I am describing here were done at the HILAC of the Lawrence Berkeley Laboratory. This was a facility, funded by the Department of Energy and managed by the University of California. It is located in the hills rising steeply behind the campus of UC Berkeley.

This lab produced more Nobel price winners in physics and chemistry than any other institution. Most of them were awarded for nuclear physics research, often for work done in the heydays of the postwar nuclear optimism. Thus, for a young nuclear physicist, the chance to work in

What's in a second?

Lawrence Berkeley Lab was akin for a young priest being invited to work at the Vatican. I'm not sure who would gets paid less, though. But who cared? Back then, I did not. The fact of being in America, working in the famous places I read about in my youth was so heady that I did not care about such trivial things like the size of my paycheck.

Eventually I did care and left academia, with the words of the Physics department chairman ringing in my ears. His response to my complaint about salary was: "You do not have time to spend the money anyhow." To quote John Wayne – if you say this to me, smile! He did not. But he sure was right about the lack of time. I typically worked 80-90 hours per week and even more during experiments. I left the University shortly thereafter and joined IBM Research, doubling my salary.

Turning Lead into Gold. It's just a side effect

But back to nuclear physics. Prof. Huizenga's idea, developed in collaboration with Drs. Wolf-Udo Schroeder and John Birkelund (well before I arrived), was to convert a time measurement into an angle measurement. That's an ancient concept, because any old-fashioned analog clock with moving hands uses this principle.

We visually equate time with an angle – say noon with an angle of zero degrees between a vertical line and the hour hand, 3pm with 90 degrees, 6pm with 180 degrees and so on. Thus, if one has a system rotating at a known rate, then an angle measurement corresponds to a time measurement. (We shall not concern ourselves with the case where the system spins several times in the period of interest.) This was the basic idea behind measuring the time scale of these nuclear reactions. Our team studied what happens if one accelerates heavy nuclei to medium speeds (a few percent of the speed of light) and let them collide

What's in a second?

with other heavy nuclei. Depending on the details – types of nuclei involved, speeds and how they collide - vastly different things can happen. If the nuclei aren't too heavy, if it is a direct hit and the speed of the incoming nuclei is just right, the incoming projectile may just get swallowed by the target nucleus. This outcome is called nuclear heavy-ion fusion. The newly created nucleus may survive if its formation wasn't too violent and if it is not too heavy. Indeed, a whole zoo of super-heavy nuclei has been discovered using this technique.

If the nuclei are too heavy to ever fuse, but are colliding with enough energy so that their surfaces touch, a very different phenomenon occurs. Our team called it *strongly damped reaction*. Other teams called it deep-inelastic collisions. As the nuclei touch, they exchange some of the protons and neutrons from which they are made. Since the nuclei can't fuse – they are too heavy – they eventually will part their ways again, but now they are changed. They lost or gained nucleons.

Assume, for example, that the target is a nucleus with 82 protons - commonly known as lead. During the collision, the projectile nucleus happens to pick up three protons, which are 'donated' by the target. After the collision, the target nucleus is left with 82-3=79 protons. That is gold. In other words, *turning lead into gold with strongly damped collision is easy*. It just is not very cost effective, if one may say so. In another collision, the target may gain protons (or neutrons). What starts out as well defined atomic numbers for target and projectile become broad, Gaussian distributions.

This exchange of protons and neutrons exerts a heavy breaking force on the colliding nuclei. It is as if two coal trains are coasting past each other on two tracks, and, while doing so, crews on the trains furiously shovel coal from one train to the other train. Each lump of coal carries

What's in a second?

with it some momentum from its parent train, which gets absorbed by the receiving train. Since they are moving in opposite directions, each lump slows down the receiving train a little bit. Equate lumps of coal with protons and neutrons and the trains with the nuclei and you have a perfect analogy of the process.

The rate of energy loss during strongly damped collisions is stupendous. I once calculated that the rate of energy loss during the collision of just two tiny nuclei exceeds the total power generation of the United States. Too bad that the sign is wrong – it is energy loss, not gain!

We were interested in all aspects of these powerful collisions, not just their timing. But we figured out a way to measure quite accurately how long such a collision lasts.

Imagine playing a pool game with sticky balls. If a projectile ball hits a target ball in a glancing blow, they may stick to each other for some time, rotate as a pair and may eventually separate again. Nuclei repel each other, being positively electrically charged. It is easy to measure the total angle of rotation by looking at which angle the projectile emerged from the reaction zone. We could figure out – in ways I do not want to get into – how direct or glancing the impact was, and we could calculate the rotational speed (RPM) of the touching nuclei. Then a simple division (rotation speed divided by rotation angle) would give us the reaction time.

There were many details which made it a lot harder than I make it out here – especially the effect of electric repulsion before and after the nuclear surfaces touch- but fundamentally the concept was that simple. No fancy quantum mechanics was needed to measure this reaction time – just as you do not need to use quantum mechanic to get the time by looking at your fashionable analog watch.

What's in a second?

These are, to my knowledge, still the shortest times which were ever directly measured [20]. We do not know if this will ever lead to practical applications. Right now it doesn't look so.

But who would have guessed that Olaus Roemer's first measurement of the speed of light in 1676 (by observing the phases of Jupiter's moons) would lead to a magic box in your horseless carriage which is giving you turn-by-turn directions, in a sweet voice, as you are driving? I refer to the GPS, of course.

---

[20] I'm not counting times which are derived from attributing the width of a the peak in an energy spectrum to a time via the Heisenberg Uncertainty Relation. I do not consider this a real measurement of time.

What's in a second?

Californium^{252} (ħ)

See also page 178

I love California. But I can't say the same for Californium. It really scares me. You'll see why it can cause some nightmares...

Few people have ever heard of Californium. It is a radioactive element – and oh-boy, is it ever radioactive. In comparison, it makes weapons-grade plutonium 239 look as harmless as a jar of peanut butter.

Californium (Cf) is an artificial element, one of the 'transuranium' elements, first discovered – or one should say, first man-made- in 1950 at the University of California. The discoverers were some of the great old men of the heroic age of nuclear chemistry – Glenn T. Seaborg, Al Ghiorso and Stanley Thompson.

The heaviest naturally occurring element on earth today – Uranium- has 92 protons. Plutonium, which is also man-made, has 94 and Californium has 98. That doesn't sound like much of a difference, but adding just a few more protons to a heavy nucleus makes it vastly more unstable.

Uranium decays, but very slowly. Its half-live – depending on the exact isotope[21] – is measured by billions of years. That's why it is still around today, long after its creation in the fire of a supernova explosion. Plutonium 239 has a half-life of 24,000 years and Californium 252 of only 2.6 years. In other words, if you got a pound of Californium today, half a pound would have disappeared in 2.6 years. But herein lies the problem. For half a pound of

---

[21] Isotopes are variations of a chemical element with differing number of neutrons. For example, there is Uranium 238 and Uranium 235. The former has three more neutrons than the latter, but both have the same number of protons (92).

Californium 252

Cf to disappear in 2.6 years, a huge number of nuclei must decay. Each decay releases energy and this hypothetical pound of Californium would immediately evaporate, just from the heat of its decay.

Fortunately, nobody has ever tried to make a pound of Cf. Today's price of Cf^{252} is $27Million per gram. Even worse, a tiny speck of Cf^{252}, the size of a grain of salt, glows white hot and it emits enormous numbers of neutrons, fission products, gamma-rays, alpha-particles, beta-radiation – the works. You do not want to be close to a visible speck of this stuff. A single microgram[22] emits 170 Million Neutrons per second!! In comparison, you can hold a pound of weapons grade plutonium in your hand for a few seconds. It just feels like a very hot potato.

Unfortunately, I have been close to Cf^{252} – in fact, I chased it with a wet towel. You see, the fact that it emits such a cornucopia of radiation makes it the Swiss army knife of nuclear calibration sources. Most detectors will respond to at least one out of the zoo of particles, which Cf^{252} emits. Thus get yourself a bit of Cf^{252}, mount it in front of the detector you want to calibrate and expose the detector to the radiation coming from the Cf.

That's exactly what we did for calibration in the good old days of our nuclear experiments in Berkeley, using the noble old HILAC accelerator. Such an experiment is an exhausting affair. It takes a week to set it up and then more weeks of around-the-clock data taking. Accelerators are complex, expensive machines – beam time on the HILAC costs as much per hour as flying a smaller jet. Thus you can't go to your hotel and sleep – running the experiment is a fulltime, 7x24 affair. Needless to say, at the end of such a 'run', our entire team of about four to six physicists was totally exhausted. It was worse than being a young MD – at least they get to sleep every other day.

---

[22] I microgram = 1/1,000,000 gram

Californium 252

On this particular experiment, our allotted beam time ended around midnight. But this did not mean that we all could go and sleep. It was still necessary to do some post-run calibration of the detectors, using Cf^{252}. For some reason I ended up with this task on that run. I do not remember whether I volunteered or perhaps I was the most junior guy on the team and got stuck with the job – it doesn't matter. The calibration could be done by one person, so there was no need for all of us to hang around.

The task entailed opening the big vacuum chamber, removing the target and replacing it with the precious Cf^{252} source. Then I would close up the chamber, turn on the detectors, and let calibration data accumulate, shut everything down again and remove the Cf^{252}.

We needed only a very small amount of Californium for this calibration, far less than a grain of salt. But it had to be deposited in an extremely thin layer on top of a carrier; otherwise it would not have been a precise calibration source. The carrier we used was a very thin layer of carbon film. It was stretched over a hole in an aluminum strip which replaced the target. (See also page 62ff).

The carbon film was just a bit sturdier than a soap bubble. A slight whiff of wind could break it. A small amount of Cf^{252} was deposited on this flimsy bit of carbon film. Do you see the potential for trouble ahead? Incredibly enough, that whole contraption was the standard arrangement for using Cf^{252} as a calibration source. This must have originated in the good old days of Berkeley (and Dubna) when real men spiced their drinks with radioactive isotopes. Just kidding, I hope.

All alone, in the wee hours of the night, I mounted this fragile Californium source in the vacuum chamber, pumped in out – which took an hour – then did the calibration run. The spectra looked good, and I was sooo

Californium 252

ready for bed. By now, it was about 3am and I had not slept for a long, long time.

I shut the electronics down, rotated the target holder so that the Californium source would not face the incoming air stream directly and carefully cracked the chamber's air valve. Venting had to be done slowly, since there was the omnipresent danger of blowing the carbon film. I had vented the chamber many times before and knew how far one could crack the valve without blowing our targets to bits. Another two hours elapsed while the chamber was slowly filling with air. Sweet sleep was only an hour away – do not rush it now. Finally the hissing sound of air entering the chamber stopped. I carefully lifted the big domed lid off the chamber and looked inside, still holding the dome. When I got my first glimpse of the target ladder, it felt as if someone had poured icy water down my back. The thin carbon film covering the hole in the Aluminum strip wasn't there anymore.

The film had broken, in spite of my careful, slow venting. Now the Cf^{252} was floating through the air, on wings of Carbon film. As my eyes focused, I saw little black pieces of carbon eerily floating in the air of the chamber, ready to be picked up by the ventilators in the experimental cave.

It is funny how time seems to slow down in such a tense moment. What should I do? Slam the dome back down onto the chamber and trap the Cf^{252} inside? Too late – the rush of wind caused by a quick motion of the big dome would have scattered the floating pieces of carbon film even more than they already were. I was thinking furiously. There was no time to call for help. I had only seconds to do something or face the debacle of Cf^{252} spreading all over the experimental area and beyond.

Then it hit me. An old towel was hanging over some piece of equipment near by. I do not know why it was there, but it was a godsend. I carefully put the lid on the floor, grabbed the towel and poured a bottle of water over it. Many people in California carry bottled water, as did I.

Then, with the moist towel outstretched, like an entomologist hunting a deadly species of butterflies, I went after the little fragments of carbon film floating in the air. The moment I touched a piece, it immediately stuck to the wet towel. Within minutes I had caught them all. I carefully put the towel into the vacuum chamber, put the lid back on and, still shaking, dialed the Lawrence Berkeley Lab health physics department. These are the guys who, in any nuclear installation, are responsible for radiation safety.

Within minutes, they showed up, wearing gas masks, rubber gloves and carrying bright yellow Geiger counters. They carefully scanned the room for remaining pieces of Cf^{252}. Its high radiation came in handy now, because it would give away any errand pieces. But they found none. The wet towel had done the trick. I had no radioactivity on my hands, either, and it would not be too difficult to extract the valuable Cf^{252} from the towel. So, in the end, no lasting harm was done, and even better, the calibration data looked good.

By 7 am, I arrived at the Hotel Durant, just down from the Berkeley Lab. I would have been more than ready for a good stiff drink after this close encounter of the radioactive kind, even at this hour. But the bar was closed and there was nothing to do to head for bed and try to sleep and not have nightmares about deadly butterflies.

Californium 252

A Walk in the Woods: Karen

See also pages 179-181

As one can guess from the previous stories, I was the proverbial nerd in high school and clueless around females. Well, maybe all men can say that to some degree.

This sorry state of affairs continued during my university time. Physics students seem to have a lot in common with monks. They are spending very long hours in strange places where women are seldom seen. But eventually, when I turned thirty-one, I started to have serious doubts about spending the rest of my life in academia.

It seemed that having a university career and enjoying the better things in life were mutually in-compatible – for reasons of time and money. In this rebellious state of mind, I finally made the decision to do something about this mysterious other sex.

The first order of business was to find a place where one could find examples of said sex. After some internal brain storming, it seemed like a good idea to take a cooking class offered by my university. Not that I have any interest in cooking (still don't), but it seemed a likely place to meet females. So I marched into the appropriate office to sign up for the class, only to find that there was no slot left. What the heck, since I was here anyhow, I might sign up for something else. This turned out to be a hiking class. Now I already knew perfectly well how to hike and camp, but it still seemed like a fun thing to do.

The course consisted of a few evening classroom sessions, followed by an actual walk in the woods. At the first evening meeting, most of us were already seated in a basement room of the University of Rochester. Somewhat late, a female student arrived. She was a tall blonde, late twenties, in a well-fitting brown airline uniform, which nicely accentuated her pretty figure. The emblem on her breast pocket said Eastern Airlines.

Since I already had a private pilot's license, this young woman immediately caught my eye. Her name was Karen with a very complicated last name, even worse than mine. I tried to talk to her, overcoming my considerable shyness, and found it surprisingly easy. She seemed to be fun loving and laughed easily.

During the various evening classes, I tried to impress her, but this is always difficult when one is just another student in the same class. I do not know how much of an impression I left on Karen.

Finally, the day of the actual trip arrived. It was a cold mid-September afternoon when a chartered bus discharged our group of cold looking hiking students and an annoyingly chipper instructor in the Adirondack mountains of upstate New York. But the day turned into a pleasant Indian summer afternoon, which one often finds in the autumn of New England. We walked about a mile with our packs and then made camp. Since I knew how to do that, I finally had a chance to prove my usefulness to Karen and her female hiking companion.

Karen told me later that I seemed to be hanging around her campsite a lot, but in a nice and useful way. In the morning we woke up to a very cold and foggy day. It was hard to get out of the sleeping bag. That's the time when the thought of a hot cup of coffee is what motivates one to get up - even if one is not much of a coffee drinker at other times. It's not even so much the thought of drinking it, but holding the hot cup in one's cold fingers.

I do not remember much of the rest of the two-day trip, except that I talked a lot with Karen and that it was generally a pleasant outing. But nothing particularly interesting happened, except that we came across an impressive beaver dam and spotted its creators.

A Walk in the Woods: Karen

After the trip, I did not call Karen right away. When the entire class met a couple of weeks later for a farewell dinner, Karen seemed outright cold. I did not know what to think. This – plus the fact I had met another lady, also named Karen - distracted me for three months, until after Christmas. I even took Karen II up for a flight. That was relatively easy, since her father was a pilot. Thus she wasn't afraid of going up in a small plane. Soon it became clear that Karen II wasn't interested in any relationship and my thoughts went back to that shapely tall blond Karen whom I had met in the woods.

So I called Karen I again, right after Christmas and asked if she wanted to meet again. Her answer was that she had a stiff neck! Well, that seemed like a poor excuse and I thought that was the end of our not yet even existing relationship.

But low and behold, right after New Year 1982 the phone rang and it was Karen I ! She apologized for turning me down a week earlier and asked if I wanted to meet her. We did, over a very nice dinner, and I learned a couple of interesting things. First, her stiff neck a few days ago had not been an excuse at all – she had even worn some kind of neck brace for a few days. It was understandable that she did not want to meet anyone with this thing around her neck.

Second, after the hike, another fellow, who was also interested in Karen, had told her that I was married with five children! She believed him, of course, and that's why she had been so cold during the group get-together. That bastard! With this out of the way, we made quick progress in our now developing friendship.

Karen lived in a cute cottage right on the shore of Lake Ontario. She invited me to come for a visit, and I did, bringing along my dive gear to snorkel in the wintry cold lake. What a romantic fellow. Getting wet and cold was a waste from a diving point of view, since all I saw under

A Walk in the Woods: Karen

water were rounded pebbles stretching endlessly from the beach. But it impressed on Karen that I was a somewhat adventurous fellow, in spite of being a nerd. Best of all, it was very nice and warm in her house after that lake dive.

We became close friends and more. When she told her mother about me, something funny happened. Karen had mentioned that I was a scientist of German descent, and her mother[23] certainly noticed my strong accent when we talked on the phone. Given the typical movie depiction of mad scientists with flowing white hair and funny accents, her mother's question was entirely natural. She asked Karen, with grave concern in her voice
"How old is this man?"
She pictured a 60-year-old professor. In reality I was only two years older than Karen.

Soon after we got engaged, Karen wanted to show me her Caribbean, which was like a second home to her. She had lived a short time on the island of St. Croix, which is part of the US Virgin Islands. But she soon left the island because of its horrendous crime rate. It is astonishing that the British Virgin Islands, next door, have hardly any crime to speak of. There is a cultural lesson here, no?

Married

Karen picked the island nation of St. Lucia, in the southern Caribbean, for our honeymoon. As we were planning for the trip, I asked with some concern how much my flight would cost me. After all, I was making very little ($29,000 per year) at the university. I wasn't concerned

---

[23] I do not know why there are so many jokes about mothers in law. My personal experiences with the mothers of both Karen and Anita and my new love were just wonderful.

A Walk in the Woods: Karen

about the cost of her flight, because as an Eastern Airlines employee she could fly on standby for (nearly) free.

Karen looked at me, very astonished, and then started laughing very hard. I did not get it. What was funny about being concerned about the cost of an airline ticket? Still hardly being able to speak, Karen explained that spouses, parents and kids of airline employees could fly at the same negligible rates she could. I had not known that. Karen explained that all female airline employees worry about being married just for this benefit. The fact that I did not even know about this when we got married made her day. Not that she really had any doubts, but… Later she showed me am Eastern airlines T-shirt. It said simply: "Marry me, Fly for free."

Technically speaking, it wasn't free. A flight in economy class did cost $6 one-way to any Eastern destination. First class tickets were $12. Well, a roundtrip to the Caribbean for the two of us, going first class, added up to a whopping $48.

All this cheap flying was standby. In the eighties and nineties, it was easy to get a standby seat. Today, with computerized yield management, getting a standby seat is much harder. A rigorously enforced condition for flying standby was that men had to wear a jacket with a tie and women had to wear dresses. The stores in airports selling fancy clothing make most of their income from airline employees who need to get a jacket or dress in a hurry.

We stayed at the Anse Chastanet hotel in St. Lucia. To this day, this is one of my most favorite hotels in the world. Guests stay in separate small octagonal 'cottages', which are very open and airy. The cottages spill down a very steep forested slope to the sandy beach far below. An open restaurant serves excellent food. But you have to fight for it with aggressive tropical birds, which fly without any shame into the restaurant and demand their share.

A Walk in the Woods: Karen

On the beach is a small dive shack and it is possible to do a reef dive right off the beach, although the local reef is not the best.

As we were there, a boat with a crew of badly sunburned Germans arrived. They were all men, on a sailing holiday away from their wives. It was an annual event of the Hamburg Yacht club. Even with this promising pedigree, they were a rather hapless bunch of sailors. One of them had his leg in a cast, because he had fallen through a rotten dock on Dominica. When we first saw them, they had just beached their dinghy and promptly headed for the Ticki beach bar of the Anse Chastanet hotel. But they had been too lazy or too anxious for a beer to secure their dinghy properly. It promptly got swamped by incoming waves. Yet they had a good time, drinking lots of Jamaican Red Stripe beer and singing loud German drinking songs. I was rather embarrassed for my fellow country men. That feeling disappeared soon after I joined them at the Tiki bar to help them dispose of lots of beer. Karen shook her head and went to our cottage.

A few miles to the south of the hotel are the *Pitons*, which are the most recognizable landmarks of the entire Caribbean. These are two pointy, sugar cone shaped mountains raising sheer out of the deep blue Caribbean sea. At the foot of the smaller, but steeper cone lies the beautiful town of Soufriere. This is the French word for sulfur, and the name is well chosen. Nearby is a crater, which is accessible by car. In this crater, current volcanic activity is very evident in the form of strong H_2S gas emissions, given the whole area a strong rotten egg smell. Bubbling hot mud pools add to the experience of an active geothermal area. When we visited Soufriere in 1983, it was a picturesque, but decaying town.

But a few years later, the movie 'WATER' was filmed in Soufriere. It featured Michael Caine as the governor of a fictitious Caribbean island where oil seems to

A Walk in the Woods: Karen

have been discovered. It is a great ironic comedy, portraying the Caribbean very well. In the movie, a pompous mid-level British official visits the island. In preparation for his visit, the town is painted and generally prepped for the important visitor.

Well, I was in Soufriere recently (late 2007), a few years after the movie was filmed. But it had had a strong positive effect on the town, which is now as spic'n span as any Caribbean town can possibly ever be. By the way, the big botanical garden on the outskirts of Soufriere is just magnificent.

Our honeymoon in St. Lucia started my own love affair with the Caribbean, culminating in a long-term sailing trip with Karen in this delightful arc of islands. To the very day, I prefer it to the South Pacific islands, even though the latter are easier to get to from California.

Karen and I were married for wonderful 14 years, during which we shared many adventures and travels. I often quote Karen's battle cry for traveling:

It doesn't have to be fun, but it has to be memorable.

A Walk in the Woods: Karen

Windjammers

See also page 170

Windjammer is a term of endearment for big sailing ships.

The biggest and fastest windjammers were designed towards the end of the 19th century – sleek four-masted and steel-hulled ships, designed for speed in a race for profit. They were built to bring goods from the Atlantic seaboard to the West coast. The trips of these great ships were followed in the newspapers of the day like sports events in our time. The Cutty Sark was the most famous of these magnificent ships.

A cruise line, Windjammer Barefoot Cruises, operates a number of these great old sailing vessels. The company currently (2008) owns four ships (S/V *Mandalay*, *Legacy, Polynesia* and *Yankee Clipper*), which mostly cruise in Caribbean waters. My first exposure to sailing was on board of one of these ships, the good old S/V[24] *Flying Cloud* out of Roadtown, Tortola, British Virgin Islands.

The *Flying Cloud* is a steel-hulled Barquentine, built in 1936 with a length of 208'. A Barquentine is a three-masted sailing ship, with the foremast rigged square (i.e. sails perpendicular to the long axis of the ship) and the other masts rigged fore and aft, which means that sails are in line with the ship's long axis. For practical purposes, most propulsion comes from a 320 HP auxiliary Diesel engine. The hollow third mast serves as a smoke stack.

The sails are raised –mostly- for show. I love the good old *Flying Cloud* and am very fond of her, but she is slow. But in the rare cases - when the wind freshens enough so that one can shut down the engine, raise most sails and

---

[24] S/V Sailing Vessel, M/V Motor Vessel, R/V Research Vessel, S/S Steam Ship, HMS Her Majesty Ship, RMS Royal Mail Steamer.

blast Beethoven from the shipboard audio system, life is very good, indeed. The combination of great classical music, swelling sails and a sturdy vessel heaving underneath one's feet is a truly uplifting experience. One's chest fills with romantic dreams of seafaring and the promise of the ocean. Like emeralds on a blue string, islands with such intriguing names as Fallen Jerusalem, Ginger, Cooper and Salt are appearing on port as the grand old ship sails west-by-southwest on the sparkling blue waters of the Sir Francis Drake Channel.

The passengers are encouraged to participate in raising the sails and steering the ship. I will never forget my first turn at the big old steering wheel. The Captain told me to steer her 'steady as she goes', with a heading of 245°. A magnificent old Royal Navy compass, as big as a dinner plate and marked prominently in the old-fashioned way with 32 points, rather than 360 degrees, served to guide the helmsman (currently me). Fortunately, the more modern degree scale was also there, in a very small font. The captain used this scale. Two big iron spheres, painted green and red flanked the compass binnacle. Their job was to compensate for magnetism of the steel hull. 500 years of European seafaring history seem to be very real when one stands in a place like this.

Initially I just stood there, holding the big wheel for show and feeling heroic. Then, slowly, ever so slowly, the compass started to deviate from the assigned heading. 244°, then 243° passed underneath the lubber line of the binnacle. By now I was counter steering, but it did not do any good. I kept turning the big wooden wheel, which was hard work, but it had no effect. When the compass showed 236°, the huge sails started to make funny noises and people started to look in my direction.

The ship's master was nowhere to be seen. How could he just disappear in a time of crisis? Finally, the *Flying Cloud* started to pay some attention to my efforts. It started to turn right, as it should. But when we approached 245 ° - and I had neutralized the rudder in anticipation of being back on the assigned heading long before that - the big ship showed the same stubbornness as before. It sailed right through (pun intended) 245° and was heading with considerable eagerness towards 250°. By now I started to get the idea. I cranked in counter rudder, promptly overcorrected and found myself again heading towards 240° and embarrassing noises from the rigging.

As time passed, I thought I was getting the hang of it. It was about time, my arms were tired from working the big steering wheel. After about 30 minutes of this, the Captain stopped by again. By now I felt pretty good of my steering skills and told him so. He nodded gently and suggested that I take a look astern. My ego deflated. There, etched in the calm water of the ocean, was the sine wave of our wake, like an enormous winding snake going clear to the horizon!

"They do not pay me enough for this," I muttered and headed to the main mast to get a rum punch and a few refills.

The food was served family style in a big mess room, with lanterns swinging overhead from the low ceiling. The swinging lights weren't particularly helpful for passengers with weak stomachs. It wasn't uncommon during the first night's meal that a diner suddenly put down her silverware in haste and disappeared to sacrifice to King Neptune. It is important to do this business on the leeward side. 'Nough said.

So much for the company's brochure, which claims that seasickness hardly ever occurs on sailing ships because the sails keep them stable. That may be true if the sails are up and nicely filled with a fresh wind. It is definitely not true when the ship is anchored. Then the high center of gravity and moment of inertia of tall masts amplifies this rocking motion.

Windjammers

But soon everyone passes the *mal de mare* phase and gets the hang of seaboard life – in particular the free flowing rum swizzles in the afternoon.

There were many shipboard games. An all time favorite for drunken sailors were the *boat races*. Two rows of mats were laid out on deck. These mats were considered the 'boats'. The teams sat on the mats, forming a long row, as in a rowing shell. Each team member received a bottle of Guinness Stout Ale. *(Guinness is good for you).* The boatswain fired a starting gun, whereupon the first person in each team started to swig his or her beer as quickly as possible. When the bottle was empty, the second person could start his bottle and so on and so forth. The team won whose last member first emptied his bottle won.

So far, so good. But there was a shortcut allowed. The bottle had to be empty before the next team member could start his – and it was acceptable to pour the foamy Guinness over one's head, instead of drinking it. There was a lot of pressure on the loosing team to resort to this less than dignified way of emptying beer bottles. This presumes that anything about boat races could be said to be dignified.

In the end, both teams and the deck were awash in slippery, foamy dark Guinness (*which is not good for you*). After the race, the teams usually resorted to jump wholesale overboard to rinse off the smelly Guinness Stout. (*this is good for you.*) Hopefully they remembered whether the ship was at anchor or not. The Captain got disgusted if he had to send a launch after racers tumbling in the wake of the *Flying Cloud*. Fortunately, at the speed the ship was going, the launch crew had time to swig their Guinness (*it's good for you*) before embarking on the rescue mission.

One day, my wife, Karen, and I were leaning over the left reeling, watching some gleaming white sailing yachts passing us by. Then, it was still the left side of the boat for me, rather than the port side of the ship. Never call a *ship* a boat, her Captain will never forgive you.

"This sure looks like fun. How hard can it be to sail such a yacht?" I wondered aloud.

"Why do not we look into it when we are back in NY?" my dear Karen said, always open for a new adventure. So we did, which opened a new chapter in our life.

Sailing Class (ħ)

See also pages 170, 182-184

At the time, we lived in Westchester, which is the county just north of New York City. As one drives from the NY airports north and crosses over the Whitestone bridge, one soon enters Westchester County. A few miles north of the bridge is an exit off the Hutchison Parkway to City Island. That's where we headed on our quest to find a sailing school.

City Island it a funny little place. It is indeed an island, jam-packed with seafood places, funky small seaside businesses, boat yards and other maritime enterprises. Hidden away in a small side street was Steve Colgate's Offshore School of Sailing. It turned out that this school had a number of branches in the US and one in the British Virgin Islands – just the place where we had sailed on the S/V *Flying Cloud* a few months earlier.

We went in and talked with the nice staff – nice for NY standards, that is. They told us that it was possible to go from zero knowledge of sailing to the qualifications to skipper a 40' long yacht in 10 days! This sounded too good to be true, but we found out that it wasn't. We signed on.

A few months later (1987) we found ourselves once again in Roadtown, Tortola, BVI, lounging around the swimming pool of our hotel. It was built on a small hill overlooking the harbor, with a great view from the pool. But we were actually attending class – as we were listening to our first lesson about sailing, given by a young Offshore instructor with a good sense of humor. Twelve sailing novices were present, including their spouses.

The instructor started his lecture, but he quickly lost me. This was a bit unexpected, since I had actually read the compact textbook, which Colgate had published. It had been mailed to us when we signed up for the course. We would find the mismatch between our knowledge and the level of instruction to be an on-going issue. While we were still trying to figure out where the wind was coming from (hint – the hairs on your neck are good indicators), the instructor was discussing the fine points of the Cunningham tension. What is a Cunningham anyway and why do I care? The real answer is– you do not care, unless you are racing.

After the first poolside lesson, we were split into two groups and practical lessons began. We started hands-on training on a 26' high performance open sailboat. The boat was fast, but the presence of all the sail tuning gadgetry was a big problem. The boat was so cluttered with essentially irrelevant gadgets that it was hard for us novices to separate what mattered from the minor niceties of sail tuning. Later on we moved to a big 40' Hunter cruising yacht. The Hunter had a much simpler rigging and only on it did I truly learn what makes a sailboat work. It is not rocket science.

The principles of sailing have been described in many textbooks, but let me summarize it here for the benefit of a non-sailing reader.

The old, stately ships of Columbus' area sailed like a leaf blown before the wind. They could only sail downwind or –at best- at a small angle away from the wind. This begs the question -how could they possibly go to America *and come back*?

Answer – they used the fact that wind always blows from Africa *to* America within the trade wind zone (the latitude of the Caribbean), and *from* America to Europe in the middle latitudes of Spain and England. Thus the ships slowly worked their way down the coast of Africa until they hit the trade wind belt, drifted before the wind to the Caribbean, then worked their way northward, to Virginia and drifted back. They never knew very well where they were in an east-west sense, but sooner or later they would

Sailing Class

hit the Caribbean islands or Europe, respectively. Hopefully not at night – and that is not a joke.

It was much later before European sailors learned to sail upwind (against the wind). It is never possible to sail directly into the wind, but one can sail at an impressive angle –say 45° – against the wind. Thus, by sailing first 45° to the left of the wind direction, then turning 90 degrees and passing through the *eye of the wind*, one will end up sailing 45° degrees to the other side of the wind. By repeating this zigzag maneuver, a sailboat can make progress against the wind.

This 'upwind' maneuvering is considerable work, though. The boat bounces roughly into the waves, leans hard against the wind, the rigging is straining and the wind blows hard. All this fuss comes about because the forward speed of the boat and the wind speed add up to a much larger 'apparent' wind felt on deck. The old-fashioned 'downwind' sailing - Columbus style- is much more relaxed. It is said that gentlemen never sail to weather (upwind). If you plan to circumnavigate the earth, you want to do it in such a manner as to maximize the downwind legs.

I haven't discussed the magic, which allows a boat to sail at any angle against the wind. The following analogy may help… Imagine a wedge shaped piece of steel sitting on a greasy glass table. Now you take a pencil and push down on the wedge. What happens? It will try to escape from the vertical push of the pencil and scoot out sideways from under the pencil.

That's exactly the same mechanism which converts the sideway force of the wind into a forward motion. The wind pushes against a slanted surface (the sail) and the boat, which cannot escape sideways - because its keel precludes any significant sideways drift - is 'squeezed' forward. Voila, you have upwind motion.

Sailing Class

The angle of the 'wedge' is clearly important for this to work well. That is why the angle of the various sails is continuously adjustable, using the most important control lines of a boat, which are called sheets. A sheet is tied to the swinging end of the boom (or sail if there is no boom). If one pulls on the sheet, the angle between the sail and the boat's long axis is reduced. If the wind is abeam (directly from the side), a 45° sail angle is optimum, and if it comes from behind, one leaves the upwind realm and enters the old-fashioned blown-like-a-leaf downwind region. Wind coming mostly from ahead of the boat ("close hauled") always requires a small angle of the sail.

If you followed the description of the steel wedge being squeezed between the greasy glass table and the pencil point, it should be fairly obvious that the forward speed of the wedge can be faster than the vertical speed of the pencil, provided the wedge angel is smaller than 45 degrees. The same is true for a boat – a boat can move *faster* than the wind speed! That's highly non-intuitive, but is actually done by iceboats, which are skating on frozen lakes. In practice, the best speeds for waterborne boats are obtained if the wind comes roughly from abeam, i.e. perpendicular to the boat's long axis.

From this discussion it should be clear that the underwater shape of the boat is critical for its upwind performance. This shape is responsible for preventing the boat from drifting sideways.

There are two kinds of sailboats – centerboard boats and keelboats. The former capsize easily but do not sink. The latter, with a lot of heavy weight at the bottom of their keels, sink but rarely capsize. Take your poison. Large boats are always keelboats. If water enters them, they sink in a hurry. There have been cases where sailors forgot to close the forward deck hatch, took on green seas and the boat sank below their feet in minutes. There is a startling

Sailing Class

photo in National Geographic, showing a sailboat sitting upright on the sea bottom, the sails still flying in an underwater current. Following a pre-launch checklist in a sailboat –like in a plane- is a good idea. Key item - make very sure that no lines dangle overboard, which could foul the propeller just when you need it most, i.e. in a crowded marina!

All these simple concepts slowly became clear, buried under a mass of nautical slang and lectures about the fine points of sail tuning.

But learning about navigation was great fun. It came easily to Karen and me, since all pilots learn the same techniques. Most near-shore navigation is based on compass headings and bearings to and from nearby points of reference, such as summits of islands and points of land. The boat starts from a known point (hopefully), and then by keeping track of time, speed and direction, the navigator gets an approximate idea where the vessel is going. By taking bearings to known points of land, he can crosscheck and refine the position. As one gets more experienced, one gets a lot more modest about the precision with all this works.

A green ensign, when asked about the ship's present position, will point with a sharpened pencil to a spot on the chart (map is for cars) and say proudly: "We are here." The grizzled old salt will chew on his pipe for awhile, squint at the horizon and then make a vague circle with the pipe stem on the saltwater stained chart and say "We could be somewhere around here." But the old pro won't get his islands confused, whereas the green navigator will confuse Salt Cay with Pirate Point, believes to be precise to within hundred feet, yet is off by three miles. If he avoids the rocks lurking just below the surface, it will be by luck.

Of course, today everyone has GPS and this is all for the old-timers. Or is it? There is still a stern warning to be found on most nautical charts: *"The prudent mariner will not rely on any single aid to navigation."* This is still true, but GPS has become so good and reliable that this warning has lost much of its sting. I literally trust GPS technology with my life when flying certain types of bad weather instrument approaches. But these aviation GPS systems are far more sophisticated and reliable – and cost ten to twenty times more - than the GPS systems used on boats. In practical terms my personal rules for relying on GPS for maritime navigation are: have three independent GPS on board, two of which should be handheld and waterproof, have more than enough batteries or other sources of redundant power on board and third, realize that GPS will tell you correctly where you are, but the charts may be based on ancient, incorrect data and can show reefs and islands at wrong locations.

The error is virtually always much more severe in the longitudinal (east/west) direction than in the latitudinal (north/south) direction. More about this in the story about the South Pacific.

Back to our sailing lessons in the friendly Virgin Islands. Our little band of students progressed from the fancy, open 26' racing boat to the much bigger, more sedate and simpler 40' Hunter cruising boat. While the Hunter is full of systems – like marine toilets and stoves – which add complexity to the overall boat, it was fun and simple to sail. I fell in love with big, stately cruising boats, but still don't care about racing.

Graduation trip

On the last day of class, we were given the task to sail from Roadtown Harbor to the Indians (a group of ocean rocks) and back, with our sailing instructor watching, but hopefully not interfering. Just following along this outage gives a good overview what a simple sailing trip in the beautiful Caribbean – in good weather – is like. See the chart of the BVI islands on page 170.

One of the crew – that was yours truly – got the job of being navigator. Having a PhD sometimes is an advantage when it comes to avoiding real work - like raising sails. I plotted the straightforward course from the breakwater of the Roadtown harbor to the Indians, calculated headings (corrected for the twin compass errors of variation and deviation), measured distances and estimated times. In reality, we could see the destination shortly after leaving the harbor. But the proper navigation discipline was needed to identify the Indians in the first place. In addition, one still has to know the boat's position at all times because there could be obstacles lurking under the water's surface. For example, right after leaving the harbor, one had to be on guard for the Denmark banks south of the Roadtown harbor exit.

Allan, who worked for USAir as a pilot, was our helmsman out of the marina. Under the watchful eye of the instructor, he pushed the 'Decompression Lever' into the closed position to enable the small Diesel engine to start. This is a T-shaped handle in the cockpit, connected to valves in the cylinders of the motor. When pulled out, the engine cannot develop any compression and is unable to start. Forgetting to close this lever is the main cause of marine Diesel engines not starting. If they turn over good, fuel is clean and the decompression lever is closed, they will always start. I know from experience that it sometimes hard to get them to stop, though.

The 27 HP, 3-cylinder[25] Diesel started immediately. Some deck hands cast off the mooring lines and a favorable wind pushed us gently away from the floating dock. Allan put the engine in gear, using a single lever, which controls both power and transmission settings. These are only

---

[25] That's not a typo. Many engines with odd numbers of cylinders have been built, for boats, cars and especially for planes.

Sailing Class

forward, backward or neutral. The weak but always exciting throbbing of a marine Diesel under our feet became more noticeable and slowly the boat made headway along the crowded rows of boats. At the exit of our row, we had to make a very hard left turn to enter the main marina channel, all the while being pushed along with a quartering tailwind.

Sharp turns in a big, heavy sailboat are always a bit tricky – you need some water speed to get a good leverage on the rudder, yet you must go slowly in a crowded marina. The trick is to give short, strong bursts of power while the rudder is already turned. This will efficiently swing the boat into the desired direction, but the boat will not pick up a lot of speed.

Allan was too cautious in revving the engine and the instructor had to intervene. Together they got the boat lined up with the main channel and soon we had a clear course out of the marina. Slowly we motored along the cruise liner dock, passed along good old *Flying Cloud* – Karen and I waved to her- and soon thereafter we entered the wide, open area of the outer harbor.

When clear of conflicting traffic, we turned the yacht into the fresh wind. It was time to raise the two big sails. Allan steered the boat directly into the wind, using minimum forward speed. This would take pressure off the mainsail and allow the crew to raise it. The top of the heavy sail was already tied to a strong Dacron halyard, which is the line used to raise sails. It loops over the top of the mast. At first, raising the main sail is easy because only the narrow tip of the sail is lifted off the boom. But soon the crew had to make use of the halyard winch to continue raising the sail. Whenever the inexperienced helmsman let the boat deviate from the exact upwind course, the wind exerted a lot of sideways pressure on the big sail and precluded any further raising. Loud cries from the struggling halyard crew made the helmsman aware of the errors of his ways. But eventually the entire sail was up, gleaming white in the tropical sun.

As the designated navigator I had the responsibility for getting us to the Indians. The wind came over the left (port) bow. " Fall off (turn) 20 degrees right and steer a heading of 201 degrees!" I told Allan.

He turned the big destroyer-style wheel and the boat obediently turned right - unlike the stubborn *Flying Cloud*. The boom, just above our heads, moved sideways and soon strained against the heavy sheet (line) limiting its travel. The big boat started to heel and picked up some speed towards our destination, which was visible 5 miles away as a group of spindly rocks.

We could have turned off the engine now, but we were too timid. We still had to unfurl the big triangular front sail, called the jib. In case we ran into any snafu, it was good to have the emergency power of the Diesel at the ready.

Releasing the jib was far easier than raising the main sail. Modern jibs are wound tightly around the foremost rigging line of the boat, which runs from the top of the mast to the bow. Therefore the jib doesn't have to be raised, but is simply unwrapped. There are two sheet lines connected to the free end of the jib, called port and starboard jib sheets, respectively. These are brought astern to two hefty winches mounted on the sides of the cockpit. When the jib is in use, one sheet is very tight, wrapped around its winch and transferring the force of the wind onto the boat. The other sheet is idle, just loosely wrapped around the winch on the opposite side of the boat.

One of the crew members prepared the jib sheets as discussed and then released a thin line, which prevents the jib from unfurling accidentally. The wind immediately got under the big jib (more properly called Genoa because of its size and length) and it unfurled with a bang in a second

Sailing Class

or two. The boat felt like it was leaping forward, healed more and left an impressive, hissing wake.

Allan shut down the Diesel. He pulled the decompression lever, the Diesel died and the loud shrieking of the engine alarm got everyone's attention. But that is normal and is silenced by turning the starter key off. I am always slightly tense when turning off a Diesel on a sailboat, even after thousands of hours as skipper of big sailboats, but this feeling lasts only seconds. Then peace and serenity sets in, as it gets quiet and one feels the boat being pulled through the water by mother nature itself.

I gave Allan a new heading, a few degrees more upwind. Karen, who was strong, took some turns on the sheet winch to haul in the jib more tightly. The knot (speed) meter was broken – this was a school boat, after all– but I reckoned we were moving along at 5 or 6 knots, leaving a beautiful, foamy wake. This should get us to the Indians in an hour.

The instructor demonstrated his trust in this motley crew by climbing up on the boom and resting in the shallow depression (page 184) made by the power of the wind against the main sail. I do not know, if I were him, I would not have done it. Some error by the helmsman and he would have been flung overboard faster than Ahab could have shouted "Thar she blows!"

But everything went smoothly and other boats had the good sense to stay clear of a boat with a big "Sailing School" banner prominently displayed on the main. Soon the Indians and Pelican Island were growing noticeably bigger. The instructor told us not to plan on anchoring, but just to pick up a mooring. We would anchor at a place called Little Harbor on our way back.

Having done my job as navigator – tough job, that is – I got to be part of the mooring pickup team. We went to the heaving bow of the boat, close to where the sharp end of the boat knifed through the undisturbed water.

Sailing Class

Below the anchor chain hatch we found a heavy docking line. We tied one end of the line to a cleat and kept the other end on the ready. We would use this line to connect us to the mooring. The mooring is a permanent anchor, linked with a heavy line to a ball floating on the surface. It is picked up by crews too lazy or too nervous to anchor, or when the water is too deep or otherwise unsuitable for anchoring.

As we approached the Indians, and after dodging a multitude of other boats, we swung the Hunter directly into the wind and turned the Diesel back on, Then we furled the jib sheet around the forestay and dropped and stowed the main sail. Now we were finally ready to pick up the mooring line under Diesel power alone.

Andreas served as helmsman. He turned the boat dead into the wind and slowly motored forward, while Peter and I jumped up and down at the bow, yelling and shouting commands to Andreas, who couldn't see the mooring ball over the cabin roof. In the general confusion, we promptly missed the mooring ball and the short line (painter) hanging from it.

We had to make an embarrassing 360° turn and come back for another try. The instructor sat on the cabin roof and did not say a word. On our second attempt, I tried to snatch the painter from the mooring ball, but we still made too much headway and we lost the ball again. The instructor finally opened his mouth, saying that we were lucky that the boat hook did not fall overboard.

I was mad at Andreas, myself and the entire stupid idea of sailing. The third attempt was finally successful–kind of. Andreas was doing his best to churn the Sir Francis Drake channel into a foaming mess while we managed to get the painter aboard and tied to our docking line. It wasn't a pretty performance, but finally we were moored.

On the way back, we anchored in a delightful little harbor on the north side of Peter Island. This cove provides

Sailing Class

much better storm protection than one might guess from a look at the chart. It has a very smooth sandy bottom, which is ideal for practicing anchoring. A single house with a prominent white roof overlooks the anchorage. It is owned by an executive from Lloyds of London. This location gives him a ringside seat on the anchoring (in)competence of many yacht skippers. Fortunately, we did reasonably well on this anchor practice run. One can make a lot of mistakes when boating and get away with it, but anchoring isn't an area to be taken lightly. I suspect more yachts[26] have been lost from anchoring mistakes than from any other cause. In any case, we sailed away quite happy from the anchoring exercise.

A hearty painkiller rum drink, or maybe two or three in the marina bar after coming back into Roadtown changed my attitude toward sailing even more.

Horatio Nelson, here we come!

---

[26] In strict nautical language, a yacht is any vessel which is used for recreational purposes. Even a rowboat!

Sailing Class

Photos and Sketches

The images appear approximately in the order of the narration. If possible, I used photos taken by myself or friends. Occasionally I used images from the web, indicated by the symbol ω. Only images which are marked as freely available were used.

Photos

Sketches

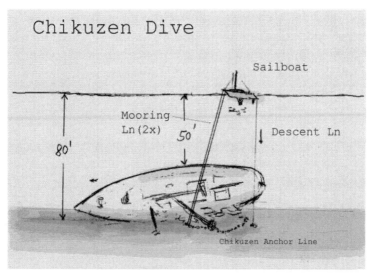

Sketch 1 Relative position of Chikuzen and our sailboat

Image 1 Chikuzen Deck and lovely Mermaid Karen

Image 2 City hall of our hometown in Germany (Berthold Wilcke)

Image 3 Maria and Berthold Wilcke (parents)

Image 4 Practicing Rhinotillexis.

Image 5 My robot mouse – STERN Magazine Foto (1968)

Image 6 Family outing in Napa valley, painted by Berthold Wilcke

Image 7 Mediterranean town Korcula, painting by Berthold Wilcke

Image 8 Rhönlerche glider near summit of the *Wasserkuppe*

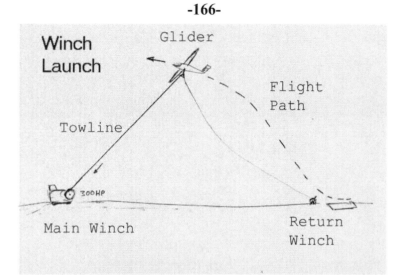

Sketch 2 Winch launch method for sailplanes.

Image 9 Our LS4 sailplane - 33 years later in California.

Image 10 Luftwaffe F104G Starfighter (ω).

Image 11 Luftwaffe Schneeberg Tower, Fichtelgebirge (ω)

Image 12 Top end of Oak Ridge Van deGraaff accelerator (ω).

This impressive accelerator is 100' tall and produces DC voltages up to 25.5 Million Volts.
The photo is the property of the Oak Ridge National Laboratory.

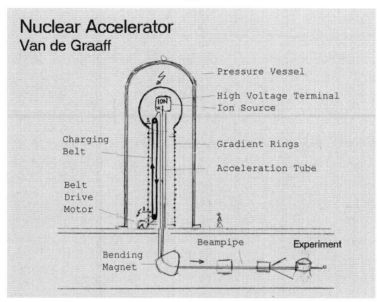

Sketch 3 Sketch of a basic Van deGraaff nuclear accelerator.

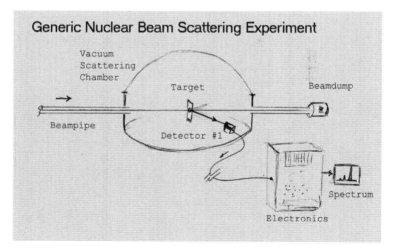

Sketch 4 Generic nuclear accelerator experimental setup.

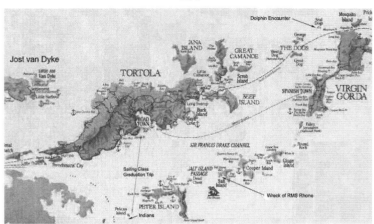

Image 13 Map of the British Virgin Islands.

Image 14 Map of Albuquerque to Los Alamos area, New Mexico

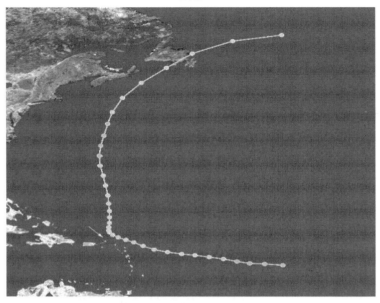

Image 15 Path of hurricane DEAN in 1989. (ω)

The sudden turn to the north of Tortola (arrow) is clearly visible. It saved this crew.

Image 16 Aftermath of hurricane BERTHA in our BVI marina.

Image 17 The one-way airport of Los Alamos and Jemez volcano.

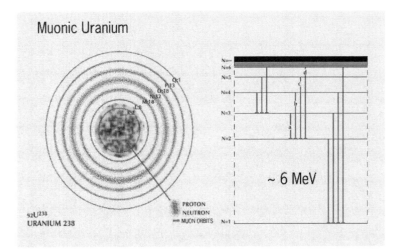

Sketch 5 Conceptual sketch of muon capture by a very heavy nucleus.

Note that the muon is so heavy that its smallest orbit is mostly <u>inside</u> the nucleus. This leads to interesting consequences (see page 87).

Image 18 A Cockroft-Walton high voltage source (ω).

This generator is similar to the one in the Los Alamos LAMPF research facility. It is used to give the protons a small initial push (a few Million Volts) to inject them into the main accelerator structure .

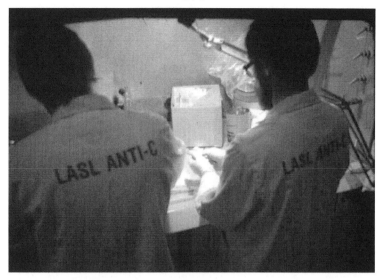

Image 19 In Los Alamos, building a nuclear fission chamber.
Dr. Wolf-Udo Schröder (left) and author (right). LASL ANTI-C stands for Los Alamos Scientific Laboratory Anti Contamination Unit.

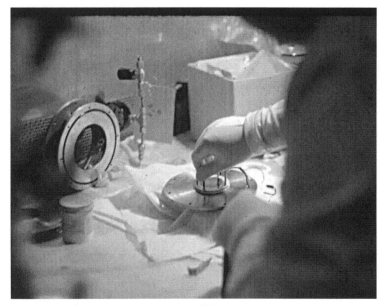

Image 20 Assembling our Plutonium^{239} fission chamber.

Image 21 Meeting in Fujitsu HQ, raising money for HAL.

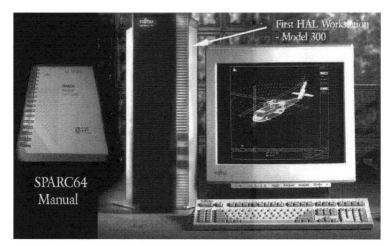

Image 22 First SPARC64 Manual + HAL Workstation Model 300

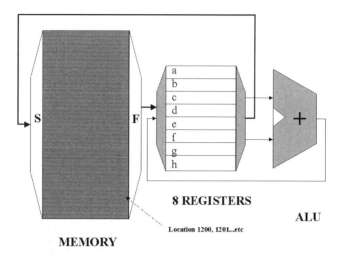

Sketch 6 Dataflow of an extremely simple Central Processing Unit.

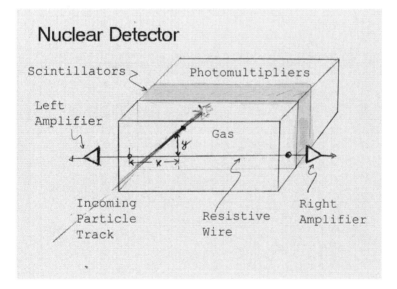

Sketch 7 A sketch of the surprisingly capable nuclear detector.

Image 23 Two of these detectors in use at the Lawrence Berkeley Lab.

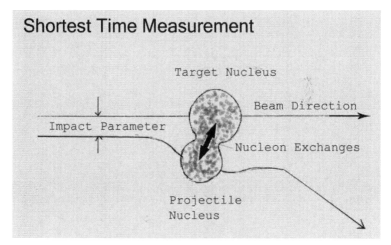

Sketch 8 Fast moving nuclei collide, rotate and exchange nucleons.

Image 24 Friends from nuclear physics days.

Future Profs. Dr. Wolf-Udo Schroeder (left), Dr. Dieter Hilscher(right) and future Los Alamos Lab Director, Dr. John Browne (background).

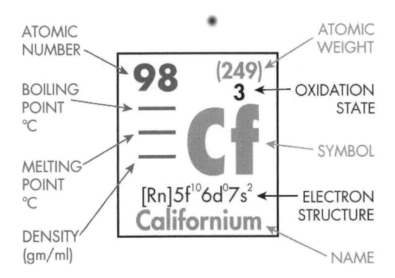

Sketch 9 Chemical symbol for Californium 252. Hot Stuff.

Image 25 Karen, 1993, as Manager of SATO, Westpoint, NY.

Image 26 Karen (left) in the cold Adirondack woods, NY. (1982).

Image 27 Years later, Karen with my father in Köln, Germany.

Image 28 Wedding in Ravello, Amalfi Coast, Italy.

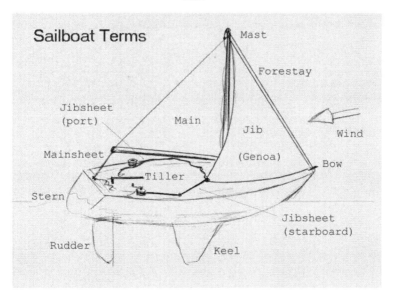

Sketch 10 Nautical terms for sailboat parts, used in this book.

Image 29 Graduation trip with Offshore Sailing School.

Image 30 Author (left) and sailing instructor with big grins.

Image 31 I'm having fun while Karen is working hard.

Image 32 The instructor demonstrates trust in his students.

Image 33 Living the good life. Karen and our boat in a secluded tropical cove.

Image 34 Our boat off an uninhabited island in the Caribbean.

Image 35 I'm hiding from a tropical rain squall – wet, but happy.

Image 36 View from our deck. SCUBA tanks in the foreground.

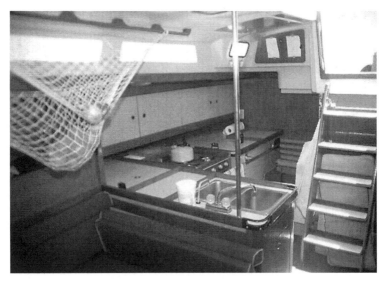

Image 37 Galley of our boat. Karen kept it Bristol ship-shape.

Image 38 Just another day in paradise. Sailing voyage 1996.

Image 39 Navigation is a tough job, but someone got to do it.

Image 40 Nanny Cay, long before Hurricane Bertha struck it.

Image 41 Karen going shopping and doing laundry – by dinghy.

Image 42 One of my not so favorite tasks – painting SCUBA tanks.

Image 43 Karen loved all animals, but Angel fish couples were her favorites. It seems they reciprocate – or are just interested in a can of cheese.

Image 44 Mermaid and Dolphin near Seal Dog Island (see page 170). See the story on page 357 why my wife was wearing this cute dive suit.

Image 45 A Suzuki Samurai on a nearly level road (for a Samurai).

Image 46 Samurais and tropical Islands are made for each other.

The white strip in the background is the runway of the Virgin Gorda Island airfield. It's inaugural flight crashed due to strong cross-winds.

Image 47 Victor 256 – IBM's first general purpose message-passing supercomputer which we built in Yorktown Heights, NY (1986 -1989).

Image 48 The huge IBM *ASCI Purple* supercomputer at LLNL.

See story on page 233 about the bitter battles we fought before the message-passing computing model was accepted.

Image 49 IceCube, an experimental IBM supercomputer.

Image 50 Winter in Mahopac, NY, circa 1988.

Image 51 Karen and me in Mahopac, circa 1986.

Image 52 Karen flying over New Mexico, enroute from NY to CA.

Image 53 Flying along the Hudson river, long before 9-11 2001.

Image 54 Karen on our ferry flight, from Kansas City to NY.

Image 55 View from a Bay tour – San Francisco airport from 3500'.

Image 56 Flying and hiking combined: Karen high above May Lake, Sierra Nevada, CA.

Image 57 Mammoth Lakes airport, ready for exercise (2007).

Image 58 Left instrument panel of the Bonanza A36, flying at 15,500'.

Image 59 On top of Half Dome, Sierra Nevada, CA.

Image 60 Bonanza over Monument Valley rock formations.

Image 61 Over Utah, in a high-wing Cessna.

Image 62 Off-road in New Zealand, with Anita. Note engine snorkel.

Image 63 Off-road in Red Rock country, Sedona, AZ (2007).

Image 64 Dr. Anita Borg

Dr. Anita Borg, on the title page of the issue of the San Jose Mercury News in 1999. The issue featured a multi-page article about her and her work. This article caused me to meet and eventually marry her.

Image 65 Anita, relaxing in Melbourne, Australia.

Image 66 Anita's very own special encounter with dolphins in Hawaii. This photo was made public by her Institute: The boss at play!

Image 67 Flying Tiger Moths in southern Australia.

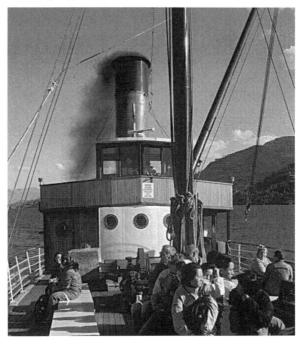

Image 68 Steamship TSS Earnslaw, New Zealand.

Image 69 Anita in her beloved Porsche Boxter.
Fun car to drive, except it kept loosing important parts.

Image 70 View from home at 2000', with dramtic Föhn clouds draped over the Pacific coastal range, just a few hundred meters away.

Image 71 On the Kaiser Franz Joseph glacier in New Zealand.

Image 72 Circling Sailing Vessel *Windstar* in Bora Bora.

Image 73 Author or pirate?

Image 74 'HMS' Diamond Rock off Martinique.

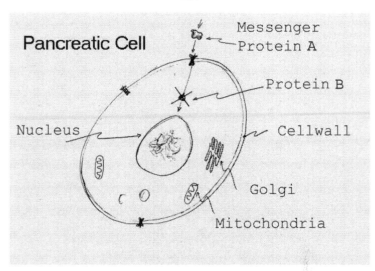

Sketch 11 Cell of pancreas and protein 'relay race'. (see text).

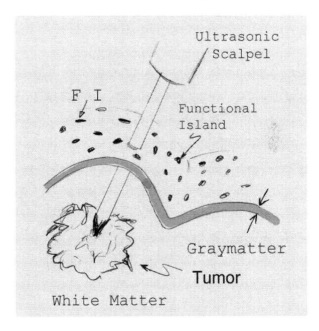

Sketch 12 High tech brain surgery (see text).

Image 75 Ultralight Takeoff, Costa Rica. Engine quit seconds later.

Image 76 Minor mishap with our first Skyhawk.

Image 77 Matterhorn, seen from a Zermatt hotel, CH.

Image 78 Camping on a Nevada dry lake, with Ron Labby.

Image 79 Thunderstorms building over the Caribbean sea.

Image 80 Bonanza up high, author wearing an Oxygen cannula.

Image 81 Dive boat in Truk lagoon, with 52 warship wrecks below.

Image 82 Finally, getting close-up pictures of sharks in the Bahamas.

Image 83 'The difference between men and boys..' Jet purchase.

Image 84 Sailplane pre-purchase check. Dr.Wolf Weber at right.

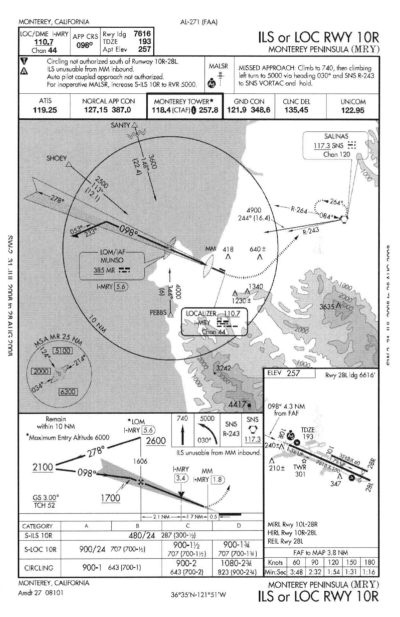

Image 85 FAA Instrument Approach Plate for Monterey ILS 10

18° 41' S
174° 03' W

Image 86 Karen, backlit in *Swallow's Cave*, Kapa Is. Tonga.
I nearly drowned just before taking this photo (pg. 291)

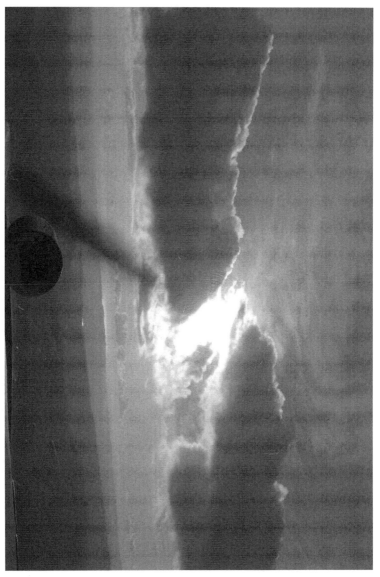

Image 87 Magic of Flight

Flying towards the Pacific ocean, which reflects the sunlight (below the propeller blade). Near Monterey Bay, California.

Image 88 Anita poses on the rudder blade of RMS RHONE (pg. 363)

Another previously published photo.

Image 89 Anita giving the acceptance speech for her Heinz Award Library of Congress, Washington, DC, 2002.

A Sailing Voyage

See also pages 170, 184-191,208

It was pretty clear that a two week course in sailing wasn't enough to truly qualify us to rent a big yacht on our own – even though bareboat companies like the Moorings or Sunsail would accept these skimpy qualifications. So we decided to buy a small boat and practice near home.

Karen, who managed the airline ticket office of West Point Academy, was entitled to become a member of the West Point Yacht Club. That sounds glamorous, but even better was the fact that the annual club membership fee was only $83 per year. The Boston yacht club charges slightly more.

We found a 23' replica of a northeastern pilot boat. It was cutter rigged, meaning it had two jibs, not just one as most sailboats. These pilot boats were used by harbor pilots, who raced to intercept incoming sailing ships, offering their harbor guidance services. The pilots, naturally, were very motivated to own fast boats, because the pilot who arrived first had a good chance to snag the business. Our boat was a fiberglass replica of such a pilot boat, called the *Venture of Newport*. Unfortunately, it never had heard of its heritage, because it was so slow. On the other hand, perhaps her skipper did not know what he was doing. Maybe that's more likely.

Karen and I kept *Venture of Newport* for two seasons, moored abeam the spectacular WestPoint Academy in the swift running Hudson river. Sailing there was quite challenging, since the river, like the Rhein river, had cut deep into the mountains. This made for unsteady winds. Big and fast freighters motored up and down the Hudson. It was essential to stay out of their way.

Theoretically, a sailboat has the right of way over a motor ship, but in practice –and especially in a confined waterway- this means nothing. You better get out of the ship's way or you are driftwood.

To make matters worse, the small 10 HP Honda outboard engine had the disconcerting habit to suddenly stop running, without any warning or apparent reason. It took me the entire summer of 1988 to figure out its problem. When I finally did, it seemed like a miracle that that poor little engine could run at all and I withdrew all the curses I had heaped on it. It had to do with a missing Woodruff key in the ignition system. Some idiot had forgotten to install it.

Well, that little boat was good and cheap training. Sailing doesn't have to be expensive. We bought the *Venture of Newport* for $4500 and sold it two years later for the same amount, even though it had been damaged by a collision while it was moored out in the river. It suffered a hit and run accident, which left a nasty gash in the gunwale of the boat. With the experience gained from that little cutter, we felt confident in setting off by ourselves in the Caribbean and we did this for several years.

In 1996, a couple of years after we had sold HAL to Fujitsu and golden handcuffs were off, Karen and I decided to go sailing for a year. We did not want to do a big transoceanic crossing, rather spend time in an interesting area with many islands and interesting dive sites. We quickly ruled out the South Pacific and decided to head for our beloved Caribbean. We both felt more comfortable there.

We got ourselves a 41' Canadian-built C&C boat called *MarLyn*. It was strong and very fast, with a hefty 8' keel. Fortunately, I managed to hit ground with this deep keel only once, and it was not much of an event. The application of enough raw engine power got us out of this

Sailing Voyage

predicament. In general, this is not a good way to deal with a grounding, but I got away with it this time…

MarLyn was built for cooler climates and not for the tropics. Its ventilation could have been a lot better, but we survived and got used to it. Unlike more modern boats, it did not have a dive platform, only a swim ladder. This made it a lot harder to get into and out of the water, especially for Karen wearing her mermaid suit. However, these problems were small compared to the good sailing performance of this sturdy boat. We frequently passed bigger boats. Even though I do not care much for sailboat racing, this felt great. Shorter passage making is safer, too, as short term weather forecasts are more accurate.

Voyaging was a wonderful, but surprisingly busy lifestyle. We usually got up at dawn, sailed, dove, and took care of the many domestic chores, which are far more time consuming on a boat than ashore. Our boat had no dishwasher, food shopping or getting compressed air for Scuba tanks was an expedition - and what do you do with garbage? We would not throw it over the side. The days usually ended with Karen's delicious dinner aboard or – rarely- ashore. I wrote the ship's logbook, dealt with video equipment and other electronics, maintained our Scuba gear and did the navigation planning for the next day.

It may sound very funny, but I loved cleaning dishes during this trip. Unless we were anchored in a dirty anchorage, I threw the dishes and silverware into a sturdy nylon net bag, jumped into the dinghy and raced at full throttle through the anchorage, with the net bag dragging through the water. This sojourn cleans dishes extremely well. It was usually well after midnight before I fell exhausted into my narrow bunk. Karen was already asleep in hers. We had no good sized bunk on *MarLyn*, so romance was relegated to the deck in very dark coves.

Sailing Voyage

We sailed among the Leeward Islands, centered on our beloved Virgin Islands. Of the many islands in the Caribbean, our favorites are the British (but not the crime-ridden US) *Virgin Islands*, *Dominica* for its spectacular mountains and jungles, the *Caymans* for their exceptional diving, *St. Lucia* because of Soufriere and the Pitons, *Grenada* for its Careenage (inner harbor) and the *Tobago cays*. We cared less for densely populated *Barbados* and *Antigua* (except the English harbor area) and touristy *St. Maarten/St.Martin*.

We had somewhat mixed feelings about the French islands. We spent some time sailing *Martinique*. With its lush jungle, *HMS Diamond rock* and the towering presence of the volcano Mt. Pele, the island left quite an impression. Her Majesty Ship *Diamond Rock* is a rock just offshore Martinique, which was held by the British during the Napoleonic wars for nearly two years. They hauled cannons up on the rock's sheer flanks, only to be overcome later by barrels of rum, which the wily French floated to the rock. See a photo of the rock on page 208.

Mt. Pele blew up in 1902, killing all but one of the 30,000 residents of the town of St. Pierre. The survivor had been incarcerated in the jail of the town, where rescuers found him. Even today, St. Pierre looks scorched by the explosion. Everywhere one sees black rocks, with rounded and melted looking shapes. That's exactly what they are. We found St. Pierre very spooky.

Diving on *Little Cayman* is spectacular. Cousteau listed it among the very best dive sites in the world. I will never forget my first encounter with the Cayman trench. Just a few hundred feet off the beach of Little Cayman is the deepest trench in the Western hemisphere. As we slowly motored along the beach, we saw a wiggly line at 15' on the depth finder. The water depth varied only slightly. Here and there, a coral block showed up as a bump on the depth trace.

Sailing Voyage

Then, not more than 1000' off the beach, the wiggly line suddenly stopped. The sea bottom had literally dropped out from under us. The chart said that we were now over several thousand feet of water. The Cayman trench is 25,200' deep. We anchored – on the 15' plateau, of course – and jumped into the water.

It was very obvious why the depth sounder pulses so suddenly disappeared. The wall drops vertically, straight into a deep blue abyss. Swimming over the edge triggered my fear of heights. It was like floating over the top of a World Trade Center tower and suddenly leaving its roof. Beautiful gorgonians and other corals covered the walls. Here and there, sand chutes cut into the edge, dumping slowly moving rivulets of sand into the abyss.

We frequently spotted dolphins while cruising the Caribbean, but we managed to dive with them only once. We were anchored near a few small uninhabited islands (Seal Dogs in the BVI, see chart on page 170) when we saw a pod of dolphins playing nearby. We quickly got in our dive gear. Karen even slipped into her mermaid suit, as she hoped to get much closer to the dolphins by wearing it. We quietly got into the water and immediately saw the dolphins frolicking near out boat. Mostly the dolphins ignored us, but a single one made a quick detour to inspect Karen. Fortunately, I was in a good position to get a stunning photo of the two ocean denizens (see photo on page 190).
Karen was so delighted with this speical dolphin encounter that she decided, still underwater, to re-investigate a career as a veterinarian after our return to the USA. If it hadn't been for her cancer, she would be a Doctor of Veterinary now…

Occasionally, the needs of civilization intruded in our blissful cruising. Even though I was very protective of our electronics, devices died all the time – even a sturdy

Sailing Voyage

Hewlett Packard calculator. The heat, humidity, and salty air on a sailboat are murder on electronic equipment. In addition, we had frequent problems with batteries and other power related issues.

In August 1996, I returned to California, since a good friend of mine, Robert Garner, and I were program co-chairs of the Hot Chips conference in Stanford. It was an unreal experience – to jump from cruising and diving with a lovely mermaid in the Caribbean to a world of nanoseconds and silicon chips. While at Stanford, the Caribbean became unreal within a day. Yet, the inverse happened after returning to the yacht. Which one is the real world?

Our voyage – which was supposed to last an entire year - was cut short soon after the Hot Chips conference. As described in 'Cancers', Karen started to feel sick, and soon we had to return to the States, only to find out the terrible news of her cancer. Transition from heaven to hell can happen so suddenly. Fortunately, the inverse is true, too.

Sailing Voyage

Ode to Samurai (ħ)

See also pages 191,201

I do like Samurais. No, I don't mean the guys yelling Banzai. Rather, I mean the unassuming, little Jeep-like vehicle made by Suzuki 20 years ago.

It was sold in the US market from 1985 to 1987. People got scared of it and the US sale of Samurais was halted soon, because it had the disturbing habit of ending up on its roof when driven fast on highways. However, it has endeared itself to me in many adventures and I never flipped it onto its back.

The Samurai is a lightweight 4WD vehicle, patterned after the original Jeep. It was designed to live a tough life in rough places, where maintenance is non-existent and highway travel is the exception rather than the rule. It can waddle through deep mud puddles; climb unbelievably steep hills -if the driver knows what he is doing- and crawl over rocks and through creeks. It even has rubber plugs on the floor - to drain water out of the cockpit after and is sometimes found equipped with an engine snorkel!

On YouTube, one can find astonishing exploits of this vehicle. I have far less off-road experience with the Jeep Wrangler than the Samurai, but from what I have seen, I'd take a Samurai over a Jeep if the going gets really tough.

There is nothing automatic about this car, except ignition timing. It has a 4-way manual stick shift and a transfer case lever, which allows to select 2WD, 4WD High, 4WD Low and Neutral. The front axle hubs need to be manually locked. Let me explain this 4WD slang as it is not entirely obvious.

Most cars have only two driven wheels, on either the rear axle or the front axle. When a car rounds a corner, the inside wheels need to turn more slowly than the outside wheels. A clever mechanical contrivance, the differential, takes care of this speed difference. The differential is one of these inventions whose working is impossible to explain in words, but becomes obvious once you see a model in action. I'm not going to try to explain it.

A 4WD vehicle must have two differentials – one for the front axle and one for the rear axle. So far so good - but what about dealing with the speed differences between front and rear axle drives? One might put a third 'center or front/back' differential into the car, but unless this is done properly, it will defeat the whole purpose of having 4WD in the first place. Say the car is stuck in the mud with its front axle. If it were equipped with a center differential, the result would be that this differential would send all engine power to the front wheels -which are now spinning uselessly in the mud- and none to the rear wheels which still could make good use of it.

That's what a differential does – it robs power from a slower spinning (or stuck) wheel and gives it to the faster spinning wheel. Therefore, *manly* 4WD vehicles have no third differentials. The front and rear axel drives are rigidly linked.

But this design is dangerous. If one drives any car on a dry blacktop road, the front and rear axles MUST be allowed to rotate at different speeds. This will make up for the slightly different tracks which the four tires of a vehicle do experience. So what happens if one drives a Samurai – which has no third differential – on a winding blacktop road in 4WD mode?

Answer - the whole drive system will freeze up. It can happen after traveling just a few hundred meters, if the road allows a good grip and is windy. A few things happen then, none good…

Ode to Samurai

Either the car becomes un-steerable and may go over the edge of the road or the wheels will lock up and skip, hop, and chatter. If one is unfortunate, there will be a loud and expensive noise heard from underneath the car, as the drive train breaks. It is important to be religious about taking a Samurai out of 4WD mode before getting back on dry paved roads.

On a dirt road, snow-covered pavement or off-road, there is enough tire slippage to prevent the drive train binding problem.

Many drivers are attracted to the concept of 4WD – it sounds so good to be able to go anywhere, any time – that car manufacturers came up with an idiot-proof concept. This is called All-Wheel-Drive (AWD) and is found on most suburban SUV. AWD do have a third (center) differential, but it is modified so that *not all* power is directed to the fast spinning wheels. The center differential is a distant relative to the torque converter, which is used in all cars with automatic transmissions. A torque converter contains two turbine rotors in a common housing. The rotors are immersed in an oil which transfers power effectively in normal operation, but allows slippage if torque differences get too large - just what is needed.

An AWD driver doesn't need to know anything about the intricacies of using a 4WD. But it is nowhere as good in heavy terrain as a real 4WD nor is it as macho. A Lexus 330 RX just is not in the same bragging category as a Samurai or Wrangler when it comes to extricate itself from a mud hole. But it would take an idiot to drive a $39,000 Lexus into the mud hole in the first place.

The hubs, which I mentioned before, are a mechanism located in the center of the front wheels and allow to disconnect the front wheels from the front wheel drive shafts. This saves fuel and drive train wear and tear if the car is driven on good roads, where rear-wheel drive mode is sufficient. But many inexperienced 4WD drivers have gotten stuck in snow or mud only because they forgot to lock the front hubs. Without these in a locked position, putting the transfer lever into 4WD mode won't do any good. Unfortunately, one often remembers the need to lock the hubs too late. Then one has to get out and find the locking knobs while already stuck in mud, sand or snow. 4WD has two modes - low and high. The low mode inserts another speed reduction gear into the power flow, further increasing the torque, but it reduces speed. In 4WD-L mode one can take the foot off the gas and the car will creep forward, like a car with an automatic transmission. That is great for crawling over rocks. If one steps on the gas, the car will still go slowly, but has enormous pulling power. 4WD-L is sometimes called the (tree) stump pulling gear.

We first encountered Samurais as ubiquitous rental vehicles on Caribbean and Pacific islands. Such a car usually looked like someone had beaten it with rock or worse, and rust was common. It is a tiny car, but it comes with big fat tires, which give it a lot of ground clearance. You just look at it and know that it is a go anywhere vehicle - but do everything slowly. It just wasn't designed for serious highway travel. Its high center of gravity and very short wheel base makes it very unstable.
It's small size is a blessing when maneuvering through forests and among rocks. The Hummer was specifically designed to follow in the tracks of American tanks, thus its great width. But it is a poor choice for most civilian off-road uses because it is too big, wide and heavy.

Over time, I got fond of the Samurai – because these poor, neglected and beaten up vehicles just do not fail. It has a small 1.3-liter engine producing 60 HP. The starter motor seems to have nearly as much power as the engine. I'm kidding. But the strong starter motor heartily spins the engine, and it always fires right up. After many years of owning, driving and completely neglecting a motley collection of Samurais, I have never had a starting problem – or any other mechanical problem except flat tires. But that is hardly the vehicle's fault.

Low weight is another essential characteristic of a real off-road vehicle. That alone makes most suburban monsters useless for serious off-road use. A Samurai feels as if four hefty guys could carry it out of a mud hole. That is very important, because using 4WD in earnest is going to get you stuck in bad places. While I have never had a Samurai fail me, I managed to get them stuck a few times. But it takes some challenging terrain to achieve this feat.

Once I got stuck in a temperate rain forest. I never had an electric winch, but always carry a 48" Hi-lift, 150' of 3/8 line, a Come-along, nylon straps, a boat anchor and the usual pick, shovel and boards when going off-road. A Come-along is a mechanical ratchet with a built-in steel cable. It can be used to drag a car out of mud. The boat anchor is essential when dealing with sand or mud and there are no convenient trees or rocks nearby.

I was following what looked like an old forest trail. The surface was smooth and it looked like an easy drive. But at some point, the wheels would just spin. Somewhat incredulously, I got out and immediately my feet went out from under me. The ground was as slippery as wet ice. It turned out that the soil was some kind of clay, which had turned into a slick wet mess. It wasn't very deep, but the car would not go anywhere. I half walked/half crawled to the nearest tree, tied a nylon strap around it (to protect the bark), hooked up the Come-along and dragged the car away from this slick spot. It goes to show that surprises can come anytime when off-roading.

The hill climbing capability of the Samurai is amazing. The wheels sit at the very edge of the frame, thus allowing the car to negotiate steep obstacles, such as ditches or rocks. This is critical, so that the edges of the car do not hit a steep obstacle before the tires have a chance to crawl over it.

There is a large public (55,000 acre) off-road area in central California, south of the Pinnacles volcano. It is called the Clear Creek Management area and is a Mecca for two and four-wheeled off-road buffs. It is located near the San Andreas Fault, in an uninhabited mountain range. As one approaches the area, one sees what looks like snow capped mountains. They aren't – what looks like snow are exposed ridges of asbestos! A 14-mile long tongue of asbestos, close to the surface, makes the area unusable for normal uses like farming.

The asbestos, acting like a sponge, soaks up the winter rains and releases the water as the perennial Clear Creek. But do not drink the water of this creek, as clear and beautiful as it looks. It is laced with needle sharp asbestos crystals. This is a great off-roading area, but you do not want to visit it when the wind is blowing. Then the air is full of asbestos needles. The forest service posts updated airborne asbestos levels, so you can decide for yourself whether you want to have fun or risk asbestosis.

The area is a fascinating mixture of serene mountain forests, dramatic drop-offs and bare asbestos ridges. An old friend, Mike Blasgen and I flew there one day. I kept a Samurai at the nearby King City airport. We drove up the Clear Creek canyon and then I pointed up to a steep mountainside, leading out of the canyon. Mike dryly said "You are kidding, aren't you?"
I wasn't and just pointed the boxy snout of the Samurai towards the hill, put it in 4WD-L and off we went. The climb out of the canyon was a non-event. The Samurai just is a mule. But it was still an uncomfortable feeling. You want to lean forward, fearing that if you lean back the car will tumble end-over-end back down the hill. But it won't

do it as long as its long axis is aligned with the hill gradient.

However, never, ever try to cross a steep hill sideways. The car WILL topple sideways and tumble down the hill. I wear a motor cycle helmet when driving the Samurai on these kinds of slopes.

I bought a few Samurais – they all seem to cost around $1500 - and kept them at various small airports. Cheap ($21) solar panels plugged into the cigarette lighters keep the batteries charged, even if the car is not driven for months. In my experience, vandalism is not a problem when leaving cars for years at small California airports. The Samurais have served me faithfully for years without doing any maintenance – no oil changes, no nothing except the mandatory bi-annual California emission checks. It is hard to have more mechanical fun for less money than with a Samurai.

Ode to Samurai

Embarrassing Talk in Yale? (ℏ)

See also pages 192, 193

Most people think that scientists and engineers are of the cool Mr. Spock kind. No emotions shall enter the scientific discourse, and invariably the truth will victoriously emerge. Nope. Nothing could be further from the truth – at least the part about the emotionless progress of science and technology. I do believe, however, that we do progress towards the truth, which could be defined as the sum of all invariants under arbitrary coordinate transformations.

This story is about a technological debate, which has been raging for decades among computer scientists. Now (2008), it is entering again into a hot phase. We are talking about parallelism, or the use of multiple computers to solve a task.

Technological discussions are even more heated than purely scientific ones, since in addition to ego, reputation and research funds, real profits and the value of stock options are at stake. I have been deeply involved in the battles revolving around parallelism on and off since 1986 and made friends and enemies as the result.

To see why parallelism is subject to debates, consider a couple of jobs. Let's assume workmen are digging a ditch. If one workman takes ten days, then it sounds reasonable that ten workmen can do the job in one day. But what about a thousand workmen? Can they really finish it in 10/1000 of a day or in 12 minutes? Not likely – it will take them more than 12 minutes just to get the shovels and agree who works where. Then they will get in each other's way.

Consider that a woman needs 9 months to deliver a baby. Does that mean that nine women can do it in one month? No – but if they start one month apart, then they can deliver one baby per month for nine months. These examples illuminate the problems of getting a bunch of computers to work on the same task.

In the eighties, most computer scientists believed that the best way to build a parallel computer was by 'sharing memory'.

The concept is to use one very large memory and share it among all the CPUs (as described on page 112ff) , which do the actual arithmetic and logic manipulations of the data. An analogy is to give all the workmen only *one* shovel, but it is a very big one which they must share. If you have a problem believing that this is a good way to speed up the ditch digging job, compared to giving each workman his own, human-sized shovel, then we are on the same page.

To the very day, there is nearly religious acrimony between the big shovel crowd and the little shovel crowd. In computer science terms, these are the shared memory and the message-passing (or clustering) crowds. When I got interested in this, in 1986, the big shovel crowd ruled the roost. It consisted mostly of computer science theorists. These are people, who are very smart, but they keep themselves mostly busy with neat, analyzable small problems and avoid dealing with the big, apparently intractable problems of real world applications. Their conclusion was that sharing a big memory was the better way to program a parallel computer.

But there was a developing counter current, driven mostly by physicists who always have very big numerical problems to solve. We realized that, in real life problems, there are many opportunities to find *easy* parallelism. In the ditch-digging example – not only are the ditches so long that a thousand workmen can work comfortably without getting in each other's way, there are hundreds of ditches to dig, and there are also dams and roads to build. Nearly all real life problems abound with many easy opportunities to put huge numbers of workmen (or computers) to work.

Most computer scientists, on the other hand, wrote clever papers how hundred workmen could manipulate their big shovel and did not realize the abundance of easy parallelism in real world problems. They only studied the problem of digging a single, short ditch.

I stumbled quite innocently enough into all this. From our university nuclear research work, we still got tall stacks of experimental nuclear data tapes, waiting to be analyzed. One should think that Yorktown Heights Labs, the HQ of IBM's glamorous Research division, had plenty of compute power available to tackle such tasks with ease. But that was not the case, at least in the early eighties. Several thousand scientists shared just a few expensive mainframes.

But at this time, the IBM PC was starting to become very popular. Thus, I got interested in ganging many small computers together to help solve this big data analysis problem. I analyzed thirteen different nuclear science applications and found immediately easy opportunities to parallelize them all. This was only a paper exercise, but since I understood the problems very well, there was no doubt in my mind that the conclusion was absolutely correct and far reaching.

It was time to build a real computer based on these findings. Rather than using the ubiquitous x86 PC processor, I started an –initially- modest project (Victor) which used special computer CPU chips (Transputers) designed by Dr. May of Inmos for the explicit purpose of building parallel computers. As a European product, they were the subject of derision by the US computer science crowd, but by golly, they worked and they were easy to use. Fortunately I had a very supportive manager, Dr. Eric Kronstadt, who recognized the opportunity to build scalable computers. Today Eric is the Director of the supercomputing work in IBM Research, which has – in the form of the Blue Gene machine – produced the fastest supercomputer on the planet. It is a little shovel machine, of course.

With a budget of only $50,000, which was hard to get because it was so non-mainstream, we built a 32-way machine, called Victor 32 in 1986/87. It worked well right off the bat, thanks to the great engineering expertise of Dick Booth, an IBM engineer from Rochester on assignment to Yorktown and Dr. Doug Joseph from Research.

At the same time, a large group of people built a shared memory (big shovel) machine, called the RP3. It was heavily advertised and had a budget exactly one thousand times as large as ours - 50 million dollars. It never worked well, because large-scale big shovel machines are very hard to build. No, make that stronger – *good* ones are unbuildable for rather fundamental physics reasons.

But soon people found out, through the grapevine, about the existence of the nicely working Victor 32. Soon programs in earthquake simulation, ray-tracing graphics, back-propagation neural network, waveform-accurate circuit analysis and others were created and running on our machine, all done by a small group of dedicated early users from within and outside IBM Research.

The success of this cheap and simple message-passing Victor machine in running real applications – while the RP3 was fumbling – was noticed and I soon found myself in charge of a mission to build much larger message-passing machines. The first one was an improved 256-processor version of Victor, which cost a few million dollars. It used much faster Transputer processors and we added mass storage capability in the form of sixteen SCSI disk nodes.

Eventually I ended up with the Vulcan/TF1 project in my department, too. This had been started, independently, by a brilliant mathematician and computer engineer in Yorktown, Dr. Monty Denneau. He called it originally the TF1 project, which stood for Teraflop 1. Monty had been responsible, with a small band of dedicated colleagues, to build an entire succession of successful special purpose message-passing machines and continues to do so to the very day. I don't think that IBM ever really thanked Monty enough for what he did for the company over all these years.

All of this led eventually to the creation of the IBM SP Supercomputer product line, which dominated supercomputing in the latter part of the nineties. The SP and its successors were little shovel (message passing) machines and three billion dollars worth of SP and SP2 systems were sold. That was 30 times higher than my initial "sales projections" (which were just wild guesses). When the big money rolled in from SP sales, I had left IBM for HAL and therefore can't take any direct credit in the big success of the SP. But my long, tenacious and often very bitter fights for the adoption of the message-passing model certainly paid off for IBM.

The RP3 project was quietly shut down.

Yale

The battle between shared memory and message-passing (or clustered) supercomputing was not easily won. I vividly remember a seminar at the Computer Science department of Yale University, which is located in New Haven, CT, not very far from IBM Research in Westchester County, NY. I had been invited to give a talk about our Victor and Vulcan work, and took the opportunity to hammer home my conviction that big real life problems nearly always are easy to parallelize. During the talk, I showed thirteen examples, using real physics problems. The mood in the lecture hall grew hostile. Finally, one gentleman jumped up, red in the face and sputtered: "If you were right, it would mean that there is no need for computer science research in parallelism."

Embarrassing Talk in Yale

I do not remember my answer, but it probably wasn't diplomatic. A few days later, my manager in Yorktown called me and said that some people had found my talk in Yale embarrassing!

Well, I'm glad to report that the term embarrassing has firmly entered the language of parallel computing. Problems of the easy nature discussed above are now commonly called: '*Embarrassingly parallel.*' I suspect, however, that the term was coined somewhat earlier by another physicist, Prof. G. Fox, and was not the result of my talk at Yale.

While evangelizing the message passing architecture, I met a great physicist, Dr. Dan Auerbach, at the IBM Research Laboratory in Almaden, California. His background was molecular dynamics and he was also the Director of the Science and Technology Department of Almaden. Dan had come to the same conclusions, i.e. that real life problems contain lots of inherent parallelism, which can be put to use without the awful complexities of sharing memory. He and a small band of colleagues had built, from scratch, a parallel machine called SPARK. It was a very impressive system, which achieved 95% (!) efficiency on a real-life molecular dynamics code and was even faster than the multi-million dollar Cray-1 supercomputer.

Dan invited me to give a talk at Almaden and this led to a life-long friendship, during which I learned a lot from him. He hired me back into IBM after the big sailing voyage. Today Dan is the CTO of a promising energy startup located in Santa Barbara, CA.

In the mid-nineties, I found myself again involved in parallelism, but on the wrong side of the battle. At HAL, the marketing team insisted that our customers wanted a shared memory machine, and my team, responsible for architecture, reluctantly embarked on designing one. Our machine, called R2, worked, but it was very complex – as all big shared memory machines are. In the end the customers did not want them after all, because big shared memory machines are inherently rather unstable. Any corruption can easily spread throughout the entire machine. Marketing had lied.

This was a case where management and stupid marketing pressure caused me to do something against my better judgment. This was also absolutely the last time I ever gave in to external pressure like this. Life is too short to waste it on non-sensical projects.

It also convinced me for good, without the shadow of a doubt, that building a *big* shared memory machine is dumb.

Today, the enormous success of Google has demonstrated how far the message passing (also called clustering or scale-out) model has come. The incredible performance of the Google complex, which solves thousands of complex searches every second, is made possible by millions of standard PC class machines working together, exchanging messages and not sharing memory except on a very local level.

In the future, parallelism will emerge out of its niche in supercomputing and enter personal computers. This is inevitable because new high performance CPU chips have multiple CPU engines (cores) on them, rather than a single core. In this very specific case –but which is commercially extremely important - it may even make sense to share memory, because personal computer CPU's inherently connect to only one memory bus. Therefore it is not a stupid kludge as in a big shared memory machine. Thus the techno-religious battle of parallelism will go on.

What did I say about the importance of emotions in science and technology? This was a dispassionate discourse, no?

Ignition Keys

Like for most teenage boys, the dream of owning a car was a big part of my late teens. In Germany, first car ownership typically occurs several years later than for US kids. But I learned whatever I could find in the public library about cars and earnestly advised my parents that the VW Beetle was the worst car they possibly could buy. They did buy one anyhow.

A red FIAT 128 was my first car. I had to wait to the age of 23 before I could afford it. In spite of the dreadful reputation of Fiat cars, this was a delightful little car with a surprisingly sporty 55 PS (HP) overhead cam engine of only 1.3 liter displacement. It gave me hardly any mechanical problems, not counting those I caused myself.

For example, once I removed the carburetor – mostly for curiosity - and heard one of the brass nuts securing the carburetor to the intake manifold go 'clink-clink' as it disappeared deep into the bowls of the engine. Made from brass, there was no way to bring it back with a magnet. I was terrified and for months, I wondered what would happen. Would the engine blow up some day? Nothing noticeable ever happened – the nut must have left the engine without fuss. Or it never left it and was riding happily up and down a piston for years. One of the unsolved mysteries of youth.

Like all young men, I liked to show off my car's ignition key. But it did not particularly impress any young ladies. It said FIAT, a far cry from the galloping stallion of Porsche or the prancing horse logo of that other Italian car company starting with F. But it triggered my lifelong fascination with ignition keys. They are symbols of freedom, adventure and the good life.

Well, car ignition keys are easy to understand. They turn an engine on or off and unlock the steering. But what about other vehicles, more expensive and sexy than even a Ferrari or Porsche? Does a Cessna or Bonanza airplane have an ignition key? For that matter, what about an Eclipse jet or a Boeing 737? What about a sailboat? Or a balloon or a glider? Or a nuclear reactor or submarine? I do not know the answer about the last one, but can talk from experience about all others.

Yes, a single engine Cessna airplane, like a Skylane, has an ignition key, which is combined with an ill-fitting door key. If one surmises that a $300,000 Skylane sports a distinctive ignition key, in a league with that Ferrari prancing horse, one would be mistaken.

First and foremost, the original Cessna key has been lost. I'm the proud owner of one of the 16 original ignition keys ever made by Cessna. Ok, I'm exaggerating. One gray haired airplane mechanic claims to have never seen an original Cessna key until he saw the one for my beloved Skyhawk. Airplane keys are usually copies of copies of copies, fitting sloppily into the locks. It is always a bummer if they fall out of the ignition switch while flying!

They are also small and look about as impressive as the key to a desk drawer. One often needs to get copies for airplane keys, as mechanics like to have their own and loose them all the time. I know from experience that it is a bad idea to tell the guy in the hardware store that this is an airplane key. Two reactions are common. Either the store clerk giggles in disbelief, or he refuses to have anything to do with this key. I have learned to stop bragging about airplanes and instead mutter something about a lawnmower when the guy with the apron asks what this is for.

You do not have that problem with Boeing keys. Airliners – at least the Boeings- do not have any ignition keys at all. Yes, they have external door locks, but the airplanes were hardly ever locked in the old days. Now, of course, after 9/11, they all have cockpit doors and thus door keys ultimately control the use of the plane.

Ignition Keys

Incidentally, jets engines do not have ignition systems in the ordinary sense. Rather, they have igniters, which are turned on only during the starting process or if the going gets tough in flight. The igniters function similar to spark plugs, but with much higher energy discharges.

Larger piston plane with multiple engines, like a Beech Baron or DC3, do not have an ignition key either. Each engine has two magnetos, so four magnetos have to be controlled. This makes too much of a wiring mess at the backside of a multi-engine ignition lock. Thus, four separate toggle switches are used instead of ignition keys. It always feels very satisfying to run one's hand over a long row of hefty cockpit toggle switches and go click, click, click, click, click…

Gliders clearly can't have an ignition key (except for motor gliders). Instead, locks on their trailers are their security devices.

Sailboats tend to use two types of keys. If they have an auxiliary engine, it has a combined engine/alarm key. A padlock tends to secure a washboard like arrangement of boards, which prevents people from entering the cabin. Any nuclear device I have ever seen is festooned with security devices, including multiple switches and interlocked with various sensors. No need to go into details here. That makes sense, of course.

Still, what do you think will impress that young lady more when you whirl it around your finger? A Ferrari ignition key or a Boeing cockpit door key? If only Boeing would start making igniter keys. Now that would be something.

Ignition Keys

Wild Boars

As we were trying to make HAL successful, I had an interesting experience involving real bullets, not the usual verbal ones.

Wild boars in California are not endangered. Far from it – they multiply like rabbits. With the absence of natural predators, the population of wild boars increases steadily. In the late eighties, it was estimated that about 80,000 wild boars were roaming in California, causing significant damage to native plants and animals.

The wild boar of California is a cross between native feral hogs and far more aggressive European wild boars. The former are descendants from domesticated pigs, which escaped from rural farms in the foothills of the Sierra Nevada and the coastal mountains. These were relatively good-natured.

The European boars were released deliberately, 90 years ago, into the uninhabited St. Lucia mountains of California. This is a wild and beautiful area, which extends for over 100 miles south of Monterey. Much of it is designated wilderness area, where any form of mechanized travel – even mountain bikes – is prohibited. It is so extensive that satellites are used to monitor it for wildfires. Several times, while flying over it (that doesn't count as mechanized travel), I reported wildfires to Air Traffic Control. They always courteously confirm such reports, but rarely give you feedback if the fire has already been reported. Still, it can't hurt to report.

One of my favorite mountains in the Los Padres/St. Lucia range, right at the edge of the wilderness area, is Cone Peak. A good dirt road, suitable for any AWD or 4WD vehicle, leads to a trailhead at 3500'. A steep hike of only two hours gets one to the summit at 5155 feet. That doesn't sound very high, but Cone Peak is right at the edge of the continent and the view down the steep slope dropping far below your viewpoint into the Pacific is breathtaking. There is a sandy underwater shelf off the coast and the usual dark blue or green Pacific looks here more like Bahamian waters. From the summit, one has a magnificent 360-degree view. Except for a tiny piece of the California Coastal Highway, visible way below, one could be on an uninhabited planet.

Back to wild boars…
The aggressive European boars and the local feral hogs interbred happily, giving rise to a very aggressive hog population. Karen and I found that out the hard way in the mountains bordering Silicon Valley, only a few minutes from our home. We were chased by a wild boar into a tree. It seems that I never quite forgave the hogs this rather humiliating experience.

A year later, a friend of ours, Bob Carlson, who owns a small winery in the up-and-coming wine country around Paso Robles –invited us to participate in a wild boar hunt. Paso Robles is about 160 miles south of Silicon Valley. Karen, who is fond of all animals, declined, but I agreed.

There is very little paperwork required for hunting wild boars in California. The state encourages hunting boars for various ecological reasons. In 1995, all a hunter had to do was to pay $7.90 and get a booklet with five boar hunting tags, i.e. the right to kill five boars. There is no season for wild boars, or rather they are in season year round.

Wild boars are fearsome creatures. They can run up and down hills at amazing speed, all day long. They have big husks and are well armored. Hogs are strong, stocky animals with thick skins and a one-inch thick cartilaginous plate under their shoulders. This plate is an excellent bullet stopper. A high velocity, lightweight bullet – like the cartridge used in the M16 military rifle- would just disintegrate in this plate and only succeed in making the hog angry. The best caliber is a heavy, medium velocity round, like the standard NATO caliber of 7.62mm.

The three of us met in Paso Robles – I flew there in my Cessna - and we stayed overnight at his ranch, drinking his good Cabernet Sauvignon and telling stories. Very early the next morning, Bob drove us north onto a military base called Fort Hunter Liggett. This is about 50 miles north of Paso Robles, near King City.

The base is on a vast area of California hills covered with chaparral, large meadows and scattered stands of live oak trees. I had fond memories of it from various off-roading trips in this area and visits to Cone Peak, which is west of the Fort. We took off at 04:00 from Paso Robles, and arrived at the entrance of the Fort at daybreak. There were no guards at the entrance back then, although this has changed because of the second Iraq war.

We drove west along the paved main road, then got off the road and crossed a shallow creek, ascending a gentle valley covered with widely scattered stands of Live Oak. Fortunately, by now it was bright enough to see where we were going on this off-road travel. Wild hogs like brush, Bob explained, and we were looking for a stand of it. After criss-crossing the hillside for a while, Bob suggested that we get out of the jeep and continue by foot.

We had not walked very far when Bob, who had considerably experience hunting boars, found a spot with boar scat. He suggested that we stay here, in a slight depression, and see what would develop. As we were waiting there, I had time to think the situation over.

What was I doing here? I do not particularly desire to shoot wild animals, and there were numerous stories of hunters being hurt by injured and angry hogs. Pigs are aggressive animals, they are strong and the tusks of wild boars are dangerous weapons. Many dogs have been killed by cornered pigs, as have been hunters. Bob did not bring his dogs to the hunt for this very reason.

We waited as the sun slowly rose, but there was no sign of boars. Soon it was 9 am and it was getting quite hot. We debated what to do. Boars aren't necessarily asleep during the day; they may forage for food any time. Still, animals are most active at dawn and dusk. We decided to wait it out until evening and see what happened. Fortunately, we had brought a good supply of water, food and -ahem- beer. We told stories in the sparse shade of the live oak forest, dozed and had generally a good time, boars or no boars.

In the evening, our luck turned. We were still talking when Bob's friend pointed down the gentle hillside to a group of six boars. All of them were adults. They moved slowly, stopping frequently to dig up the ground in search for roots and small animals. It was still bright, and my rifle had a scope with a big aperture. Seeing wasn't a problem. By now, the three of us were lying prone, with our rifles pointing towards the unsuspecting boars.
"Take the meat sow on the right," Bob whispered to me. It was a medium sized boar in a thick, dark coat, rooting around in the ground.

My heart was in my throat. I never had killed a major living being before, and now it was my turn. Yet, it seemed now impossible to back out if it now – a mixture of morbid curiosity and macho pride precluded that. I raised my rifle, a Remington 700 chambered for Winchester .308 cartridges, and put the cross hairs on the shoulder of the unsuspecting sow. It seemed like an easy shot. She moved slowly, and it was not difficult to keep the cross-hair centered on her shoulder. But the longer I waited, the more uncertain my aim got.
"What are you waiting for?" Bob whispered.
I held my breath and squeezed the trigger. I barely heard the discharge, but remember seeing the boar jump on

impact of the bullet. She spun around, but wasn't dead at impact. Oh, no, I thought. That's exactly what I feared – a wounded boar, mad as hell – and I couldn't blame her. A moment later, another shot rang, and then another.

By now, the small herd was in confusion and retreated into the thick bush nearby. That is, all but two. 'My' sow kept turning around herself, but it looked like her end was near. Her motions got slower and slower, and finally she fell to the ground. It was a sickening sight, and I did not feel the least bit proud of having killed a wild boar. I may have felt better if it had been a male boar, but killing a sow felt very wrong. One of my hunting buddies had scored a direct hit on a male boar, which was lying motionless on the ground, hit by two bullets.

I will spare you the details of the field dressing. Sufficient to say, we drove the jeep up to the spot where the killing had occurred and dressed the two animals in the glaring light of the Jeep's headlights. What a disgusting job – I will never do that again.

But I looked forward to the venison, which I like to eat. But it was a disappointment, too. The meat of both boars was tough and stringy and had, in my mind, a funny taste. Shall we say it was on the wild side? It is likely that we did not do a terribly good job in cleaning and dressing the two boars.

That's all the hunting I'll ever do. While the actual hunt can be exciting, the aftermath is something I can do without.

Pilot's License – New York (ħ)

See also pages 194,195

Flying – like mountaineering – holds a powerful sway over some people. For those who feel it, no explanation is needed. For those who do not, no explanation is possible.

I do not know who first said this about mountaineering, but it is very true. Flying fascinates me and I am getting more, not less, addicted to it with increasing age and financial resources. But becoming a pilot did not come easily and it took me a long time to get over my fear of leaving solid ground and worries that a wing might fall off. Maybe this is part of why it is a source of endless fascination.

This is the story how I got into airplanes with engines. Back in 1974, I had soloed a simple glider in the mountains of the Rhön, Germany. A few years later, after moving to the United States, I found myself knocking on the doors of flight schools at the municipal airport of Rochester, NY. My intent was to get a private pilot's license for single-engine aircraft.

As a young postdoctoral fellow this was not easy. But at least it was a lot cheaper than back in Europe, where it costs about three times as much to fly as in the USA. I carefully compared prices and went with the cheapest outfit, called Key Aviation. They charged about $35 per hour (in 1977) to rent a very small two-seater airplane. This rate included fuel. The FAA regulations require a minimum of 40 hours of flight time before one can get the private pilot's license. Hardly anyone gets the license in such a short time, except in sunshine states like Florida - and only if one has no distractions such as work. The national average to obtain a private pilot license is 66 hours. I needed 83 hours to get my license. A lesson from this endeavor for me was that low price and good value isn't the same.

Private flying in the USA relies heavily on the so-called Fixed Base Operators (FBO). A typical FBO is a combination of flight school, plane rental company, maintenance shop, plane dealer and gas station, all wrapped into one business. The curious name is a reference to the post World War I days of the barnstormers, who made a living by flying beat up old planes, usually rickety Jennies, from town to town and selling rides. The price for a 10-minute ride was always $5. The more reputable operators stayed at one place and were called Fixed Base Operators to differentiate them from the roving barnstormers. This name survives until today.

Key Aviation was a typical FBO, run by a very crusty old chap. Come to think, most small FBO's are run by very crusty old chaps. I remember once complaining to him that some radio did not work. He just told me "Son, all what you need is a compass and an oil pressure gauge. The rest is bureaucratic nonsense."

His statement impressed me, kind of. But I was young and impressionable. In reality, it was hogwash. But among pilots there is a certain reverse psychology at work. Nobody is proud about driving around in a beat up old clunker. But many pilots are proudly flying old crates – this is seen as manly as *driving* high performance *iron*.

These last two terms need some explanation. Experienced old pilots are often called drivers, rather than pilots. "Bob is driving a triple-seven" means that Bob is the Captain of a Boeing 777. Again, this is some form of reverse psychology. Someone uses the term driver if flying has become so commonplace to him that he can compare it to driving a car. I barely have enough flight time today (a couple of thousand hours) to be called a Bonanza driver.

Iron refers to serious planes, like any Boeing jet airliner. *Crate* can either refer to a rickety old plane or to shipping containers– as paying the ultimate compliment of "He can fly the crate the plane was shipped in".

Key Aviation wasn't using the usual Cessnas or Pipers, but rather the sleek looking line of Grumman single engine planes. Like many Grumman's, they were named after cats with names like Trainer, Lynx, Cheetah and Tiger. Grumman built highly regarded Navy planes such as the Hellcat, Wildcat and Tiger cat. The old nickname of the company was Grumman Iron Works because their planes were so sturdy.

Their line of private planes has the look of miniature fighter planes. The wings are mounted low; the canopy slides back and you enter the cockpit from above, as in a fighter plane. One can even fly them with the canopy partially open, just like one can see in movies like Pearl Harbor, Midway or Tora Tora Tora. These planes were made from aluminum - glued, not riveted- and had a reputation of being relatively fast and unforgiving. This was particularly true for the original version of the two seater trainer, A1A.

All of this, plus the low rental price, attracted a good friend, Wolf-Udo Schröder and me to learn to fly at Key Aviation. The FBO occupied a small shack and hangar on the south side of the Rochester airport. That's where General Aviation (GA) was based. The airlines use the north side of the airfield. Let me explain the term GA. All of aviation is divided into three sectors: scheduled airlines, military and everything else. GA is the latter and as such includes private and corporate flying, search and rescue, soaring, air ambulances, law enforcement, agricultural uses, charter flights etc.

In Rochester, the airlines used runway[27] 4-22, whereas GA generally used the shorter runway 7-25 on the south side of the field.

Aviation has a certain snobbishness to it. There, I said it. If you are a pilot, you are part of the club. If not, you are an outsider. The prospective student probably will encounter this snobbishness when he first enters an FBO. Unfortunately, about 95% of the time it is a guy. This number hasn't changed since 1920, which is a shame.

If the FBO were a car dealer, he would insist that the staff pays attention to a prospective customer. Not so in an FBO. The old timers will continue chatting among themselves, and the girls behind the counters are likely to ignore him as well. When he finally manages to attract some attention, people will be friendly to him, but it will take considerable effort before he is accepted as an acolyte of the only true calling.

Well, I was in the same situation, but eventually managed to get someone's attention. The fact that I already had soloed sailplanes three years earlier helped to break the ice. At least I seemed to be serious about this flying thing, in spite of my funny accent. Actually, having a strong German accent doesn't hurt when flying in the USA. The reputation of the Luftwaffe as a formidable enemy is still perpetuated by American movies and books such as 'Memphis Belle'.

In the seventies, there were still many old timers around who fought bravely in the skies over Europe. All of them love to talk, and the stories are often scary, sad, sometimes funny, but always fascinating. Now, that I am

---

[27] These numbers are the compass headings of a runway. Runway 4 and 22 refer to the same strip of concrete, but used in opposite directions. 4 means that a plane landing on it is flying a course of 40 degrees. The runway pairs are obviously always 180 degrees apart, e.g. 4-22, 7-25 etc.

grey haired and an experienced pilot, US veterans who are getting a bit confused about years often ask me if I flew Messerschmitts in the war. Nope, I wasn't even a glimmer in my parent's eyes then. But at least I sat in a replica Messerschmitt, in Germany, just six weeks ago. This beautiful plane is being restored by the president of the Zellhausen Aeroclub, Harald Wiegand, near Frankfurt.

Udo and I both signed up for the cheapest planes available, 2-seater AA1A Grumman trainers. They have a 100 HP engine and short, stubby wings. I was assigned to a young flight instructor by the name of Alan. Today my first advice when a young person asks about learning to fly is always the same: your flight instructor is more important than anything else. Make sure you trust him, that he is a decent teacher and that you two get along. If not, do not hesitate to fire him. Yes, that's right. He works for you and you can fire him as your instructor. Part of this strong advice was based on my rather bad experience with Alan. He was a young lawyer and instructed only part time.

Incompetent Flight Instructor

I will never forget our first flight together. It was a cold day in the early Rochester spring. We signed out the plane, got the key and logbook and walked out to the little red two seater, tied down on the flight line. My first logbook says that it's tail number was N9253L. I just (2008) checked in the FAA aircraft registration database, and it was registered in 2007 to a Maj Holdings LLC located at 218 Kimberley Ct in Thomasville, NC. That means it is now flying for 37 years, which is not unusual. It is also scary what one can find easily on the internet.

Alan walked around the aircraft and taught me, a bit on the cursory side, how to preflight this plane. One checks for fuel levels in the two tanks, oil level, tire pressure and loose flight control surfaces. Then one shakes the wings and listens for funny noises, looks for cracks and records the tachometer time of the plane. Alan declared the plane flight worthy and we climbed in. We fastened our seatbelts, which to the very day, even after thousands of take-offs, is still an exciting moment.

Alan hit the starter button. The little engine barely turned over. This was to be expected. The batteries in all planes are small and are barely adequate when cold. But fortunately the engine coughed, sputtered and finally started. Alan called Rochester ground control for taxi clearance to runway 25, received permission and we began to taxi.

That was my job. Taxing a plane is often harder than flying it. Planes, which are so elegant in the air, are ungainly ducks on the ground. Most do not have steering wheels. Rather, one steers with the feet. Turning the yoke in front of you, as if it were a steering wheel, does not alter the ground track of the plane. The Grumman had to be steered with differential braking. The two rudder pedals are connected to two independent brake cylinders. If one steps on the top of a rudder pedal, the main wheel brake on that side of the plane activates and the plane pivots around this brake. By dancing on the top of the rudder pedals, one can steer a plane in more or less a straight line. But it is not so easy.

In some planes, the rudder pedals are connected with springs to the nose wheel. That makes steering a bit easier than in the Grumman.

I zigzagged, barely in control, along the yellow line of the taxiway, with Alan yelling in my ear. We did not use headsets then, and cockpits are very loud. Many older pilots are quite deaf. Today, active noise-canceling headsets have solved this problem.

Eventually, we arrived at the run-up pad near the beginning of the runway. Alan explained how to do a run-up before takeoff. In a run-up, one verifies all instruments, wiggles the control surfaces and checks the engine. The ignition system is one of the major differences between car and airplane engines. Ignition is the most failure prone part of any piston engine. Aviation piston engines have two completely independent and self-contained ignition systems, each feeding one of two sparkplugs per cylinder. The centerpiece of each system is called a magneto which is completely independent of battery, alternator, radios etc. The battery can fall out of an airplane and the engine will keep running. For the ignition check, one increases the engine RPM to 1700, turns one of the magnetos off and watches for a slight drop in RPM. Then one repeats this with the other magneto. This positively demonstrates that two independent sparkplugs are firing in each cylinder. In a more complex plane, there are dozen's of other items to set and check, but there is not much to do in simple trainer like this Grumman.

We received our takeoff clearance from the Rochester control tower on frequency 118.3 MHz and I taxied into position at the beginning of the runway.
"You do the take-off!" Alan yelled. I advanced the throttle, which is a big black knob sticking out of the dashboard. The little 100HP engine howled and we started moving.

As we were gathering speed, following more or less the white runway centerline, Alan started slapping my right hand, with which I was holding the yoke. He did not say anything, just kept slapping my hand. Had he gone nuts? Was I trapped with an insane instructor? We reached 70 mph and it was time to pull the nose up. This is always a glorious feeling I never take for granted. You manipulate some controls, and magically the earth is falling away below you. Pure magic!

As a university student, I drove every day over a stretch of four-lane highway, which was ascending a hill. Each time, I had the strong vision of pulling on the steering wheel and somehow, magically, the car would levitate into the air. The highway and the other cars would drop away and the car and I would soar above it all. Now this recurrent dream had become reality.

If Alan would only stop slapping my hand! I yelled at him, asking what was going on and he yelled back, saying that I was supposed to use my left hand for steering. In a sailplane, which is controlled by a stick, the right hand is used. I did not know about this left hand control business and it takes time to get used to.

Soon the big Rochester airport was below and behind us. We turned left, towards the south, and flew at a couple of thousand feet above the farmlands and fields surrounding Rochester. In the distance I could see the green hills surrounding the pretty glacially carved Finger Lakes of upstate New York. Alan told me to level out at 2500' and soon we were droning along in straight and level flight, heading for the practice area.

There we began our 'air work'. I learned how to turn the plane without losing or gaining altitude, change speeds and adjust power and engine settings for climbs and descents. Alan asked me to demonstrate a stall during this first flight. I thought that this was rather early, but obeyed his order, as any -somewhat intimidated- early phase flight student would have done.

Stalling an airplane got nothing to do with the engine stopping. Rather, it is the wing which 'stalls' and looses lift. This occurs when the angle between the wing and the on-rushing air is too big. This angle is called the angle of attack and is one of the most important concepts in flying. Imagine driving along on a highway and holding your flat hand out of the window. If the hand is parallel to the wind, you will only feel air resistance pushing your hand backwards.

But if you rotate the wrist so that the hand forms a small angle – say ten degrees – with the wind, you will feel a strong lifting force. That's the same force, which lifts the plane into the air. But if you rotate the hand much more – say to 60 degrees – the lifting force is gone and you will feel only a strong force pushing your hand backwards. Your hand has 'stalled'. The universal cure for a stalled wing is to reduce the angle of attack by pushing the control yoke or stick forward. In addition, in a powered plane, one adds power to pull the plane out of the stall. This helps too, even though pushing the yoke or stick forward is the primary fix for a stall – and it is a nearly universal cure for any aerodynamic ailments of a fixed wing plane. (It is not true for helicopters, which can crash if one does this).

A sailplane has no engine, which helps to pull it out of a stall. Therefore one must push the stick forward more briskly to reduce the angle of attack and regain flying speed.

Alan reduced the engine power and instructed me to pull back on the yoke. The nose rose high into the sky, the little plane shuddered and its nose dropped sharply. Knowing that pushing the yoke or stick forward is the cure for any stall, I did so with gusto. Alan lost it. He screamed at me. "You are going to kill us! What are you doing?"

In hindsight, I know (a) that I surprised him with my brisk forward yoke motion and (b) that he was a incompetent flight instructor. First, moving the yoke forward is *always* the right thing to do in a stall, and a flight instructor is not supposed to loose his cool if a student, the first time he does a maneuver, doesn't do it optimally. Unfortunately, it took me several flights with him to recognize his incompetence – or fear of flying? – and fire him. Soon thereafter he stopped flight instruction and focused on his law school. For sake of his clients, I hope he is a better lawyer than flight instructor.

If you ever learn to fly, do not hesitate to get rid of a bad flight instructor. There are more out there than one might guess. Nevertheless, the vast majority of instructors is enthusiastic about flying and they try their best to convey their love of aviation to the neophyte.

There are basically two types of flight instructors. The first is young, fresh out of school, has little real world aviation experience – maybe only a couple of hundred flight hours – and is probably building flight hours to qualify for an airline job. The second is the grizzled, grey-haired guy who may have another career, but loves teaching and flying and has had lots of real world experience. Ideally, you want both instructors. The former are up to the most recent fine points of the aviation regulations. The latter may be a bit fuzzy about these FAA rules, but thousands of flight hours and surviving in general aviation planes have him them when something may be legal by the FAA rulebook, but dangerous in real life. The opposite situation exists, too. The graybeards teach you the weather tricks, the rules of thumb, how to get the best cooperation out of air traffic control and the many other fine points of a very challenging and complex profession.

Incidentally, it is not a coincidence that so many private pilots are medical doctors. It is not just their availability of discretionary funds, but both activities demand intelligence, excellent judgment, the ability to multitask and a bit of arrogance and self-confidence. I mean the latter in a positive sense. It takes some arrogance to cut into a patient or take the controls of a flying machine.

Many aviators eye MD-pilots with some envy. The Bonanza is popular with doctors, and is often called the 'fork-tailed doctor killer'. This term refers to the distinctive V-shaped tail of the original, smaller Bonanzas.

My second flight instructor, Bill, was a great example of the gray haired, crusty old type. He was a freight dog – that is he flew charter flights, loaded to the brink with cancelled bank checks – in all kinds of weather. Doing this in the cold northeast, using beaten-up old twin piston planes teaches you a lot about aviation survival. He

-258-

taught me many lessons about real world flying. Unfortunately, the hazards of his profession eventually caught up with him. I heard years later that he had been killed in a crash, but do not know any details. One problem with flying with him was his schedule was so unpredictable. This, combined with the general somewhat – shall we say easygoing – attitude to maintenance of the FBO and the frequently poor weather on the shores of Lake Ontario led to cancellation of many lessons and long delays between flights. The result was often that the first part of a lesson was a refresher of the last lesson. Another red flag in evaluating a flight instructor is if he wanders into the pilot's lounge and casually asks: "So what did we do the last time?" If this happens more than three times – fire him[28].

Flight training took its usual course. After hours in the practice area, getting to know the plane and flying it with some kind of predictability, we returned to do 'pattern work'. That is learning to take-off and land, again and again and again. Taking off is pretty easy, once one knows how to taxi the plane at slow and high speeds. Just taxi with full power and when the proper speed is reached, pull on the yoke and off you go.

Landings

Landing is a tricky and –if done well- an extremely satisfying business. If one thinks about it, landing is a nine-dimensional problem! You want to bring the plane to a certain x-y-z spot in space – the touch down zone – with a certain speed vector (three dimensions in velocity space) and a certain attitude in space (roll, bank, pitch). No wonder this takes a lot of practice.

---

[28] Only male flight instructors ever seem to do this.

As the plane turns onto final, you control power and pitch of the plane for a certain speed, sink rate and attitude. Then you carefully adjust power and pitch so that the desired touch down point remains stationary in the windshield. If it sinks below your reference point – like a flyspeck on the glass- you are too high and need to reduce power. If the plane gets too slow, pitch forward and add power. It is a constant balancing act between pitch and power settings. If there is a cross wind, one needs to do additional things with rudder and ailerons to keep the plane on the extended centerline of the runway.

If the aviation gods smile on you, you will be rewarded with the sweet chirp-chirp sound of tires gently touching the runway. Even better, if this happens in the touchdown zone and without side-ways drift. But there always remains an element of luck in a beautiful landing. More often than not, a landing is not perfect. Fortunately, landing gears are quite sturdy and can take a lot of abuse, which is dished out on a regular basis by students and occasionally even the most experienced drivers.

There is the hoary old saying that any landing you can walk away from is a *good* landing and any landing after which you can use the plane again is a *great* landing. I've witnessed a couple of *good* but not *great* landings, but – touch wood- have never committed a *good* one yet.

Unfortunately for pilots, passengers seem to judge a pilot's skill entirely by the landing. In reality, the important tests of a pilot occur in other phases of the flight – such how the weather is handled. But that is invisible to passengers. All passengers know is that a sweet chirp-chirp landing is good. In reality, in gusty wind conditions, you want to plant the plane firmly on the ground and a gentle chirp-chirp is not desirable.

As I was learning to fly in Rochester, a crew of an airliner (the airline's nickname was Useless Air) committed a *good* landing on runway 22. They came in hot and high in a DC9. That means they were both too fast and not low enough to stop the plane in time before running out of concrete. I happen to watch the event and could see right away that the proper course of action should have been to abort the landing and go around for another try. But they did not. The DC-9 hit runway 22 about in the middle, rather than within the first 1000' and was going way too fast.

The jet ran over the end of the runway into the grass and mud beyond. The nose wheel collapsed immediately, digging a deep trench into the soft grassy ground. Nobody got seriously hurt, but the two pilots lost their jobs within the hour. That was quite deserved. Right away, a paint crew showed up and painted over the logo of the airline. That is standard practice after a crash. The DC-9 was towed to a hangar on the GA side of the airport and the turbines and main avionics units were removed the same day. Then the plane was left unattended in the hangar for weeks, an easy target for exploration by curious aviation students.

Slowly I was learning to do landings to a somewhat predictable standard. This is never a linear progress. Sometimes one does a few acceptable landings in a row, and then there is a period where one can't do anything right. But eventually, the day of my first power solo arrived. It always comes as a surprise. Bill and I did a few touch and goes, then he directed me to stop on a taxiway, declared he couldn't stand flying anymore and jumped out. "Take her around three times by yourself. Without my weight, it will climb faster and float longer," Bill said and disappeared.

Fortunately, I saw he was holding a handheld radio transceiver. So he could call me if needed. In somewhat of a daze, I taxied to the runway, asked and received permission for takeoff and soon found myself on downwind, staring down on the familiar sight of Rochester's runway 25. Before I could get used to the empty seat to my right, routine reflexes took over and I made two *great* landings, followed by a nearly good one. Basking in the glow of the first power solos, I taxied to Key Aviation and received the obligatory cut-off from my shirt, a photo and a handshake. That beaten up red trainer never looked so good!

Non-pilots often assume that the first solo is the crowning achievement of the private pilot training. Nothing could be further from the truth. My first solo occurred at about 15 hours, i.e. it took me 68 another hours before receiving my private pilot's license. After the solo, we went on to practice cross-country flying.

Now all the interesting aviation topics arrived in full force – weather, navigation, air traffic control services, fuel management and so on. In between, I went up solo to practice touch-and goes and do air work like stalls, slow flight and other maneuvers.

Spins were absolutely, positively not part of our air work. The little trainer was not approved for spins – and that was NO in big, capital letters. It was nearly impossible to get it out of a spin, which means that the pilot would end up in a crater of his own making. Only one person ever recovered from a spin in this type of plane and it took him 12,000' vertical feet. That is about the maximum altitude the plane can climb to. He was a very, very lucky fellow. Anyhow, I do not like spins. The windshield fills with a rapidly whirling earth, and the whole sight and sound is confusing and disconcerting. Give me straight and level precision IFR cruising any day!

In these days, GPS did not exist yet and Loran boxes were so big and heavy that it was used only on ships. Thus old-fashioned pilotage, dead reckoning and VOR or ADF navigation was used in aviation. *Pilotage* is navigation by looking out the window and seeing where you are – with the help of a map, of course. *Dead reckoning* is navigation by using compass, map and a clock to figure out where you should be, given the direction and speed you are flying. These two are usually combined. Dead reckoning gives you the approximate idea where the plane (or boat) should be and pilotage pins it down(or not).

VOR radio navigation has been the backbone of air travel for the last 50 years and is only now supplanted by GPS. Airlines still rely heavily on VOR navigation. An airplane can determine with good accuracy bearing and distance to such a station and the entire system of airways is based on connecting such VOR stations.

After a few cross-country flights with my instructor, I was signed off by him for my first cross-country flight. It was a simple flight, from Rochester to Ithaca, NY. Navigation was easy until it was time to find the darned airport! That is known as 'the last mile problem' ;-)

I looked all over to find that promised strip of asphalt, which I knew had to be near by. It had always seemed easy to see the airport with an instructor in the right hand seat – what happened now? Maybe he was giving off unconscious clues, like looking towards the airport.

Ithaca airport had a tower, and I had already announced that I was 5 miles north of the airport, which was really a wild guess. As custom dictates, I had also pronounced my status as a student pilot. Good I did so, because the tower controller came on just as I was getting frantic and said in a kind voice:

"53L, suggest turning to a heading of 040 degrees. The airport will be at your 12 o'clock, 4 miles."

Oops, this heading was perpendicular to my current course! Without the tower's help I would have flown right past the airport. It took me years to figure out the best strategies to find airports. Fortunately, the human eye slowly gets trained at seeing new shapes, like runways from the air or camouflaged animals.

The best strategy is to stay high, fly to a good checkpoint a few miles from the airport - a checkpoint that one cannot possibly miss - and figure out, beforehand, the precise heading from the checkpoint to the airport. Then, once turned to this heading, the airport should show up exactly over the nose of the plane.

Today, with GPS or when flying on instruments, all these problems have disappeared. The instruments show exactly where the airport is located. Just do not let it disappear under the nose of the plane.

Pilot's License – Part II

See also page 170

My friend Wolf-Udo and I did some of our training for the private pilot license out of Los Alamos. The town has a challenging airport, as described in an earlier story about science in Los Alamos. At the time the airport was still closed to the general public. But we learned that it was possible to rent planes owned by Los Alamos residents. We found a beat-up old mustard-brown and white Cessna 172 Skyhawk, a young and enterprising flight instructor and then we went to mix science with pleasure.

Flying in New Mexico is very beautiful. It often has visibilities, which exceed100 miles, spectacular mountain landscapes and a virtually empty sky. The only fly in the ointment is density altitude, which robbed the pretty anemic old plane of even more performance.

A plane needs air to fly and both high altitudes and high temperatures decrease the number of air molecules available to combine with gasoline to produce power and bounce off the wings to create lift. The combination of both – high temperatures and high altitudes – has a very strong effect on a plane's performance. The required runway for takeoff can double and triple.

Over the years, many planes were lost because pilots underestimated the insiduous effect of density altitude. In such an accident, the plane usually crashes right after take-off, never able to leave the zone of high lift which exists close to the ground.

Because of all this, the old Skyhawk could barely stagger into the thin, hot air of a typical Los Alamos summer day, loaded with three rather hefty guys. The plane gathered speed and barely had lifted off the ground when the end of the runway whizzed by. Fortunately, the ground beyond the mesa rapidly drops away and we could afford to sink a bit, gather more flying speed and then slowly claw our way up to the desired altitude.

Down in the canyon is an area cleared of trees – it has served as an emergency landing strip for more than one plane which did not have enough power to climb after take-off from the mesa. The presence of this emergency landing strip was reassuring to all of us.

We frequently flew across the Rio Grande valley – which more properly should be called Rio Piccolo in these parts – and practiced touch and goes in Santa Fe. This airport has long runways, is 1000' lower than Los Alamos and therefore is far safer.

At first, I did not like the Cessna 172 at all. It felt like a fat, lumbering truck, compared to the Grumman AA-1A trainer, and the force needed to control the yoke seemed immense. Today I can only laugh at this first impression – now a 172 feels like a kite, compared to the heavier planes I also fly. But then it seemed truck-like on the controls.

The wing of a Cessna high-wing airplane blocks the view for much of the sky, especially when banking in the traffic pattern around an airport. It felt like driving a truck around blind turns. Neither Udo nor I liked the Skyhawk at first. But slowly it grew on us. We knew that it is the most frequently build plane in the world (43,000) and it has a very low accident rate.

The real turning point in how I feel about this plane came when first practicing stalls in the 172. The Grumman trainer -which we both flew in Rochester- lets you know without a shadow of a doubt when it stalls. The nose drops precipitously and if you aren't very careful, a wing might drop, too. Then you had your work cut out to recover. When the Los Alamos instructor made me first do a stall, the old Cessna shuddered mildly then gently put her nose down and regained flying speed, mostly on its own volition. I looked at the instructor, speechless.
"That wasn't a stall?" I finally said.

"Oh yes, that was it," he insisted. He flew it all the time, so he should know. Suddenly I looked at the old girl with different eyes. All planes can bite when mistreated, but the Skyhawk had to be kicked and beaten before it would take revenge. Wow!

This first stall in a C172 started a life-long love affair with the C172 and its bigger sister, the C182. They aren't glamorous, sleek or fast, but you can trust them to take good care of you. For two decades I have owned Cessna Skyhawks and never regretted it. So many good memories are associated with this trusty flying steed.

Lindbergh called his delightful book about the first flight across the Atlantic in 1927 simply '*We*'. Every pilot understands immediately - he meant himself and his plane[29], the 'Spirit of St. Louis'. Flying the old Skyhawk around the mountains of New Mexico was like a bonding experience.

Today I fly fancier iron, but believe that the last plane I will ever fly, hopefully a few decades from now, will still be another trusty Cessna Skyhawk or Skylane, cruising leisurely over the beautiful countryside of the American west.

Our flight instructor was young and willing to do unconventional things. Udo and I talked him into flying with us to an Indian reservation in northern New Mexico. It had a dirt and gravel airstrip called Torreon, which doesn't seem to exist anymore. In Torreon we found out the hard way that you can land planes in places you can't fly them out of.

The flight there was uneventful and beautiful. We circled the Jemez Mountain towards the northwest, found the field and Udo did a beautiful landing. A power line crossed the approach end of the strip. For some reason, airfields always seem to attract power lines, cemeteries and

---

[29] This is called the *Aeronautical We,* a cousin to the *Royal We.*

golf courses. We got out, listened to the silence and decided that there was nothing to do but take off again. Neither a single person nor a building was in sight. That is not uncommon at rural airstrips of the American West. Here land is plentiful and it doesn't take much to build an airstrip. A bulldozer and a compass will do.

It was my turn to fly and therefore do the takeoff. A plane always should take off into the wind and downhill. But what if the two factors favor opposite runways? The pilot operating handbooks are silent about this topic. Today I know how to calculate this tradeoff using some formulas I derived. Most often, the wind is the dominant factor - at least for typical runway slopes and winds in excess of about 7 knots. But none of us knew that then.

We took off uphill and against the weak wind. I quickly pushed in the throttle, the engine roared – more like a mouse than a lion in the high, thin air – and slowly we accelerated. When we reached the 60% point of the runway, the airspeed indicator needle had not even come off the peg! That was clearly a no go.

I pulled the throttle back and braked. We came to a stop in a cloud of dust, not very far from the end of the runway. Ok, let's try the opposite direction. I swung the plane around and we went downhill, with the wind behind us. The result was the same. That was definitely not good.

There were still a few options, though. We could wait for cooler air in the evening or morning. Then the plane would climb much better. Or one of us could stay behind and we'd pick him up later by car (5-7 hour round trip). The third option was to fly out with two persons, drop one of us off at a larger airfield, fly back, pick up the next person and then all of us could take off together from the big airfield. Except, there was no big field nearby. None of the options sounded very appealing.

The instructor finally decided that he would try a takeoff himself. He used the same direction as for my first attempt, taxied the plane all the way to the extreme end of the runway and carefully leaned the fuel/air mixture until the plane's engine produced maximum power. I had not done that, and it made a big difference. This improved power allowed us to leave the ground. He held the plane at very low altitude, accelerating it in ground effect.

When the power lines were looming ahead, he yanked the plane up and over them. I was sitting in the back (safest place!) and swear that the power lines flashed by within three feet of our wheels. Whew – that was close. I never forgot that lesson. Calculate expected take-off distance *before* you land in a marginal field!

Slowly, over a period of 2 years, I accumulated enough flying hours and solo cross-country flights to qualify for the Private Pilot's check ride. This involved a lot of winter flying, which has its own share of challenges. Airports are the coldest places in town. Preflighting a plane in winter, in Rochester was no fun at all. It is a very big no-no to take off with snow or frost on the wings, and it has to be carefully brushed or scraped off. That is a long, tedious task in the teeth of an icy Canadian winter wind blowing across Lake Ontario. Did I mention that I love California?

One preflight task involves draining fuel samples from various points on the wings and belly of an airplane. Then one can visually check for the presence of water, kerosene or dirt. The most frequently used fuel is dyed blue (100 Octane Low Lead) and water shows up as distinct little drops rolling around at the bottom of the clear fuel sample cup.

One cold Rochester morning, I did this chore once again. Drawing fuel from the left tank, I did not see the telltale drops of water and should have been satisfied. But some sixth sense warned me. 30 years later, I do not quite remember what it was. Maybe it was so surprising to find no water at all – which was uncommon in these old planes with brittle fuel gaskets – or the color did not look right or maybe the gasoline smell wasn't strong enough. In any case, I got suspicious, poured some fluid on my palm and sniffed. No gasoline smell whatsoever! I put a drop on my tongue – no biting sensation.

It was water! The whole damned cup was full of nothing but water! I drained another one, with the same result, and then a third one. That was enough for me. I marched back to the FBO and got the owner involved. This time he took me very seriously. He came out and started draining the tank himself. Cup after cup, nothing but water. When gas finally started appearing, we had drained about a liter of water from the tank. The other tank contained several cups of water, too.

This was a potentially lethal situation. If the reminder of the fuel system contained enough fuel to start the engine, taxi and begin the take-off before the water hit the engine, the engine would have quit right after takeoff. This is a common occurrence and usually fatal. For once, I found the FBO seriously concerned about a maintenance issue. Unfortunately, we never found out how all this water got into the tanks. It may have been a combination of melting snow, leaking filler gaskets or prolonged sitting – who knows.

Checkride

Finally the big day of the flight test arrived. The examiner was a friendly man but with a tough reputation. Any flight test starts with an oral examination. He asked good and interesting questions. For example – if a plane, with its engine stopped, can glide a certain distance from a certain altitude, how far can it possibly glide if someone had loaded it up with so much stuff that it was twice as heavy? Surprising answer – there is no change to the gliding distance. You just have to fly faster.

Then he asked more questions about v-speeds to fly, engine operations, airspace and finally gave me a distant airport as a destination. My job was to plan a cross-country flight there. I did, and we finally went flying. We took off and headed toward the first checkpoint of our trip. When I had found it, he declared that weather had closed our destination and we needed to divert to another airstrip, south of Rochester. I had not been there, as it was a very small field. I calculated the necessary course and fuel requirements.

Fortunately I found the airfield without trouble. Go ahead and land, the examiner said. This was surprising, since this is usually not part of the check ride. The strip was long but awfully narrow. It was a handful to keep the plane on the centerline of the runway. The examiner seemed satisfied. We took off again and he asked me do some stalls and hood work.

A hood looks like an oversized ballpark cap that limits your view to the instrument panel and prevents you from looking out and see the horizon. All this worked out ok, and he asked me to fly back to Rochester and land. He did not let on how I had done. On final, he told me that he would land the plane. He made a beautiful landing, holding the plane off the runway until the tires chirped on the concrete. Was this a good sign or a bad sign? We taxied to the usual tie down spot, shut the engine down and he congratulated me to passing the private pilot test ride.

What a relief! His main criticism was that I was rather sloppy about staying on the centerline of the runway on take-off. That was the reason that he made me land on the narrow strip. He wanted to see if I could keep the plane under lateral control. He admonished me to always stay on the centerline, even on wide, big runways and spoke the traditional words that a pilot's license is a license to learn.

Pilot's License-Part II

After passing the check ride, a newly minted private pilot is legally qualified to take non-paying passengers to the air. The problem many of these hopeful new pilots face is that nobody in his or her right mind wants to go with them! This reluctance seems particularly pronounced with most members of the prettier sex. For weeks, the new pilot will hector friends, bribe colleagues and beg family members, only to be turned down again and again. With some luck, he can talk a flying buddy to go with him.

In my case, I managed to talk one of our female graduate students – Arden- with whom I was on good terms, into becoming my very first passenger. I checked out the plane, got the keys and proudly marched to the little red plane sitting on the field. I confidently climbed on the wing, stuck the key in the lock and turned it. Rather, I tried to turn the key, but it would not turn. Knowing that airplane locks and doors are cantankerous, flimsy things, I wiggled and pushed, twisted and cajoled that stupid lock. It was a no go. The sliding canopy just would not open. I got hot under the collar. What an impression this must have made on Arden. Here is this new pilot and he can't even get into the plane! After several minutes of vain attempts, I admitted defeat and slinked back to the FBO. It turned out that somehow the wrong key had been given the tag for this airplane, thus it wasn't my stupidity. Still, I never could quite get over this and nor could Arden. I have absolutely no recollection of this flight, nor were there any more flights with her later.

The lesson for any newly minted private pilot is: fly for your own enjoyment and never try to push a non-flyer to go up with you. Come to think, this is always a good rule, independent of how many flight hours one has accumulated.

The FAA is rightfully very concerned that private pilots never fly passengers for profit. This is the domain of pilots with commercial or airline transport (ATP) ratings. Private pilots can share operating costs of the plane if the use of the plane is incidental to the trip, but not in any other case. The FAA comes down very hard on private pilots who even slightly violate these rules.

The commercial rating is actually surprisingly easy to obtain, compared to the instrument rating, which is an orthogonal measure to the pilot's pyramid shown below.

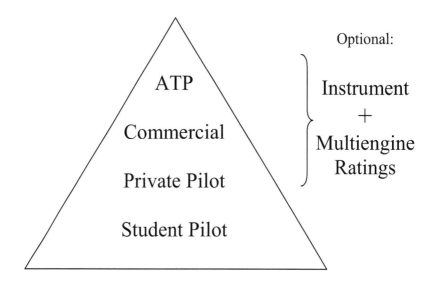

He could be an ax-murderer! Dating Dr. Anita Borg

See also pages 202,203,206,207

After Karen, my first wife, died, I was in a funk for about two years. I did not quite realize it at the time and thought that I handled the loss quite well, but was kidding myself. There were no professional accomplishment during this time to be proud of – I just did not care. Nor were any new adventures or travels happening in this time. I barely remember these years. It goes to show how important attitude is for living life well.

All that changed when an old friend of mine, Gary Hoffman, dropped an issue of the San Jose Mercury News on my office desk. The 'Merc' is the main newspaper of San Jose and, implicitly, Silicon Valley. Gary was under strict orders from his wife, Furong, to give it to me and insist I should read a specific section. It was about a woman in high technology.
"Yeah, yeah, I will read it if Furong insists,"
I muttered, not very enthusiastically. My desk was covered with work related stuff, which needed attention.

But a few days later I picked up the newspaper. It was a Sunday supplement, several pages thick. Its cover page showed a large picture of a very attractive, gray-haired lady. She looked very spunky, standing on top of a pile of computers. The title said "Mother of Inventions" The lady was Dr. Anita Borg, founder and Director of the Institute for Women and Technology.

I read it with growing interest. Anita had observed that, for all their progress, women were still vastly under-represented in technology professions. As a student of physics I knew that fact only too well. Female physics students are as rare as hen's teeth. The ratio was much better in computer science, but still only one third of all computer science PhD were female. Only the life sciences had achieved parity. Dr. Borg had made it her goal to do something about this problem – and she did it with energy, enthusiasm, provocative insights and a wealth of new ideas.

For example, she felt that there were many devices, which could be designed better using women's input. A provocative quote of hers became a favorite of the many reporters covering her and the institute: "The Palm Pilot is a great gadget. But what if it were designed for a woman's – rather than a man's – breast pocket?" That was her style – outrageous, insightful, funny and always thought-inspiring.

She made many remarks about technology and gadgets, which resonated well with my increasingly critical thoughts about the same issues. I kept reading. She was divorced. Then I turned the page and saw a picture of hers, standing under the wing of a Cessna 150 aircraft. The caption stated that she was a pilot! That did it – I now really wanted to get in contact with her.

I mulled it over for nearly half an hour and then wrote her an e-mail. This was 1999, and search engines already made it easy to find contact information. In the e-mail I said a few words about myself, that I admired her work and commented that her critical remarks about the uselessness of many technology gadgets reflected my own attitude as a recovering early adaptor for gadgetry. Then I added a hook in the form of a postscript: It said:

"… but there are exceptions. The Gamin 430 is an absolutely marvelous device."

Two days later Dr. Borg replied to my e-mail. As she told me later, she received many such e-mails, but especially the postscript about the Gamin 430 triggered her curiosity. She did not know what a Gamin 430 was, but suspected that it was a device related to aviation, even though the e-mail had not said anything directly about

He could be an ax-murderer

flying. Her hunch was correct – the Garmin 430 was and still is a bench mark for aerial GPS navigation systems. We exchanged a few more e-mails and soon agreed to meet in person. I suggested flying to Yosemite Valley, which she found to be a great idea. The staff of the institute was aghast.

"You do not know this guy and getting into a plane with him? He could be an axe-murderer for all you know!"

But her staff was behind the times. Anita had looked me up on the web and concluded that few axe murderers are employed as senior technologists at IBM. So she did not see much risk.

We met in San Jose and drove to the airport where I keep a Bonanza A36. As she later wrote:

"I had expected that we would rent a little two-seater somewhere to fly to Yosemite-Mariposa. But then we drove up to his hangar, in which was this big, powerful Bonanza. This was not what I had expected." I realized that Bonanzas can be better than Porsches for dating.

Our first day together was a romantic dream. We flew to Mariposa, where I kept a 20 year old Volkswagen Vanagon. Having had somewhat of a hippie background in the sixties, Dr. Borg – by now Anita – found that very neat. We drove along the winding Mariposa river, marveled at the rushing waters and talked and talked. We talked about our lives, ambitions, idols, technology, work, travels, and adventure. We wandered under the tall waterfalls and the towering granite walls of Yosemite Valley and had a late lunch at the Awahnee Hotel, which is one of the most romantic places in America.

We took off from Mariposa, using the last daylight. That was important to me, because I really hate to take off from that airport at night. Its runway 26 points directly towards a nearby hill, which has no lights whatsoever. It is a nightmarish feeling to hurtle towards this invisible obstacle without knowing for certain if one is going to out climb it. I know that feeling from experience.

As we cruised home, over the dark flat expanse of the California central valley, the full moon rose in the east. Little did I know at the time that Anita found few things more romantic than moon light. We flew home in silence, perfectly content, contemplating the possibilities this day had opened. After landing, however, I did not hug or kiss her. She liked to tell her friends the story that I saluted and clicked heels, making fun of my German background. That story is absolutely not true!

Cancer and Wedding

This wonderful day led to a whirlwind romance. We got married a year later, unfortunately over-shadowed – and accelerated – by the fact that she was diagnosed two weeks before with a deadly brain tumor, already in its final stage. The oncologists in Stanford sent her home to die in a few weeks – and made some outrageous claims, which nearly sabotaged our insurance coverage, with six figures at stake. The details are too painful to recount here.

Fortunately, the head of Neuro Surgery – Dr. Michael Berger- at the University of California in San Francisco disagreed with the Stanford opinion, performed two complex brain surgeries and gave Anita three active years to enjoy life. Dr. Berger was our real hero – not only for the surgeries he performed, but other things he did related to this case.

As an aside - Anita received X-ray treatment after the surgery, too. The doses were very high, over 1000 REM per treatment, if I remember correctly. If this had been a full body irradiation, it would have been deadly. But it had the interesting side effect that for a few days after the brain irradiation Anita turned very hostile. It took a few treatment cycles before we realized the causal relation.

He could be an ax-murderer

Anita and I got married on the Saturday between Dr. Berger's decision to operate and the actual surgery on the following Wednesday. It is funny how a wedding, which is the source of so much stress for most couples, becomes a quick, fun affair if you know you'll be on the operating table in a life-and-death surgery a few days hence. We invited 50 friends and had a great wedding in Anita's house, overlooking the Bay of San Francisco.

The three years were wonderful, except I found it hard to get used to being called Mr. Borg all the time. Anita did not change her name, of course. It would have been silly to do so, since she was so well known.

Now her institute has been renamed as the *Anita Borg Institute* [30] and is thriving under the able leadership of Dr. Telle Whitney. The Anita Borg fellowships, underwritten by Google, have become a token of excellence. They are now a major career achievement for young women going into computer technology.

Living with Anita was rather interesting. Ok, that is an understatement. She was a bundle of energy, fun loving, liked to kayak and dance (here we parted ways) and was equally adept at deep strategic discussions or planning a prank. It is easy to see why she became a mythos among women in her field. Fortunately, her enormous contributions were recognized with many honors. She received two Dr. h.c. in addition to her own PhD.

We had fun kidding around how she would be addressed in Germany, where even a woman who has no doctorate, but is married to a Doktor, is addressed as Frau Doktor. We figured that the proper title sequencing would

---

[30] www.anitaborg.org

He could be an ax-murderer

be Doktor Doktor Doktor Frau Doktor Borg. My European friends never quite understood why we found this so funny.

Another major honor she received was the Heinz Award for Technology, Economy and Employment in 2002. This is a big deal. The Heinz awards were established in 1993 by Teresa Heinz in memory of her late husband, Senator John Heinz. The awards are given annually to honor leaders in the area of greatest importance to the senator. These awards are slowly becoming a social sciences equivalent of the Nobel prices. It was a true honor to meet Mrs. Heinz. From all what I have learned about Senator John Heinz, he must have been a truly outstanding human being. The text of her acceptance speech for the Heinz award is included as an appendix.

Anita liked Europe and we spent a lot of time in France – where she was supporting an archeological dig at the medieval town of Nuyeres – and in France and Switzerland.

She liked to drive fast. That shouldn't come as a surprise. A physicist friend of hers owned a Porsche Boxter, and when he moved overseas to work at CERN, she bought it. She looked great in her maroon sports car, driving up and down the twisting roads in the mountains bordering Silicon Valley.

The car was fun to drive, but a maintenance nightmare. All kinds of important things broke or fell off. Well, it was a first year production car. We knew it was a risk. Today Boxters have a good reputation for quality. But I will never forgive it that it broke down on the day we were to receive the word on the type of Anita's cancer. At least the task of having it towed home distracted us from the disastrous news she had just received. I sold it soon after her death, and the ignition system failed completely a day after the sale. This Porsche had a perfect track record.

He could be an ax-murderer

She taught me the basics of kayaking and we spent hours paddling along the wild coast of California near Monterey. These were very happy moments. Having a deadly cancer doesn't destroy joy in life – one just lives more for the here and now and enjoys the little things life has to offer.

One of the 'little' things in her life was a two-seat Cessna 150, which I had bought her as a birthday gift in 2001. She couldn't fly alone anymore, but, as always, the task of piloting a craft through the air makes all other sorrows appear unimportant. Such is the magic of flying.

Anita was a great cook, too, and loved to entertain. Her house in the coastal hills overlooking the Bay of San Francisco was often a place for great parties. She loved to dress up and got herself a turquoise mermaid suit tailored once she learned about Karen's great experience with hers. She had a lot of fun diving with dolphins, manta rays, large turtles and other critters in the Caribbean, South Pacific and Hawaii.

At the same time, she was leading her institute as much as her slowly deteriorating capability to read and talk allowed. She demonstrated that receiving the diagnosis of suffering from an inevitably fatal cancer is not a reason to sink into despair, but to live life to the fullest and make the best out of it.

Her reaction is on par with that of R.J.Mitchell, who was diagnosed with a fatal abdominal cancer, yet managed to design the fabled Spitfire fighter, which so successfully defended Britain against the Luftwaffe attacks.

I am so glad that many thousands of women are every year affected by her work. She will be remembered by thousands for a long, long time. Among these are the young women who have received the coveted Anita Borg Fellowships, which are funded by Google.

Thanks, Alan Eustace!!

He could be an ax-murderer

Who'll Come a' Waltzing Matilda With Me

For a few years, my office mate at the University of Rochester was an unflappable Australian physicist from Perth – Dr. John Birkelund, now with Kodak Research. He was a great physicist and a guy one could steal horses with. Ever since knowing John, I had a fondness for Australia. When I first visited it, I fell in love with this amazing place. This story is a little tribute to down under...

Waltzing Matilda is an Australian folksong – and Australia's unofficial national anthem. As I'm writing this, I'm listening to a rousing rendition by the Australian folk singer John Williamson and furiously trying to transcribe his words:

> *There once was a jolly swagman camped by a billabong,*
> *Under the shade of a Coolibah tree,*
> *And he sang as he watched and waited 'til his billy boiled,*
> *"Who'll come a-Waltzing Matilda, with me?"*
>
> *Down came a jumbuck to drink at the billabong,*
> *Up got the swaggy and grabbed him with glee,*
> *And he sang as he stowed that jumbuck in his tucker bag,*
> *"You'll come a-Waltzing Matilda, with me."*
>
> *Waltzing Matilda, Waltzing Matilda*
> *"You'll come a-Waltzing Matilda, with me"*
> *And he sang as he stowed that jumbuck in his tucker bag,*
> *" You'll come a-Waltzing Matilda, with me."*
>
> *Down came the squatter, mounted on his thoroughbred.*
> *Up came the troopers, one, two, three,*
> *"Whose is the jolly jumbuck you've got in your tucker bag?"*
> *"You'll come a-Waltzing Matilda, with me."*
>
>
> *Waltzing Matilda, Waltzing Matilda*
> *" You'll l come a-Waltzing Matilda, with me?"*

Waltzing Mathilda

"Whose is the jolly jumbuck you've got in your tucker bag?,"
" You'll come a-Waltzing Matilda, with me?"

Up got the swaggy and jumped into the billabong,
"You'll never catch me alive," said he,
And his ghost may be heard as you pass by that billabong,
" You'll come a-Waltzing Matilda, with me?"

Waltzing Matilda, Waltzing Matilda
You'll come a-Waltzing Matilda, with me?
And his ghost may be heard as you pass by that billabong,
"Who'll come a-Waltzing Matilda, with me?"

Waltzing Matilda is a tribute to the Aussie's sense of independence, dislike for authority and their love for the bush. I just love the song and the country.
The lyrics may need some translation to the Queen's English:

A swagman (or swaggy) is an itinerant farm worker. He has wrapped up all his belongings in a roll, his Mathilda, and he is walking (waltzing) with it. The song got nothing to do with dancing whatsoever! A billabong is a pond in the bush, and he sits there, watching water in his pot (billy) boil. As we waits, a sheep (jumbuck) comes to drink and he grabs it and stores it in his bag. Just at this moment a landowner (squatter) on a thoroughbred horse comes by, along with three troopers. Rather than allowing himself to be arrested, he jumps into the billabong and drowns. He is independent to the end – very Australian. The term for landowner is telling. In other English speaking countries, a *squatter* means someone illegally living on land. In Australia it means an established landowner!

The Australian language and customs are a source of endless wonderment. For example, a man is a *mate* or a *bloke*, a woman a *sheila*, a small child is an *ankle biter* and an English gent is a *pommy bastard*.

Waltzing Mathilda

The ending ...*ie* is a frequently used term of endearment, as in "I will have a *stumpie* (small beer) with the *shrimpie* on the *barbie*."

Beer, of course, is the national drink of the Aussies, even though the growing of wine in the southwest near Melbourne has made great progress. The best-known Australian beer is Fosters, delivered in bloke-sized blue and yellow cans and –incidentally- advertised all over the Caribbean. I like Fosters and am engaged in an endless quest for actually finding Fosters when cruising in the Caribbean. Most of the time, the little shops in the Caribbean do not actually have it stocked and this bloke has to settle for a Red Stripe from Jamaica. Fosters shows a great sense of humor in their advertisements, making fun of the Australian language. One example is an ad depicting three surfboards leaning against each other on a beach. The byline says "Australian for board meeting."

Anita and I have both been invited a couple of times to New Zealand and Australia to give talks (and some attempts were made to lure us away from California, but sorry mates, no dice) and greatly enjoyed the experiences. Melbourne is a lovely city, which reminds me very much of Europe. It is located at the lower Yarra River. A beautiful aquarium and great restaurants can be found along the banks of the Yarra. Melbourne's network of electric trolleys gives it a very continental feel. It is the second most important city in Australia, and Melbourne is engaged in a good-natured rivalry with Sydney.

Canberra is not taken very seriously by Australians. While it is the capital of Australia, it seems to be seen as outsider. A frequently heard joke:
" Canberra? Aye mate, that's eight suburbs in search of a city."
This attitude towards Canberra reflects the overall attitude of Australians towards their government. It is there, but not to be taken very seriously.

Outside the cities the bush is awaiting. That word simply means anywhere, which is not in a town. It has nothing to do with vegetation. While Aussies pride themselves on their bush, the vast majority lives in cities. But the closeness of the bush (by definition) and its importance in Australia's history makes it a towering presence in the nation's conscience. It includes the endless stretches of thin forests, lovely smelling stands of Eucalyptus and Coolibah trees, the mind-bending reddish deserts and the gentle rolling ranges covering the periphery of much of Australia.

The interior is a place, which has to be seen to be believed. A big part of Australia is taken up by the *Null Arbor* plane. That's Latin for no (null) trees – and they mean it. Up north is the *gun-barrel highway* – a dirt road as straight as a gun barrel. There are few places better for off-roading than Australia – and in many places it is not an idle luxury, but the only way to get somewhere, except by a bush plane.

Until recently, flying was minimally regulated and affordable. But after 9/11, the Australian authorities, in a very un-Australian show of panic, clamped down on the freedom of the air which was such a big part of the Australian experience. That is too bad, particularly now that GPS has solved the Australian navigation problem. Old-fashioned navigation by pilotage and dead reckoning over a featureless bush is not for weak sticks[31].

The Aussies seem to be more proud of their animal kingdom than anything else except Waltzing Mathilda. But they do no brag about the grandeur of a million cockatiels taking to wing or the hilarious experiences with cockatoos descending on a campsite, demanding handouts. No, they

---

[31] Common term for bad pilots

are inordinately proud that they have the most poisonous, aggressive and dangerous bunch of critters around – and this did not just start with Crocodile Dundee.

I'm never quite sure what is true and what are tall tales when Aussies order another *pint of piss* (large beer) and regale the innocent from abroad with wildlife stories. These invariably feature monster saltwater crocs's, scorpions which can kill with one look, deadly stone fish, a tiny, blue-ringed octopus whose bite will kill and – horror of horrors - killer *'roos* loose at night.

The latter refers to the big kangaroos which bound about carelessly and in surprisingly large numbers. A collision between one of these *buggers* and a car is bad news for both sides. That's why a lot of Australian 4WD cars sport sturdy iron 'roo bars mounted over their grill. It is supposed to deflect the 'roo. Once I watched a large group of kangaroos hanging out on a public golf course along the great ocean road in southern Australia. They seemed quite dumb as they paid no attention to the golfers whatsoever. Nor did the golfers - except they tried to play around the many big droppings the 'roos had left on the grass.

It is a wonderful country to travel in. The natives are friendly, there are beautifully kept campgrounds all around – or you can camp off in the bush, and nobody will complain. But watch out for the killer animals.

PS – a piece of advice when you are male and drinking at an Aussie bar: never empty your glass and put it on the counter upside down.
That means: *"I will take on any bloke in here."*

South Pacific Penguins

See also pages 201,203,204,205

The first time I saw a penguin in the wild was in the South Pacific. It had yellow eyes and carried a briefcase. Well, the latter is not quite true, but it should have. It was near Dunedin, on the scenic South Island of New Zealand.

Anita had a good friend there, who is a professor of biology at the university of Dunedin. She is an expert on the New Zealand yellow-eyed penguins and works hard to save them, as they are an endangered species. Their daily routine involves commuting between their nests, which are hidden in bushes and hunting for fish during the day.

Late one evening Anita's friend drove us in her old Defender 4WD to one of the lonely beaches on the southeast coast of the island. It is the South Pacific, all right, but here it feels already cold and faintly hostile. Somehow it seems very plausible that the icy shores of Antarctica are your next stop if you'd head south from this beach. Not far away, giant Albatross birds have their nesting colony. A cold wind blew in from the grey ocean as we made ourselves comfortable in a small hole near the beach.

The penguins were certainly out there – we could see their heads bobbing on the water - but so were surfers. They might scare the penguins from going ashore, the professor said. Finally, as it got darker, the surfers got out of the water. Now the penguins should dare to come home. I had a sensitive Sony PC110 video camera set up on a tripod, but I was still worried that it would get too dark to film the penguins.

We waited and waited – and finally they came out. First one, then two, then a whole group of penguins. They jumped out of small breaking waves and most landed upright on the beach. The penguins fear crossing the broad sandy beach. They know that they are vulnerable to land-based predators as they do it. The group of penguins stood at water's edge, looking around nervously. They scanned the beach up and down, again and again.

Finally, one of them summoned the courage to try it. It quickly waddled, upright, across the 200' wide beach. Penguins can't run, they move in a fast shuffle. Soon all seven were on the move. They looked like a bunch of New York commuters in dark suits. Only their briefcases were missing. In their urge to cross the beach some of them fell down, but they got up within seconds. There was no way they'd dawdle on this open beach. All made it to the safety of their suburbia homes. If they had seen anything which had spooked them, they would have turned around and spend a long night in the cold water, exposed to sea lions and sharks.

Linus Thorvalds, the creator of Linux, visited a penguin sanctuary 20 km south of there and fell in love with these birds. That's the origin of the penguin mascot of the open source software movement. One can see why he picked these cute birds for the mascot of Linux!

Like virtually everyone who visits New Zealand, Anita and I fell in love with this country. It is such a delightful combination of charming old England towns, towering mountains, lonely jungles, pastoral landscapes and a fascinating Maori culture. The Western edge of the island is dominated by the aptly named Southern Alps. I have seen many mountain ranges which look impressive on a map – just judging from their altitudes- but are disappointingly smooth and boring in real life. This wasn't the case with the Southern Alps.

Like the European Alps, southern New Zealand is a kingdom of sharp needles, towering peaks and glistening glaciers. Best of all, a network of little airports provides many jump-off points for impressive low-level sightseeing flights over and around the great peaks of the Southern Alps. During one of the flights we circled Mt. Cook, which is the tallest mountain in New Zealand at 12,313 feet. It was 50 feet higher a few years back, but a piece of the summit broke off.

We landed on the Kaiser Franz Joseph Glacier as passengers in a Jet Ranger helicopter. It was very strange to find the name of an Austrian emperor given to this magnificent glacier near the antipodes of Europe. Flying low over the glacier, one could see how the initially smooth ice flow cracked as it dropped over an increasingly steep terrain and turned into rugged crevices and icy steps. It was an exhilarating flight.

Yet I always feel strangely conflicted when flying in a plane over such wonderful mountain landscapes. All my life I've been hiking in mountains and feel very challenged by them. Shortcutting all this effort by using a plane or helicopter seems a bit like cheating.

In the center of the South island, on the shores of Lake Wakatipu, one can find Queenstown. This is the capital of outdoor nuts and it puts California to shame. All kinds of wacky activities were invented here. The most famous is bungee jumping, which was started here by a few wacky kiwis jumping off a bridge over a deep canyon near Queenstown, with a rubber cord tied around their ankles. Hang-gliding, triathlon, off-roading – you name it, it is pursued near Queenstown and on Lake Wakatipu.

An ancient steamer - the TSS Earnslaw - is carrying tourists across the lake. It was carried in parts, overland, to the high altitude lake and re-assembled here. It's mission was to transport sheep, but fortunately the smell is finally gone. The engine room is open to the public. Big boards explain the detailed workings of the twin 500 HP triple-expansion steam engines. Key parts of the machinery were painted in bright colors and cross-referenced to the boards, making it easy to understand the workings of everything. Triple expansion means that the high-pressure steam from the boilers first drives a small, 13" diameter piston. The steam leaving this cylinder pushes a 18" piston and finally a 22" piston. After this, the spent steam is condensed into water. All three cylinders drive the same crankshaft. It was fascinating to see all of it in action while we were steaming across the big mountain lake. I have been Scuba diving into quite a few engine rooms of major wrecks – always a dark and challenging venture - so it was a real pleasure to see live engines for a change. At full speed, the beasts had to be fed with over half a ton of coal per hour. All that coal had to be shoveled by hand into the furnace.

Until this trip, I never realized that the bridge of a traditional steamer has no direct control over the engine. The only link is by voice tube and the machine telegraph. This is a mechanical pointing device, which the bridge crew sets to the desired speeds (such as *dead stop, slow, reverse* and *full speed ahead*) The pointer is replicated in the engine room. But the officers on the bridge rely entirely on the engine room gang to execute their commands. Only the rudder can be directly controlled from the bridge. It was fascinating to look over the captain's shoulders as he worked to bring this big old 'Lady of the Lake' alongside the dock of Queenstown. It takes a lot of skill to do this smoothly.

The British used the Tiger Moth as a military trainer. It is a open cockpit bi-plane, similar to the American Stearman, but much smaller and more frugal. An in-line engine drives it, rather than the honking big radial engine of the Stearman. American planes have a compass the size of a fist. The Tiger Moth had a compass the size of a dinner plate, seemingly lifted right from a destroyer's bridge. England is a sea-going nation – and it shows in her planes, too!

We flew, in formation in these Tiger Moths, wearing heavy leather jackets and goggles. We weren't issued white silk scarfs, but they are a most useful 'fashion' accessory in flying bi-planes. Their main purpose it to keep precious body heat in, and they also lubricate the neck as one swivels it in search for other planes. Otherwise the skin on the neck will get raw very quickly, chafing on the leather jacket's collar as you scan the airspace. Flying with the wind in your face and with an unobstructed view to the ground is far more dramatic than experiencing the same flight in a modern plane. I can see why flying open biplanes is so addictive.

The spectacular Milford sound is on the west coast of New Zealand. Rudyard Kipling called it the 8th wonder of the world. The sound is actually a deep fjord. Fjords are defined as glacier carved valleys filled by the ocean and can be found in many places, not only in Norway. Captain Cook – who missed few things – sailed past the entrance to Milford Sound without realizing what he missed. The opening of the sound looks innocuous from the sea, but once you make your way into it, it is a spectacular landscape of ocean and vertical rock walls.

We arrived at Milford sound in a small *Twin Islander* propeller plane, which Anita and I had chartered. There is a small airstrip (MFN) at the end of the fjord. Landing there is interesting. One motors up the fjord, at low altitude and so close to the right rock wall that the starboard wing seems to touch it. Then one passes over the beach and enters a narrow valley. The airport is visible below, apparently unreachable.

But do not loose trust in the published approach procedure. Continue to fly up the valley, with very tall vertical walls towering over you on all sides. Then, fortunately, the valley widens again and provides just enough room for a steep turn to reverse course and line up for runway 29. A river guides one to the airport. What a way to arrive in Milford sound! Once on the ground, the best plan is to take a trip on one of the excursion boats, which ply the waters of the sound. They provide a magnificent view of Mitre Peak, which towers over the inner part of the fjord. It looks like a bishop's hat, hence the name. It is hard to believe, but it has been climbed. Looking at it from the sea, it seems like an impossible feat. But New Zealanders love to do these kinds of things.

By the way, the best way to see New Zealand is with a Diesel camper van. They are readily available and the country has a great network of spotless campgrounds. This is what Anita and I did. But just beware of the birds, especially the fearless Kea parrots. They hang out near campgrounds and will rob you blind, given halfway a chance.

South Pacific Islands

See also page 216,205,161,207,213,161

Tonga

At 25 degrees southern latitude, north-northeast of New Zealand's is the ancient Kingdom of Tonga. It is the only island group in the South Pacific, which has never been under the control of a colonial power. Tonga is a proud nation of very big people. It is still an absolute monarchy.

This fact is noticeable to the casual visitor. The airline of Tonga had three planes when we visited. The problem is that any member of the royal family – and there are many members – can commandeer any plane for his or her personal use. Thus traveling in Tonga contains always an element of randomness. Handing out packs of cigarettes simplifies traveling in this country.

Karen and I chartered a bare-boat (just the boat, no crew) from the Moorings. The company has a charter base in the northern island group of Vava'u. The main town and harbor of Naiafu is located at the end of a long, winding fjord. The *Paradise Hotel* overlooks this idyllic harbor and is popular with the expatriate community. Some of these are colorful characters with great stories to tell, but many have succumbed to the stupor of the tropics, cheap rum and Kava.

Hemingway would feel right at home at the expansive bar of the Paradise hotel. It was finished with beautiful mahogany wood, as a nautical bar should. This is where the sailor's expression of being *'Hard aground on the mahogany reef'* originated. Of course, that means being drunk as drunk can be.

I was anchored (not yet hard aground!) at the mahogany reef of the Paradise Hotel when I first saw the Southern Cross. But it is not much to look at – it is a disappointingly small and unimpressive constellation. But the view of the large and small Magellanic Clouds was fascinating. They are only visible on the southern hemisphere. These are two mini galaxies, about 200,000 light years from our home galaxy, i.e. the Milky way. That is less than 10% of the distance to the nearest full-size galaxy, the Andromeda nebula (2.5 Million light years). Interestingly, recent measurements have shown that the Magellanic Clouds are not gravitationally bound to our galaxy. They are just paying us a visit.

We checked out our 32' Beneteau sloop and set off among the islands of the Vava'u' group. This first sailing outing in the South Pacific felt differently. It was far more alien than the familiar surroundings of the Caribbean.

The waters between the islands are rather poorly charted. Once we were sailing fast over a stretch of ocean south of the Vava'u group. There the water should be deep and no obstacles were shown on the chart. Yet, suddenly I saw some coral heads going by on port, only a few feet below the keel. That surely catches a skipper's attention! If one hits a coral head at hull speed in a heavy keel boat, the result can be a quick sinking.

In addition, the entire island appeared to be shifted a few hundred meters in the east-west direction, compared to the chart. That is not unusual in the isolated islands of the South Pacific. Many charts in use today are derived from 19th century soundings by the British Navy. Since longitude measurements relied on accurate, shipboard clocks (chronometers), any error in knowing the correct time – not unlikely after a long voyage to an outlying island like the Tonga group – translates directly into a longitudinal position error. The effects are large–a one-minute chronometer error, at the equator, translates into a 15 nautical mile error. Still, navigation in Tonga wasn't a problem. The islands are close enough that one can see several of them at the same time and work out -from bearings taken with a handheld compass- the boat's true position relative to the islands. Also, the entire island group is shifted west by a fixed amount, thus it was easy to apply the longitudinal correction factor once and for all.

Some underwater features –such as sand banks and coral reefs do change over time. The Tuamotu Archipelago in French Polynesia is infamous for this. Strangely enough, the charts we used were silent about all these surprises for the prudent mariner.

Many of the little islands are inhabited. The popular image of the South Pacific as studded with countless uninhabited islands -open to exploration- is wrong. Even the smallest speck of land has an owner. One should track down the nearest chief and ask for permission to go ashore. Needless to say, this is a major hassle. Where can one find the chief, anyhow? Paul Theroux, in his rather caustic book "The Happy Islands of Oceania" describes his mixed experiences while kayaking among the South Pacific islands. As charterers from the Mooring Company we were somewhat better off, protected by the (then) almighty dollar, yet I never became as comfortable sailing down south as in the Caribbean.

Feasts are unique highlights of any South Pacific sailing voyage. Today they are mostly held for tourists, but they are still quite an experience. The food is served on big palm leaves, and one sits cross-legged in front of them. There are no chairs and no silverware. The act of shoving fish, crabs and other food by finger into one's mouth gives a surprisingly different and more intimate relationship to food.

We had a few interesting underwater experiences in the Tongan limestone caves. *Mariner's cave* is located on the island of N'uapapu, named after a young British sailor. Mariner was marooned in Tonga from 1806 to 1810, but he finally managed to return to England. The cave is hidden and can only be reached by snorkeling through a submerged entrance. Fortunately, there is always air trapped in the cave, but the ocean's wave action outside will compress and decompress it periodically. This is hard on the eardrums. As the air pressure drops, a dense fog[32] forms instantaneously. Being in this cave is a ghostly experience. The only light in the cave enters through the underwater entrance, bathing the cave in deep blue luminescence.

Seen from inside, the underwater cave entrance has the shape of a heart. This may have something to do with a South Pacific version of the Romeo and Juliet story. A tyrannical ruler once ordered all members of a rival family killed. But a young man in the king's family, in love with a girl from the other family, spirited her into the cave. There she hid until they both could escape on a passing ship.

Tonga was not an island of love, in spite what their tourist slogan says. Cannibalism was quite common, even though today the Tongan's blame the Fijians as the main perpetrators. In Tonga, becoming a cook was an inadvisable career choice. Cooks were considered members of the lowest cast – perhaps because they sometimes had to deal with *human* food. To mark a man as a cook, his left arm was amputated – using stone knifes. Metal was not known to the South Pacific islanders, i.e. they were a genuine stone age culture. The number of cooks in a chief's household was considered a mark of his status. Some kings had a dozen cooks. Ouch. I sure hope they gave the poor

---

[32] The same effect is used in certain nuclear detectors, called cloud chambers. Ionizing particles leave tracks in saturated water vapors.

chaps plenty of Kava to drink before their graduation ceremony (see below).

It is rumored that the taste of human meat resembles that of pork. In most languages of the South Pacific the term for the edible victim is 'long pig', and cynical expats claim that the universal fondness for Spam (spiced pork) down there is a relic of old traditions.

An important tradition in the islands is the Kava ceremony. It is a drink made from the roots of the Kava plant. The traditional preparation is to have women chew the Kava roots and spit the mush into a bowl. The men drink the Kava prepared in this appetizing manner in a slow, methodical session, which lasts many hours. I tried only the modern version of Kava, which is prepared by just grinding the root. It tastes awful, like slightly spicy dishwater and leaves a numbing feeling in the mouth. I will stick with European drinks, thank you. The islanders say that the modern preparation is not as good as the chew and spit method.

On the island of Kapa is beautiful Swallow's cave. Unlike Mariner's cave, it is not hidden at all. One can take a dinghy right into this big and very deep cavern. We did one dive in this cave and I nearly drowned. The cause was sheer stupidity.
Karen had agreed to wear her mermaid suit, since I wanted to get classy photos of a mermaid floating against the blue-backlit cave entrance. We piled the Scuba gear into our dinghy and motored into the cave, where Karen secured the dinghy with a long rope to a rock. The dinghy floated about in the middle of the deep cave.

The dinghy was too small for both of us to put our gear on simultaneously. Karen slipped into her mermaid suit and soon was happily swimming underwater by herself. I could see her golden figure undulating below, clearly visible against the dark rocks of the cave walls as I was suiting up. I was in an extremely good mood, very relaxed as I put on my gear. As in aviation, bad things happen to those who are too relaxed.

I rolled backwards into the warm water, wearing my Scuba gear. But I had forgotten a few minor things. For one, the flippers, which were still lying in the bottom of the dinghy. Second, I had not opened the valve of my Scuba tank. Third, there was no air in the BC. Fourth, I had a lot on lead on my belt, because underwater photographers always do that to avoid unwanted positive buoyancy. All these factors combined and when I hit the water, I sank like a rock. That would not have been a problem per se, except I had neither flippers to push me back up nor air to put into the BC nor air to breathe. Last but not least, I got entangled in the line which arced underwater from the dinghy to the rock.

The three stooges going diving couldn't have done worse. Within seconds, my mind switched from serene and relaxed to a sense of "This can't be happening" to "That's really not good, I'm drowning here."

While I was sinking, trying to regain control of the situation and dealing with the nuisance of having no air to breath, my beautiful mermaid swam below me, playing with fish, blissfully unaware of the trouble above her. Eventually I managed to open the valve of the scuba tank on my back, find the dangling regulator and made it up to the dinghy, coughing and out of breath. Finally I joined her, with camera and flippers. Only after the dive she found out what happened. But the pictures of a backlit mermaid floating serenely in front of the beautiful, deep blue cave opening, framed by the dark walls, were well worth a little excitement. One of the photos can be found on the cover of this book.

French Polynesia

Other South Sea trips led us to Fiji and French Polynesia. For the latter visit, Anita and I landed in a big Airbus 340 on the main island of Tahiti, which is a beautiful, high volcanic island. But the main city of Papeete is crowded, noisy and extremely expensive. The French government pumps large amounts of Francs into this overseas département, perhaps motivated by a desire to retain a testing ground for nuclear weapons without triggering too many local protests. As a result, prices in Papeete are even higher than in Paris.

But it is still a magical place. The magnificent volcanic spires of the high island of Moorea are easily visible across the channel, and the aroma of French coffee and fresh croissants suffused our hotel. Next day we flew to the twin islands of Raiatea and Taháa, about 100 miles northwest of Tahiti.

Anthropologists maintain that Raiatea is the fabled mother island, from which most of the Pacific – including Hawaii – once was populated. Today it is a sleepy island, sharing a figure-8 shaped lagoon with its sister island Taháa. The famous island of Bora Bora is about 30 miles further northwest. Anita and I picked up a big 41' Beneteau sailboat from Sunsail on Raiatea and headed out into the lagoon.

Lagoons are a typical South Pacific phenomenon, not found in the Caribbean. They are created when a volcanic island slowly sinks. Corals build a ring around the island, which reaches to the water's surface. Depending on the age of the island and the rate of the island's sinking, the central volcano may still be there, surrounded by the ring of coral, or it may have entirely disappeared, leaving just a ring-shaped reef system. Raiatea and Taháa still have big central peaks.

Sailing in the narrow lagoon between the outer reef and the center island was a new experience for us. At some places the lagoon is several miles wide, whereas elsewhere it is a narrow channel or even entirely blocked. The French have done a great job in marking the complex lagoon system with sturdy, permanent markers and they maintain them well. Thus they can be relied upon, in sharp contrast to the few and unreliable buoys found in the Caribbean.

Anchoring in this lagoon was somewhat of a challenge, as it was often in 60 – 90 feet of water. That is a lot more than the ideal 10 – 15 feet depth, which one often finds in the Caribbean. A powerful electric anchor winch is important when sailing a big boat like a Beneteau 410 with a shorthanded crew (two in our case) in these waters.

Diving in the lagoon is not particularly interesting, at least not for this spoiled diver. The fish action is on the outside of the reef, where it steeply slopes into the abyss. Even better dive sites are the reef *cuts*, which connect the lagoon with the open sea. Because of tidal action, water rushes in and out of these cuts, feeding magnificent corals. Sharks are supposed to hang out in the cuts, but, as usual, I saw none of any interesting stature. Because of her brain tumor, Anita was not able to function well anymore and we did not do a lot of diving or snorkeling.

The eating in the French pacific islands was very good. The island of Taháa is known as the vanilla island. The lagoon is suffused with the lovely smell of vanilla plants, originating from plantations. Even better, every morning, a speedboat with freshly baked hot croissants and other treats circled the Taháa part of the lagoon. Anita was in her glory.

One day, we stopped at a little waterside restaurant called Chez Louise near Tiva village in the lagoon of Taháa. The proprietor – Louise- was a gregarious big South Pacific Mama. She and Anita hit it off and they talked for hours, as we were the only foreign guests that night. We ate lobster, which was prepared with coconut milk and rum cooked inside split bamboo tubes. Louise asked what Anita was doing and she only said that she worked with computers.

Upon hearing that, she told us that the week before a large boat had anchored here and a party of ten had come to her restaurant to eat. Did we know someone by the name of Bill Gates?

Now we know where he eats out in these parts.

We left the easy comfort of the lagoon and sailed over the open ocean to Bora Bora. I will never forget the incredible sight of Bora Bora, 30 miles away, when we first spied it after rounding the northern point of Taháa. The central mountain of Bora Bora is steep and sharp, like a shark's tooth. As one leaves the main reef cut of the lagoon in Taháa, it is very tempting to lay a direct course for Bora Bora. But that is a bad idea. A long submerged reef juts out from Bora Bora, waiting to impale any vessel which attempts to steer a rhumbline[33] between the two islands. This reef has claimed numerous boats and ships. Fortunately, a lighthouse has now been built on the very tip of the reef. It seems to float on the open ocean.

It was beautiful sailing, with just the right amount of trade wind to make the sail fast, but the water not too rough. Soon we sailed into the wide cut leading into the lagoon of Bora Bora. At the same time, a beautiful modern 4-masted sailing ship – the S/V *Windstar* - motored into Bora Bora's cut. What a sight that was! I dropped sails and we circled the ship, taking many photos.

Michener calls Bora Bora the most beautiful island in the world. I have to agree, at least compared to the other islands I have seen. Numerous hotels have sprung up, though, with bungalows built over the shallow lagoon.

---

[33] Straight line on a Mercator chart, i.e. line of constant compass bearings.

It is not possible to circumnavigate this island inside the lagoon. We sailed as far as possible and dropped anchor off one of the over-water hotels, feasting on the incredible sights of Bora Bora and the French food offered in the restaurants.

This was Anita's last trip; she passed away 5 months later. But she had a lot of fun on her last voyage.

Cancers (ħ)

See also page 209

Both these wonderful women – Karen and Anita – died of cancer. Anita suffered a brain tumor and Karen a pancreatic cancer. I thought long and hard whether to write this chapter or not, but decided to do it. It is a tribute to their courage and also an optimistic outlook toward progress of medical science.

Karen

Karen and I were on the long sailing voyage in the Caribbean when the symptoms of her cancer first appeared. Karen had always been very athletic, far more so than me. But as we were walking up a steep hill on the tiny island of Marina Cay[34], she complained of shortness of breath. I'm terribly sorry to say now, but I teased her for her lack of stamina. Do I ever wish I had never said that.

A few weeks later, Karen was hauling a Scuba tank out of the water to deposit it onto the deck of our boat and fell. Her back hurt badly and a few days later one of her legs started to swell. She also complained of persistent bellyaches and nausea. We weren't too concerned about the latter, since all her life she had a slight problem with seasickness and nausea. But it was getting worse. We attributed the swelling of her leg to the fall, but it would not get better, either.

---

[34] Marina Cay is a tiny island, only a few hundred meters across. A young couple bought it (circa 1935) and they built a sturdy stone house on its summit. They wrote the book 'Our Virgin Island' about their life on the island. I read it while we were waiting out a weak hurricane in that very same house, by the light of a kerosene hurricane lantern. That was more romantic in memory than it real life. The house leaked very badly.

Another hurricane grazed the island in September of 1996, and I was busy to deal with the storm. During this ordeal, Karen's health rapidly deteriorated. We decided to abort the voyage and return home. American Airlines – I will forever be grateful to them for this –agreed to give us seats on the very first commuter flight leaving the island after the hurricane. In a mad race against time, I packed up our countless belongings from the boat - in a single night! - while Karen was in pain in a nearby hotel room.

The doctor we had phoned before our return, Dr. Maurice Goretsky of Los Gatos, wasn't particularly concerned about our plight. But when he saw Karen's badly swollen leg, he jumped into action. I know now that *two* swollen legs are usually *not* a cause for concern, but a single swollen leg is a major danger sign. Her leg was swollen because the tumor increased the 'stickiness' of the red blood cells. They coagulated and clogged the major blood vessel in her leg.

The CAT scan showed a Stage FOUR pancreatic cancer, with numerous metastases in her liver. Karen's state deteriorated very rapidly. She lost consciousness within weeks and we transferred her to a hospice. But then a miracle happened. She regained consciousness, could sit up again, eat, then could stand up and even walk. Just before Christmas of 1996, she walked out of the hospice! Staff members of the hospice cried. They had not seen this before – hospice patients don't walk out.

Karen received chemotherapy with the newly approved drug (for the US) Gemzar. It had no side effects and she led a good quality life for several months. In early April, we even took a cruise – not on a sailboat, but on a big Carnival cruise ship – to Puerto Vallarta and other Mexican towns. You could barely tell that she was very sick. But less than two months later, May 28, the cancer took her life.

Pancreatic cancer is often thought of as a very painful disease. In truth, modern pain medicine can do miracles and Karen did not suffer a lot of pain. Initially she used morphine sulfate, but suffered badly from nightmares. She often spoke of elephants stampeding in her hospital room. We switched to Fentanyl, which worked very well for her. A typical Fentanyl dose is measured in tens of micrograms, compared to a few milligrams for morphine. Karen passed peacefully in her sleep as the liver slowly shut down due to the many lesions.

Her death left me rudderless for two years. I did not do much, neither professionally or in terms of enjoying life. Only after meeting Anita, passion for life came back.

Strangely enough, as long as I have known Karen, she was sure she would die of some tumor in her abdomen. How could she have possibly known so far in advance?

Anita

Anita suffered from the most aggressive brain tumor known – Glioblastoma Multiforme. The qualifier *Multiforme* in any tumor is an ominous sign. It means that the cancer is of a type which rapidly mutates. Her cancer was located near the speech center, and that's how we discovered it. For quite a while, Anita had complained about difficulties finding words. I did not take it seriously, saying that everyone knows the feeling of missing a word. But Anita strongly disagreed, saying that she knew exactly the feeling I meant, but her problem was somehow different.

Then her symptoms got worse and one day she collapsed in her office at Xerox PARC. Her staff brought her to the nearby Stanford hospital, where a CAT scan discovered a lesion near her speech center. She received steroids to reduce the brain's swelling. This restored her speech, but it was clear that she was suffering from a major tumor. A biopsy showed that it was a Stage FOUR Glioblastoma Multiforme, which gave her a life expectancy [35] of 3 months.

The medical staff in Stanford told her in no uncertain terms to go home and die. But there was a real hero in this story - Prof. Dr. Michael Berger, head of the department of Neurosurgery at UC San Francisco. He studied the MRI scans, declared that surgery was not only possible, but that he would do it within one week. He also indicated that Anita had a few good years ahead of her and would retain her speech. Every one of his words came true. I can't say enough good things about the UC San Francisco medical team. That is in such extreme contrast with the dreadful experiences we had with some departments in Stanford (not all).

The operation performed at UCSF was an outstanding example of skill and advanced medical technology. The human brain consists of a thin outer layer (gray matter), which is about the thickness of six business cards stacked on top of each other. In computer terms, this is where processors and memories reside. Underneath this layer is the white matter, which provides long-distance wiring, power, cooling and structural support. The glioma cells, which had gone berserk in Anita's tumor, are the brain's equivalent of sheet metal. It's ironic that such auxiliary cells can cause so much suffering.

Only about 10% of the gray matter is actually active in the human brain. These active cells form 'functional islands' which are floating in a sea of spare gray matter. The islands are in the order of one mm in diameter. The challenge which Dr. Berger faced was to destroy the tumor sitting a couple of centimeters below the gray matter in her

---

[35] Quoted life expectancies are the 50% points on the Kaplan-Meier curves. This means that half of a patient population will be alive at this point in time, measured from the time of diagnosis.

left lobe, without destroying the many islands of speech functionality above it.

To accomplish this, Anita was woken up -after her skull was opened - and shown simple sketches. At the same time, the surgeon touched the surface of her brain with a probe. which injected a weak DC current into her brain. Dr. Berger systematically moved the probe over the surface of her brain while she looked at a picture and tried to say what the picture was. If the picture showed an elephant, and she said the word ELEPHANT, then he knew that the current probe, at that instant, did *not* touch a functional island. If it did touch an island, she would not be able to speak.

Over a period of about 45 minutes, the surgical team *mapped* the locations of the functional islands on Anita's brain surface near the tumor. Once this map was known – and captured in a computer – Anita was put back to sleep and the actual tumor removal began. Using an ultrasonic scalpel, Dr. Berger removed with painstaking precision the tumor tissue, cubic-millimeter by cubic-millimeter. The previously obtained map of the functional islands, merged by computer with the MRI image of the tumor, guided him in doing so. It was a 12-hour operation, most grueling for the surgeon. Anita's only complaint was her sore hip, caused by lying so long in the same position.

The operation was a big success. Anita woke up shortly thereafter, lively as can be and speaking like Cicero. Instead of a three more months, Anita had three good years to enjoy. She continued to grow her institute, we traveled all over the world and I bought her a little airplane as a birthday present.

She even dove numerous times in the Caribbean and the South Pacific. One of her doctors, who was a Scuba diver himself, said that he never heard of a patient with Glioblastoma Multiforme going Scuba diving. The UCSF team was very proud of their star patient. Of course, a lot of this success can be attributed to Anita's incredible will to survive and energy and to the wonderful people at UCSF Neurosurgical Department such as Dr. Susan Chen, Anita's primary oncologist. She even became a friend of hers, in addition to her medical role.

It is strange, but being a closely involved spectator to two dramatic battles with cancer leaves me very hopeful that mankind will get this Pandora's box of dreadful diseases under control. And I do not mean with the blunt instruments of chemotherapy and surgical knife, but through a deep molecular-level understanding of cell biology.

An expert will certainly find errors in the following section, but I hope it captures the essential biological facts more or less correctly...

In Karen's case, it is likely that the root cause of her cancer was the absence of one particular gene, responsible for encoding a protein. This particular protein is short and simple, containing only 83 amino acids. It has only one role to perform – to participate in a relay race which tells the nucleus of a pancreas cell to *not* divide.

A cell in a multi-cellular organism (such as a human) is rather undecided about whether to divide or not. Mostly it waits for external instructions. These arrive in the form of proteins, which tell a nucleus either 'divide' or 'do not divide'. An adult's pancreas is bathed in a soup of proteins whose presence says to a nucleus: 'do not divide'.

But there is a problem. A cell is surrounded by an impenetrable wall, made of a fatty substance. Even a little protein molecule is too big to penetrate this lipoid wall. Rather, the message 'do not divide' is received by the nuclei of an adult's pancreas by a relay race.

Cancers

Receptor/emitter devices are imbedded in the wall of the cells. When an external protein - let's call it type A - carrying the message 'do not divide' is attached to the receptor end – outside of the cell wall- of one of these devices, it will launch the equivalent message on the *inside* of the cell wall. This message takes the form of releasing one of the small protein molecules - let's call it type B - which we discussed above. This B protein will eventually find its way to the nucleus of the pancreas cell, which thus received the message to not divide.

I find quite unsatisfying in this explanation that it doesn't account for the whereabouts of the B protein molecules. Where do they hang out if there are no A proteins around? It would seem more plausible if the arrival of the A proteins were to trigger the production of the B proteins. But that's a detail.

Back to cancer. Studies found that 70% of all patients suffering from the cancer of the pancreas do NOT have this gene, which is responsible for synthesizing the B protein. Thus their pancreas cell nuclei can never receive the external order to not divide. Left to their own devices, they very well may start doing so, particularly if their DNA is a bit damaged. This happens routinely as a cell ages.

If one were to heal a person with this genetic deficit, a rather obvious treatment strategy presents itself – at least conceptually. A virus is just a package of genetic information. It does not have the engines (the ribosomes) which are needed to convert genetic information into action, i.e. make proteins. Instead, they hijack the ribosomes in the cells of the infected host. Therefore, a potential fix for the lack of this gene, which may have killed Karen, is to create a virus, which carries just only the little bit of genetic information needed to build the B protein. If one could *infect* the pancreas of a person with this virus, the missing protein could be produced. Here the word infection has a very good meaning.

The larger message is that life scientists have made good progress in understanding, down to a molecular and genetic level, the mechanism of some important cancers. This should give us hope that major progress in the war on cancer will be seen in this century.

Flying – Dr. Jekyll or Mr. Hyde? (ħ)

See also pages 210,211,205,200,198,196,212

The flying stories in this collection - some with a hint of danger- may trigger questions about the safety of personal flying. It is worth to dedicate a story to this complex subject, where many misconceptions prevail.

Many - usually grizzled – pilots will swear on a stack of expired aviation charts that the drive to the airport is the most dangerous part of a flight. As far as private flying is concerned, this is utter hogwash. Flying small propeller planes for pleasure and business is as dangerous as driving a motor cycle. However, flying the airlines is much safer than driving a car. In the last two years, domestic airlines didn't loose a single passenger. That is truly remarkable.

Here are the actual numbers, expressed as fatalities per thousand hours. A fatality rate of 1/100,000 hours means that there is one fatality per hundred thousand hours spent *by one person* in the vehicle or plane. Thus an airliner carrying 100 persons must crash 100 times less often than a single seat plane to have the same fatality rate.

The fatality rate of the total general aviation fleet (piston powered) is about 1/100,000. That's roughly the same as for motorcycles. The Cessna 172 has the lowest fatality rate of 1/144,000 hours, whereas some older, stall/spin prone World War II airplane types have fatality rates which are 10 to 20 times worse.

In the following, I'm rounding the numbers to the nearest order of magnitude. Cars have a fatality rate of about one per million hours, i.e. are ten times safer than the piston engine GA fleet. Airlines of the developed world are better still. Their fatality rate is in the order of one fatality per ten million passenger hours. Airlines of some developing countries and commuter airlines are a lot worse, comparable to cars. The worst airline fatality rate I have ever seen was 50 times worse than that of the average Western airlines. There are also large variances with respect to general aviation. The fatality rate in Alaskan flying is four times higher than in the lower 48 states. This shouldn't be very surprising, given the weather up there. All these data are gleaned from extensive NTSB reports.

Pilots are unimaginative in inventing new ways of crashing. They resort to the true and tried techniques - stalling and spinning the plane in the pattern, running out of fuel and crashing in bad places. Other favorites are continuation of flight into worsening visibility until either control of the plane is lost or a controlled flight into terrain accident occurs. More about this later. The majority of accidents – about 75% - are pilot induced, both for airline and GA accidents.

Engine failure other than running out of fuel is *not* an important cause of fatalities, nor are midair collisions. Surprisingly, the survival probability after midair's is 50%! Still, a midair collision can spoil an entire day.

Very few accidents involve drinking or the universally feared encounters with thunderstorms, icing, extreme turbulence or fog. Pilots do a good job of staying away from these obvious killers.

As I said earlier, many accidents occur on simple short flights with a 'kick the tires and light the fire' attitude towards flight planning.

Oklahoma

That all said, let me touch upon some of the more interesting flying moments we encountered. Karen and I were moving from New York to California in our second Cessna 172. We had to go in May, which is not the best of times to cross the USA in a light plane due to the often violent Midwestern spring weather. Even worse, I was not yet instrument rated. But thunderstorms are best dealt with visually anyhow – try to spot them and get out of their way.

We made slow progress across the eastern part of the country due to the many storms popping up day and night. We finally reached Oklahoma and rested for the night in a little town east of Oklahoma City. Thunderstorms are least likely to occur just before dawn. So we took off at 04:00, launching into darkness. That helps to see lightning, too. By 05:10, we were flying directly over the airport of Oklahoma City, at 4500' altitude. It was an impressive sight – the big, empty airport spread out below in the golden rays of the very early morning.

At 06:00, with the big city 110 miles behind us, we saw a dark cloud mass ahead. I did not like its looks and called the nearest Flight Service Station. They told me that there had been thunderstorms earlier, but now there was nothing to worry about. No activity showed up on their screens. Still, what you see out of the cockpit window is what you get, and I did not like it a bit.

We located the nearest airport, a former military base with a tower and a single, but very long runway. The tower was closed due to the early hour. The automated weather reporting system said something about 10-knot winds. That's not bad, and I went ahead to land. On final, the plane wanted to drift badly to the right and it got worse as we descended. Over the runway, I had to step on the rudder as hard as I could to keep the plane roughly aligned with the runway. This was no harmless 10-knot crosswind!

We slowed down and I taxied off the runway to the apron, looking for some tie down hooks. The wind was very strong and we were anxious to secure the plane. But we found only a single hook in the concrete. We also noticed that several big hangars had parts of their sheathing missing. These had clearly been ripped off by wind. Isn't there a musical which has something to say about winds in Oklahoma? Obviously, no sane person leaves planes outside in this state.

We tied the upwind wing to the single hook and waited inside the plane. It was not a proper tie down hook, more a stub of rebar sticking out of the concrete, waiting to impale a tire. The wind kept getting stronger and stronger. We got out of the plane and grabbed the wing, in case the knot slipped. The plane shook violently in the wind, which was now a full-blown storm. We were getting desperate, hanging on with all our weight on the upwind wing. We expected to loose our beloved Skyhawk any moment.

Around that time, a black and white Cessna 185 of the Oklahoma Highway Patrol arrived. The pilot did not even try to land on the runway, which was subject to a howling 90 degree crosswind. A successful landing would have been entirely impossible. Instead, he landed on one of the very short taxiways, which connected the main taxiway with the runway. Seen from above, the runway and the taxiways looked like a ladder. The pilot landed on one of the 'rungs' of the ladder, directly into the wind. He never shut the engine down, but kept it running at enough power to compensate for the storm. In effect, he flew his plane on the ground. That's a good trick to remember.

After what appeared like an eternity, three squad cars arrived and out piled about 20 cops. They ran to their comrade's plane, grabbed the wings and walked the heavy Cessna 185 into the nearest hangar. Fortunately, they came back out and did the same for us. Too bad I did not have a camera to document the unusual experience of being walked by so many policemen into a hangar!

Everything turned out fine in the end. The automated weather reporting station at the airport was broken and reported a wind of much lower speed than what actually prevailed. It was later estimated that the wind had reached 60 knots. And the source of this mystery wind?

Flying – wonderful or dangerous?

The Flight Service Station was correct in saying that there weren't active thunderstorms around. But when mature thunderstorms die, they collapse into themselves, similar to the collapse of the World Trade Centers. This creates an intense downdraft, which hits the ground and spreads out sideways. These were the winds, which caused us this trouble. The Dallas-Ft.Worth crash of an L-1011, where Phil Estridge, the father of the IBM PC perished, was caused by this phenomenon. It is now called a micro downburst.

There are fundamentally four weather conditions, which can cause serious trouble for instrument rated pilots: *thunderstorms, ice, fog and extreme turbulence.*

It is very rare that the *lightning* causes a problem for a metal plane. A lightning strike may temporarily blind the pilots, fry the avionics and cause general mayhem in the passenger cabin. But it usually does not cause structural damage. Next time you fly in an old airliner, look at the trailing edge of its wing. Chances are you'll see small sections – the size of a large coin – patched or discolored. That's an indication that a lightning discharge exited the plane here, burning off some metal. The entrance point is usually not damaged. Fiberglass planes are a different story – they can be ignited by a lightning bolt unless a metal mesh is part of the structure.

The primary danger of thunderstorm is turbulence. The strong updrafts and downdrafts in the shaft of the thunderstorm cloud collide and create violent turbulence, categorized as strong, severe or extreme. The turbulence in a full blown, mature thunderstorm can rip any plane apart. More likely, though, is that the pilot will loose control due to turbulence and enter a graveyard spiral, which overstresses the plane's structure.

Flying – wonderful or dangerous?

Fortunately, I have never been in a thunderstorm. With the modern weather avoidance systems available now (Sferics, XM weather and weather radar) there is hardly an excuse to blunder into one of these aerial monsters. A general rule is to stay 20 miles away from a thunderstorm cell, don't try to outclimb it and don't fly through sucker holes between cells.

Icing is not much a problem for a jet, because they have the power to punch quickly through the icing layers, which are usually only a few thousand feet thick. Big jets even heat their wings with very hot air bled from the turbine compressors. But ice is an entirely more serious matter for propeller planes. It can collect on sharp points sticking into the air stream. These include antennas, which vibrate and break off. Then you are blind in the clouds. Propellers collect ice and can start to vibrate wildly, robbing the plane of badly needed performance. The leading edges of the wings and tails collect ice. This destroys the carefully engineered shape of the wing, which reduces lift and increases drag.

Old-fashioned, fat wings tend to deal with ice better than sleeker, modern wings. It is amazing how much ice an old DC2 or DC3 can carry. They often landed covered with inches and inches of ice. The worst icing is found over mountains and in billowing, convective clouds. The top of the clouds is usually where the worst icing occurs. This has hurt many pilots, who tried to climb out of the icing layer, only to be trapped in the top of the clouds. The worst icing of all is freezing rain. It can overpower even the most powerful jet in minutes. Only an immediate U-turn offers any hope in freezing rain, which can dump inches of ice onto a plane in less than a minute. I have had a few icing encounters, but none of them particularly frightening. All mountains of California create plenty of ice, as the moist Pacific winds are lifted over their slopes.

Flying – wonderful or dangerous?

Fog is rarely a cause for accidents, with one exception. Very thin ground fog is very tricky, especially at night. Seen from above, it is nearly invisible. The lights from the towns and the airport environment punch right through a thin fog layer. But on final approach, as one enters the fog and now looks horizontally through it, suddenly all forward visibility disappears. Nothing but an immediate abort of the approach will do.

Wind rarely is a problem, except when it appears as a strong cross wind at an airport with a single runway or if it slows a plane down because it is a headwind. But strong wind flowing over rough terrain – such as a mountain range – can produce severe or even extreme turbulence. The consequences are similar to encountering these in a thunderstorm. However, it is more likely that these wind-induced turbulences are encountered outside clouds. This makes the pilot far less prone to loose control and break up the plane.

The jet stream can produce intense clear-air turbulence, for which there is still no known warning. This clear air turbulence (CAT) can come suddenly, without any warning and is by far the most frequent cause of injury or death among flight attendees. This is a good reason to always keep the seat belt fastened while sitting in an airborne airliner. Not doing so is stupid.

After listing all these horrors of flight, let's remind ourselves about its wonders. Hundred years ago, when a young man decided to leave the old world, it was almost certainly a good-bye for life. How heart-breaking that must have been, knowing that one would never see one's family again! Today, it is possible to be within 24 hours at any place in the developed world. Even if one ignores aviation's enormous economical contributions, this alone has opened a sense of freedom and richness that was just unthinkable before air travel became routine for hundreds of millions of people.

Many people have become jaded by the airline traveling experience. Well, yes, taking shoes off is a nuisance, but we should put that in perspective of how life would be without the air travel option. That's particularly true in the USA, where families are scattered over several time zones. How often would they see each other if it weren't for the airplane?

The real joy of flying comes from sitting in the front office, of course. I always joke that there are *three* classes in an airliner – front left seat, front right seat and the rest. As a result of this attitude, I barely care if I sit in economy class or first class and won't pay a dime for upgrades.

Up front, one has a view on the world, which is most often beautiful, sometimes boring and occasionally terrifying. But it always puts the world in a clearer perspective. The latter hit home when I was working as an ambitious young manager for IBM in the big Research Laboratory in Westchester County, NY. This building has the shape of a big arc, which was about 3/8 of a mile long. One day, flying over it at several thousand feet, looking down on this little bent thing, it struck me how relative and small all the issues of work were if they fit into this small arc below.

From high up, one sees how man has adapted to the world, rather than the opposite - as we often like to think. Flying over California is a wonderful and revealing experience. One sees how empty this populous state of 38 million residents truly is. One can fly for hours over its northern forests, over the huge 'empty triangle' where it borders on Oregon and Nevada, over the majestic mountains of the Sierras or the high desert in the South. In all these flights, one sees amazingly few signs of human activities. One never realizes from a roadside view how empty so much of the western USA is.

Recently, a very good friend, Ron Labby, inspired by an article in National Geographic Traveler about the emptiest spots in America, and I set out to explore them by ourselves. We loaded our strong and trusty Skylane with camping gear, guns, targets, beer and other essentials and headed for a dry lake in Nevada. There Ron landed the plane in the middle of the lake bed and we made camp. We threw a smoker out of the window to determine the wind direction.

Unfortunately, the Burning Man festival happened to go on 30 miles south, so we weren't quite as lonely as we thought we'd be. At dawn next morning, a gaggle of pilots flying bush (tail wheel) airplanes discovered us and landed nearby. Nevertheless, we had a great experience, which would be hard to duplicate without a plane.

Watching from the cockpit of an airplane the sunrise over a misty, dark landscape below, or seeing islands of mountains sticking out of a blinding white sea of low clouds is a breathtaking experience, which one never forgets. I love to fly locally, over the beautiful San Francisco Bay area. The first time I ever saw the Bay was on a painting (circa 1950) by Chesley Bonestell, the father of space art. It showed a view of the Bay from a hypothetical space station and it took my breath away. As a little boy, the thought that I'd live there one day never occurred to me. I didn't even know what this painting depicted, it just looked so beautiful.

The Bay air traffic control is very cooperative, and they usually allow general aviation planes do a beautiful aerial sightseeing tour over the San Francisco peninsula and Bay. A typical Bay tour may start south of San Jose, then follows Highway 101 and swings west of the San Francisco airport. There one can look from an altitude of 3500' down on the airliners landing and taking off.

After that, one is usually vectored west of downtown San Francisco. Near the Golden Gate bridge, the plane is released from mandatory ATC control. Now one can head towards the green mountains of Marin County or fly towards Oakland and the East Bay. Everyone partaking in such a flight is awed by the experience.

In the east, the Yankee islands (Nantucket, Martha's Vineyard, Block Island etc.) are great destinations. When we lived north of New York City, we loved to visit the islands. A trip by car and ferry would have been a grueling affair, which would have used up most of a weekend just for travel.

Even a slow, 120 mph plane like a Skyhawk makes all these destinations easy day trips. Flying up Long Island Sound with the sandy beaches of Connecticut to the left, Long Island to the right and tiny sailboats on the blue water below is a great visual experience. Even better is to fly up the middle of Cape Cod, with both its shores in clear view. What a contrast to being stuck in Sunday traffic down there on Interstate 95.

The Midwest has its own rewards for the general aviation flyer. Some airports there are adjacent to shopping malls, making it possible to shop by plane. Karen and I have done it, it is a fun feeling. It is also very convenient for farmers who have their own airstrip on the farm- as many do. It is so much easier to check fences, look for lost cattle and areas of poor irrigation from a plane than by horseback.

The big rectangular fields of the Midwest make for a relaxed attitude towards engine failure. I do not worry very much about it – in well-maintained planes, engines failures are exceedingly rare- but the concern is still in the back of any pilot's mind. The Midwest weather often provides layers of beautiful little cumulus clouds. I like flying among them, dodging them for just fun. But watch out if the sheep start growing. They can turn into monsters.

Flying – wonderful or dangerous?

Even a routine flight is a cornucopia of sensual experiences. The roar of big engines, the rush of accelerating down a runway, the swerving in gusty winds, the feeling as the wing gets fat with lift and the sensation of ascending into the sky are some of the reasons pilots fall in love with aviation. As I describe in the story about Instrument Flying (page 329ff), there are few things in life, which can give a person a better feeling of accomplishment than a well-performed flight, especially when it dealt with challenges such as weather, heavy air traffic or mountains.

Up there, unless one is doing routine cruising, the mind doesn't dawdle on the routines of daily living. The sight of a runway straight ahead on final approach, especially after a tough flight or after breaking out from low clouds feels like the crowning achievement of a day which was well worth living.

Finally, a big benefit of being engaged in GA are the fellow pilots one meets. They come in all kinds of sizes and shapes, professions and idiosyncrasies – but nearly all are interesting. The majority exhibit an interesting blend of modesty (flying does that) and self-confidence (flying does that, too). There are not many stupid pilots. These generally remove themselves from the aviator's gene pool. Hopefully, they flew alone when they bought the farm.

Flying – wonderful or dangerous?

Travels in Europe

See also pages 181,211

As a native of Europe, but Californian by choice, I return to the old continent with a renewed sense of wonder. Having been married to two American women, and expect to be married to an Asian M.D. in the future, I always felt a strong obligation to show them the best of what the old continent has to offer.

Europe is a fascinating place. It is the birthplace of the Western culture which shaped the world. The scientific mindset originated here and brought us the miracles of electricity and flight, modern medicine, nuclear power and computers, consumer societies and free market economy. Nowhere else – except in Asia- have I seen such a wide variety of cultures crammed into such a physically small place. Travel 500 miles in Europe and you will have crossed major cultural boundaries, where languages, religions, architecture and attitudes undergo profound changes.

The following are a few very personal opinions about random places in Europe - positive and negative. They are in no particular order.
- Do not waste your time visiting the Black Forest. Yes, it is pretty nice with its dark evergreen trees, gentle hills and cute, but unreliable cuckoo clocks. But the far more spectacular Alps are so close. Spend precious vacation time there.
- When in Italy, visit the Bay of Naples and the Amalfi peninsula. Yes, Rome and Florence and Venice are nice and a must see, but, for my money, nothing in Italy beats the splendor of the greater

Bay of Naples and its environs. Naples itself is remarkable – but better keep your hand on your wallet, as pickpockets are everywhere. My first wife learned this the hard way. The drama of life in this town is spectacular, at least for reserved Northerners. Driving there is not all *that* difficult if you ignore everything you have learned in saner places. Do not look behind you and, if you can physically move forward, do so. It is sheer madness, yet it seems to work. But remember- the car with the bigger engine has the right of way.

Driving around the coastal highway in southern Italy, we once came across the balled-up remains of a white Fiat 770. The bodies had been removed. It was still possible to glimpse the speedometer. The needle was stuck at 122 km/h – and that was on a curvy road which a sane BMW M3 driver might have taken at 70 km/h – tops. But in spite of its automotive craziness, this is a great place.

The Amalfi peninsula is one of the truly dramatic coast lines of the world. White limestone mountains drop steeply into the blue Mediterranean and villages of white washed houses cling to the steep slopes. Romantic Mediterranean harbors, with blue-painted wooden fishing boats pulled up on the beaches, can be found in many coves.

The docks are lively with crews from voyaging sailing and power vessels, because a neat form of docking is practiced in these parts. The boats are moored side by side, with the stern facing the dock. A gangplank connects the cockpit to terra-firma. This makes the boat's cockpit a part of the overall dock community, as it is so easy to go from the cockpit on land, onto another boat and back. In comparison, the docking styles used elsewhere appear standoff-ish. Amalfi itself has a remarkable history. The compass was invented in this town, Marco Polo grew up here, and for centuries it was a thriving city state, competing with Venice.

The famous island of Capri is also located in the Bay of Naples. Known for its famous Blue Grotto, Capri is a must see, in spite of its heavy tourism. It reminds me somewhat of Catalina Island, but it is more populated and ancient. Two romantic towns are located on the island, as is the residence of Emperor Tiberius. He wasn't the most enlightened of Roman emperor's, though. His residence was known for the infamous 'Salto de Tibero', which was a particularly lofty method of execution. His palace is located high above a cliff, and the condemned were simply thrown over the cliff, taking the big 'salto' (jump). Talking about a high dive – on Capri we saw something which still puzzles me.

Capri is the home of many homeless cats. One day Karen and I were wandering along the ocean-facing side of the island and saw some boys amusing themselves by swinging cats by their tails and flinging them into the ocean. I was about to yell, in my best Luftwaffe-trained German, at the boys, when Karen noticed something strange. The cats, after being thrown in the ocean and swimming back to land (cats can swim), lined up for another ride rather than running like the devil. What are Capri cats smoking?

- Trains are a great way to see Europe. They range from local trains stopping at every little village to the French high-speed train called TGV (Train Grand Vitesse). The backbone of Europe's modern long distance train system is the ICE (InterCity Express). It is a sleek white train, connecting the

major cities of Europe on hourly schedules. The
ICE travel at up to 250 km/h (150 mph). The tracks
are so well laid out and maintained that even these
speeds aren't the least bit frightening. The trains
move smoothly and quickly, with nary a bump.
Even as an avid aviator, I love using the ICE trains
in Europe. It is a very safe mode of travel, too,
especially given the often-miserable weather in
northern Europe. An ICE trip from Frankfurt to
München (Munich) takes just 3 hours and 37
minutes, usually accurate to the minute. A big
advantage of the train system is that most major
train stations are located downtown. Tests have
shown that the ICE is the fastest city door-to-door
(downtown) means of travel for any distance below
1000 km. Only for longer distances the airplane will
win.

- Talking about Munich – of all the European towns I
have visited, this still is my overall favorite. It
combines extraordinary sights of cultural and tourist
interest with great shopping, outstanding high
technology and a unique Bavarian take-it-easy
attitude. Bavaria is, surprisingly for outsiders, the
high-tech center of Germany, but the Bavarians
have the same self-deprecating 'aw-shucks' attitude
as many Silicon Valley residents or Texans.

- What can I say about Paris? It is Europe's New
York City. Both are fascinating towns, with great
and disgusting experiences in close proximity. I like
Lyons at least as much as Paris, but am turned off
by the high crime rates in Marseille. My favorite
major French town is Grenoble, though.

- The Alps remain my favorite mountains – as much
as I love the Sierra Nevada's and the Rockies and
others. I haven't been to the Himalayas or Andes,
though. The Alps combine a breathtaking steepness

with visual appeal and mountaineering challenges, which are unmatched in any mountains of similar altitude, which I have seen. There are local areas – like the Rocky Mountains around Jackson Hole and the eastern Sierras, which are similarly impressive, but the Alps are a 1000 km long arc of spectacular mountain scenery – and they still grow quickly as Italy pushes hard against Northern Europe. The same is true for the Himalayas, as India collides with the remainder of Asia.

- The highest summit of the Alps is the Mont Blanc (White Mountain) on the border of France and Switzerland at 4,804 m (15,770') elevation. That is not much higher than Mt.Whitney (4,421m) in the continental US and much lower than Alaska's Denali. Yet it is a spectacular mountain.

  Nearby, in Switzerland, is the Matterhorn, which is the most recognizable mountain of the Alps. Its enormous pyramid towers of the village of Zermatt. Sometimes, when the sun disappears behind the mountains, the shape of the upper Matterhorn reminds me of a giant Tyrannosaurus Rex, 4.5 km tall, lurking on the outskirts of Zermatt. Well, it is said that eating too much Fondue cheese can causes nightmares. I need to test this hypothesis more thoroughly.

- The highest mountain of Europe is not in the Alps, though. It is Mt. Elbrus in Russia at 5642m. But it is not as visually spectacular as the Swiss or French Alps.

- The Swiss railroad system is unique in the world. It truly runs on time. Powered entirely by powerful electric locomotives, it is a showcase of serious civil engineering. On some routes, like the fabled Glacier Express, there seems to be hardly any naturally horizontal surface for the train to use. The train travels over a vertigo-inducing bridge, gets swallowed up by a tunnel, only to be spit out onto another bridge – and does this again and again.

- Yugoslavia is an interesting country. The landscape, history and beauty of its old towns are simply breathtaking. On the other hand, a few of its citizens appear to be – shall we say – spiteful. I had several encounters there, which are hard to imagine elsewhere in European countries. For example, after listening in a rather fancy hotel in southern Yugoslavia to a waiter's recommendation, he turned on its heels and walked away in disgust when my wife dared to reject them!

  This was only an example. Our trips to Yugoslavia made Paris seem like a sweet and welcoming place. In hindsight, there seemed to be much hatred in the air when Karen and I last visited it in the late eighties. The subsequent civil war should not have been a surprise to us. I haven't been back since, but am still fascinated by its beautiful towns and landscapes. The islands of Korcula, Hvar and the ancient towns of Dubrovnik, Split and Zadar are still among my favorite locations in the world.

- England seems to live up to all the common prejudices. The weather is rotten, the people are delightful. They are sometimes a wee-bit hard to understand. The beer is luke-warm, indeed, but the fish-n-chips are delicious. Overall, I think the English cuisine is underrated. But then I'm easily satisfied when it comes to food or wine.

- Elba, Sardinia and Corsica: In 1970, some of my diving buddies came across an abandoned old wooden lifeboat, half buried in the muck along the banks of the river Main, near Frankfurt. They dug it out with the goal of turning it into a 'yacht'. None of them had money – they were students, artists and

German hippies. Nevertheless, over a couple of years they converted the derelict hull into a ketch. This is a two masted sailing vessel. It was about 12m long, i.e. quite a substantial vessel. An ancient 40HP Mercedes Diesel engine was to provide auxiliary power.

In the spring of 1972 the 'epic' voyage began. They launched the vessel, surprisingly without sinking it. Then the 'yacht' puttered down the Main, the Rhine and the Rhine-Rhone channel to the Rhone itself. The Rhone enters the Mediterranean in Marseille. Then they headed for the Italian island of Elba. I joined up with them there, driving my mother's new FIAT 770 -with a tiny 770 cc, 30 HP engine- from Frankfurt to Italy. At Autobahn speeds, one needed to use full power to keep up with traffic - barely.

The sailing voyage was some kind of an experience, even disregarding the bra, which was flying from the yardarm. As I mentioned, the crew had quite a hippie streak. Since the boat had been out of the water for years, the wood had dried out and the hull leaked like a sieve. Let's not put too fine a point on it. The boat was in a permanent state of sinking. Getting out of the bunk in the morning required an act of moral fortitude, since the cabin sole was covered with several inches of cold seawater. It had leaked into the boat during the night. Therefore, the first duty of the morning was to man the pumps and get rid of all the water in the boat.

I acquired an everlasting fondness for Diesel engines on this trip. The old Mercedes Diesel was driving the propeller through its car transmission. The optimal gear would have been the second, but that was broken. Thus we had no choice but to run the engine in third gear. As a result, the poor Diesel was lugging all the time, running at an unfavorable low RPM. The cooling system was too powerful and the oil temperature gauge never got off its peg. The combination of the two problems is a terrible way to treat an engine. In spite of all this mistreatment – and its frequent use required by the calm wind conditions in the summer of 1972 near Elba, the old Diesel soldiered on.

Once we were motoring off the coast of Corsica, with me steering and everyone else sleeping off their hangovers from the previous night. As the resident nerd, I was slightly more sober than the rest of the crew. As we puttered along in third gear, with the poor engine running at only 1300 RPM, I happened to notice that the oil pressure needle was rapidly trending towards zero. I let out a yell, which could wake the dead or even this crew and dove into the small hatch, which provided access to the engine. The dipstick showed no oil whatsoever, just a touch of tough, gooey black stuff at its very tip. That's when I learned that Diesel dipsticks look different. The soot from the combustion collects in the oil, creating a black tar once the oil gets very old. It is a sheer miracle that this old Mercedes engine survived all this abuse. But it never failed this intrepid crew.

There is a history of antagonism between German anglers and divers. We fight over the few lakes available. The anglers fear that the divers harass or even catch fish - which is nonsense, whereas the divers fear stones which fisherman sometimes throw at them.

This explains some fun I had one day with some Corsican anglers. We were anchored for a lunch stop about 100m offshore, somewhere between Bonifacio and Porte-Vecchio. Two men sat on the beach, fishing. While the rest of our crew watched, I put on my dive gear and slipped into the water, on the side of the boat *not* facing the shore. Than I swam, using careful compass bearings, to the place where the fishing lines of the two anglers should be. I was lucky and found one of them. I grabbed it and started moving it forth and back. As the crew reported, this got the angler very excited. He thought that a big fish was caught on his line. I played with the line, swimming back and forth, while the guy on land got ever more excited. Fortunately, there were enough waves to disperse my air bubbles. After a few minutes, I had enough, found a small piece of a car tire lying on the bottom and carefully hooked it. Then I released it all to the fisherman. Did he get a surprise to find that a piece of tire was giving him the fight of his life! I bet nobody would believe his story.

White Cocoon – IFR (ħ)

See also pages 198,215

Flying is put into two categories, which are called VFR (Visual Flight Rules) and IFR (Instrument Flight Rules). VFR is when you see where you are going. IFR is if you don't. That's usually because of poor weather conditions, such as flying within a cloud[36] - hopefully not because of ice or oil on the windshield.

Flying IFR is a big deal – a very big deal. It is harder to learn to fly IFR than to learn to fly in the first place. Not just that, it is also a serious survival issue. Recent studies commissioned by the FAA have shown that the average non-IFR trained pilot upon entering a cloud will loose control of a plane in an average of 178 seconds.

The survival time is shorter if the cloud contains significant turbulence, which cumulus clouds do. These look like cauliflowers when seen from the outside. Thunderstorms are particularly enthusiastic cumulus clouds. The consequences of loosing control while flying IFR in a cloud are usually deadly. The plane will undergo some gyrations and eventually end up in a graveyard spiral. This is an ever tightening and steeper spiral in which the plane will pick up speed until it sheds some needed parts, such as a wing or tail. A sleek plane –such as a Bonanza or a jet- will pick up speed a lot faster than a dowdier plane like a Cessna Skyhawk. That's one of the reasons why Skyhawks are so safe. A pilot of one of these may even survive a loss of control accident if it happens near the bottom of the cloud. In a Bonanza – loose control and you will buy the farm, which is pilot-speak for being killed. I

---

[36] For pilots reading this, please excuse me glossing over the difference between IMC and IFR.

own both types and love them both, but I do not kid myself about which one demands more attention and proficiency.

John F. Kennedy, Jr. died this way. He wasn't even flying in a cloud, but he was in a hazy night out over coastal waters when he lost control of his Piper Saratoga. The big question is whether or not a pilot can see the horizon and therefore know the attitude of the plane. Attitude means how the plane is oriented in the sky. Is it flying straight and level? Or is it pitched up or down and/or steeply banked? A graveyard spiral is a flight condition where bank, pitch and speed simultaneously increase.

To someone who hasn't experienced it, it seems incredible that the human body can be in some completely unusual attitudes – like upside down - and not sense it. During initial instrument training, a flight student gets a convincing demonstration of that. The student wears a vision-limiting device, which blocks viewing the outside world. It only allows him to see the instrument panel. The instructor asks the student to look down and close his eyes, then takes the controls and puts the plane through some moderate gyrations. He leaves the plane in some unusual attitude – perhaps with the noise pointing up and the airspeed decaying, and then asks the student to regain control with eyes closed.

It is totally impossible. One senses clearly that things are wrong. The g-forces may jam one deeply into the pilot's seat, or one may be floating above it, just held in place by the seat belts. The revving of the engine and the increasing sound of the wind is very scary. All senses scream to DO something, but it is just impossible to figure out what one should do. Soon one enters the graveyard spiral. The g-forces continue to increase and the wind outside the cockpit takes on the sound of a demonic howl. If this were for real, you'd know that your life expectancy is now measured in tens of seconds. That would make it difficult to think clearly.

Since the view of the horizon is so essential, most planes build since 1950 have an *attitude indicator or A/I* . This is a fancy mechanical device. It contains two gyros, which presents the pilot with an artificial horizon. It is often just called the artificial horizon. The A/I sits in the center of the instrument panel, right where the pilot looks most of the time. In jets, where attitude is particularly critical, the A/I is a large instrument, 4 or 5 inches in diameter.

The artificial horizon has an upper, blue part and a lower, brown part, standing in for sky and earth. The dividing line between the two fields moves just as the real horizon outside. A symbol of the actual plane is superimposed on the instrument. As one enters -for example- a climbing turn, the dividing line will bank and drop below the plane symbol, just as the real horizon does.

Unfortunately, the attitude indicator in most small planes is driven by vacuum suction rather than by an electrical motor. The suction is created by an engine driven air pump. These things have the disconcerting habit of sudden self-destruction, whereupon the artificial horizon will fail. The A/I will die slowly as the gyros spin down, indicating a bank where there is none. Pilots have followed a dying attitude indicator into the ground.

If one catches the loss of vacuum early enough, one can cover the attitude indicator with a post-it note and use a simple backup gyro gadget, which is called Turn&Bank. This device knows nothing about up and down, only about left/right turning. It is a lot harder to use than the A/I, even though Lindberg crossed the Atlantic with only such a simple Turn&Bank. Today, the actual in-cloud recovery rate from artificial horizon failures is dismal. Conservative pilots put two attitude indicators in the panel, one powered electrically and the other one by vacuum suction. Thus there is always one working attitude indicator. I would not dream to fly a Bonanza or jet in clouds without a redundant A/I. But then I'm a chicken pilot.

There is a story, which, if true, demonstrates the incredible power to get confused when flying without reference to the real horizon. It supposedly happened during World War II in Texas - where else. A lone student in an old-fashioned Stearman bi-plane was droning along in clear air *between two cloud layers*. The big, ole Stearman was used as the initial trainer for American flyboys in WWII and had no artificial horizon.

Three advanced and much faster trainers – AT6 'Harvards' – were flying in formation and catching up with the lone and slow Stearman. The student below had not yet discovered the AT6 squadron. Their flight leader – remember, this is Texas cowboy country- told his pilots *to roll inverted* just before they caught up with the Stearman below. When they finally passed him, they were all going nicely straight and level, but upside down. The story goes that the student pilot promptly rolled his Stearman inverted, when he saw the AT6, thinking that *he* was upside down. Major King in 'Dr. Strangelove' would have been proud.

But there is a lot more to learning to fly IFR than keeping the dirty side of the plane down. Upgrading from a VFR private pilot's license to an IFR rating is considered the toughest of all aeronautical FAA ratings. It is a thinking person's game, because not only has one to keep the plane's attitude correct, one has to navigate, communicate with machine-gun speed talking Air Traffic Controllers, plan for approaches, keep up with weather, calculate fuel burns and so on. The list is endless. Many pilots think that flying single-pilot IFR in crowded airspace – say NY or LAX- is so challenging that it shouldn't be done at all. In my own experience no other activity I have ever engaged creates as much instant workload and pressure. A good, reliable autopilot is a great help – nearly a second crew member. I find everyday decisions – even difficult business ones, like killing a startup - to be of lower stress, compared to hardcore IFR flying. No wonder that so many CEOs are (former) aviators, as are surgeons.

Currently, most IFR flying is still done behind instrument panels populated with many round mechanical instruments. The pilot has to integrate the information presented by all these 'steam-gauges' in his head. A new generation of computer driven, flat-panel screens are simplifying IFR flying. These show moving maps and will, in a decade or so, use interfaces, which are far more intuitive than the traditional airspeed/altitude/attitude presentations displayed today.

One promising user interface is that of what appears to be an aerial highway of rectangular gates, which are floating in front of the plane. The pilot's job is to fly through these gates. This is so intuitive that a child could do it. But current production planes still use the very traditional presentations of altitude, airspeed and attitude, even if it occurs on a flat computer screen.

To put all this into context, let me describe a short IFR flight from the town of Palo Alto, south of San Francisco, to Monterey, CA. The total distance PAO – MRY is only about 70 nautical miles. This story is not based on a specific, actual flight. Rather, it is an amalgam of many real IFR flights in the general area. Here it is…

The weather report talks about broken clouds over the Bay area, with a cloud base at 900'. The freezing level is at 4000' and the wind in Monterey is light and variable. The California coastal marine layer (fog) has moved in and the Monterey (cloud) ceiling is reported at 250' above field

White Cocoon - IFR

elevation. That's low, but flyable when using an Instrument Landing System (ILS), which Monterey fortunately has. A couple of hours before departure, I plan the flight, using specialized IFR charts and approach plates.

For a layman, IFR charts are very boring, compared to the colorful VFR charts. A 'just the facts, madam' attitude dictates the style of IFR charts[37]. Lines depict airways and airports are shown only as little circles. The bigger airports may have little feathers sticking out of the circles. The feathers indicate the presence and direction of an ILS. This is always a welcome sign for an IFR pilot.

Nowadays, many smaller airports have new instrument approaches, which solely rely on space-borne GPS satellite signals. They work well, but it is still a scary thought to hurtle through fog and clouds towards solid earth, with no guidance other than the feeble[38] and easily disturbed signals of a constellation of satellites circling overhead. Still, I use GPS approaches all the time. They work very well in actual practice and are the only IFR approach option at most small airports.

Once I have prepared my flight plan – which takes only a few minutes – I contact Flight Service by computer or phone and file the plan. This is a standardized form, which contains all the necessary flight information – pilot's identity, the type, speed and identifier of my plane, when and where I want to go, how to get there, desired cruising altitude etc. The form also asks for the number of passengers and the color of the plane. That's in case a post crash search needs to be initiated.

As an amusing aside, in an emergency, ATC will always ask for the number of *souls* on board. They do not care to know the number of *bodies* on board, because the

---

[37] The upper right corner of the book's cover page shows an IFR chart (San Francisco area)

[38] Typical GPS Signal to Noise ratios are in the order of 1/1000 !

plane might be used by an undertaker in his line of business.

After arriving at the airport, I preflight the plane and do a last minute weather check. A wireless device like an iPhone is a great tool for doing that. The website **http://adds.aviationweather.noaa.gov** contains the aviation weather information a pilot flying in the US needs.

Before starting the engine, I announce to the 'Clearance Delivery' station at the local tower that there is an IFR flight plan on file, for a departure time of 18:30 Zulu or 10:30 Pacific Standard Time. The clearance delivery person will go look for this file, usually find it and tell me that the clearance is 'on request'. This means that she called ATC and informed them that a plane with such and such a flight plan on file is standing by for take-off.

When ATC – in Sacramento- has reviewed the flight plan, taking into account special considerations, the clearance will be relayed to me. For example, in Palo Alto, airplanes bound for San Francisco International will be overhead and this may effect the plan. Eventually I will receive, via the Palo Alto tower, the actual clearance, which gives an initial direction, altitudes and a radar transponder identifier to 'squawk'. Hopefully the transmission will end with 'cleared as filed'. That means I can expect to fly the route, which I requested. The worst news is to receive a 'full route clearance', where ATC has thrown out my entire plan and is going to give me a totally new route. There is no point to argue, mother ATC knows best.

Now I try to write down the newly assigned route without making errors. That's not so easy, because it may contain waypoints I never have heard of. But I must find them all on the chart before take-off and visualize the overall flight path. It is also a very good idea to program the entire route into the GPS and see it on a map. An accidental typo in a waypoint name may appear as a 4400 mile detour to Argentina. On a map, that's easy to catch.

Still, all this work may be for naught, since the actual route may still be modified in flight.

This time I'm lucky, ATC clears me 'as filed' to Monterey. I read back the entire clearance and the gal from Clearance Delivery confirms that I got it right. It's time to switch to Ground Control. The fellow in the Palo Alto tower cab clears me to taxi from its current position to the run-up pad in front of the runway. As this is not a good day for flying, the run-up pad is nearly empty. Only one other plane sits there, also running up its engines.

I taxi onto the run-up pad and switch quickly to the tower frequency. Listening to it will give me a feeling of the air traffic situation around Palo Alto as I sit there and do the run-up. I carefully 'flow' through the pre-takeoff checklist. Oil pressure is ok, ammeter is showing a slight rate of charge, A/I is level, gyrocompass is aligned with compass heading, altimeter indicates 3' above sea level and the vacuum suction gauge shows 5.1 inches of Mercury. I do the engine run-up, verify that the doors are locked and that the controls are free and operate in the correct direction.

The latter is not a joke – every year, a few planes crash on take-off because some controls have been hooked up backwards. This occurs mostly during maintenance, but sailplanes, which are frequently assembled just before flight, are particularly vulnerable. Everything checks out. The outside air temperature is 42°F, well above freezing. Today I fly the Skyhawk, which is equipped with an old-fashioned carbureted engine. The temperature in the throat of the carburetor is 39 °F. Good again, that's safely above the temperature where ice can appear in the carburetor. If that happens, it can choke the engine until it dies. One can feed hot air into the carburetor to clear the ice, but that reduces the power output of the engine and shouldn't be done needlessly.

Finally I call the tower.

"Cessna N1252U is ready to go, IFR to Monterey"
"Taxi into position and hold,"
the tower advises me. I add some power and slowly taxi
onto the beginning of the runway, keeping a sharp eye on
the final approach path. I want to verify that there is really
no plane on final. ATC staff makes very few mistakes, but
four eyes are better than two are.
"Cessna 52U is cleared for takeoff"! Time to go. I slowly
feed power to the 150 HP / 320 cubic inch Lycoming four-
cylinder engine. It growls loudly and stabilizes at 2450
RPM. That's about what one would expect. The airplane
accelerates quickly, as the power to weight ratio of the
plane is not bad. A quick dance on the rudder pedal keeps
the plane more or less on the centerline, in spite of the
surprisingly gusty crosswind. What did that flight examiner
say, 29 years ago in Rochester? I still need to watch staying
on the centerline.

The airspeed needle comes alive and quickly climbs
to 65 knots (75 mph). It is time to rotate. I pull crisply on
the yoke, and the plane effortlessly jumps into the air. The
bouncing of the wheels on pavement stops, but I feel a
vibration coming through the rudder pedals. Nose wheel
jimmy – well, that's an on-going annoyance with most
Cessnas. It will stop in a few seconds, no cause for concern.

The ground drops away. I turn 10 degrees right,
climbing over the power line which parallels the Bay shore.
A Stanford English professor owns a house about a mile to
the North. She is supposedly prone to complaining about
noise and the pilot community here has agreed to avoid
trouble by making this small turn towards the bay. So far,
nobody has been caught by the tall power lines. It pays for
pilots to be good neighbors, lest we get into the restrictive
regulatory mess in which European aviators have to live.

I'm glad that the cloud bottoms are not very low.
The weather report said 900', and that looks about right. It
gives me about 60 seconds after takeoff to give everything

a last glance and prepare myself mentally for entering the clouds.

Nowadays I'm far more relaxed about getting engulfed, but I will never forget that first time. It was in the late eighties, just north of New York city. With a very good flight instructor in the right seat – a former IBM Director, who had switched careers- we were racing towards a towering, solid white wall. My heart pounded, all senses screamed against doing what appeared like a suicidal act. Imagine racing a car at 120 mph into a white wall – that's how it looked. My first solo IFR flights were nerve wracking. It did not help that on my very first solo IFR flight the alternator failed.

But now, with many hours of solo IFR flights under my belt, most of them in the high performance Bonanza and not in the homey little Skyhawk, the fear is mostly gone. But I will never loose the respect for the whole enterprise of flying when you can't see where you are going. It's an amazing, unnatural act.

As usual, the bottom of the cloud is not well defined. As the plane reaches about 1000', the view of the ground gets hazy, and then disappears completely. The Skyhawk has neither an autopilot nor a second artificial horizon and ample work is cut out for me. My clearance requested to make a right turn within 2 miles of the airport, heading southeast to the San Jose VOR. This is a radio navigation station located on that airport, transmitting on 114.1 MHz. I already dialed this frequency into the navigation radio before takeoff and the needle is coming alive. The tower calls me.

"Cessna 52U, contact departure on 120.1 Have a good flight, sir."

He pronounces the frequency as one-two-zero-point-one.

"52U, 120.1, so long"

I had already dialed this new frequency in the standby window of the primary communications radio. It was expected from the clearance. A push of a button activates the new frequency.

"Norcal, this is Cessna Skyhawk N1252U, climbing through 1200."

That's it – all what needs to be said.

"Cessna 52U, radar contact. Climb and maintain 4000. Turn right to 150."

"150 on the heading, climb and maintain 4000."

I love this concise exchange of information. No ambiguities here - one follows the finely tuned traditions of aircraft control by radar and voice communication. One day – in about 20 years – this all will be obsolete, replaced by satellite guidance and avionics systems chatting directly with each other, exchanging their plane's positions. But for now, it's done as our forefathers did it, dating back to the fateful day in 1957 when two airliners collided in a cloud and their debris fell into the Grand Canyon. That's when the air traffic system as we know it was born. It has served the nation and the world very well.

For a while, the radio is quiet. The plane appears suspended in flight. Now, that the anxiety of my first IFR flights a decade ago has disappeared, a strange and peaceful feeling engulfs me as I pilot my little craft through the clouds. It is like being suspended in a soft cocoon of featureless white. White is good. If it turns grey, let alone greenish, watch out. That means that the moisture content is high and, if the temperature gradient is right, thunderstorms could be nearby. Today, that's not a problem.

I watch the needle of the outside air temperature gauge with some concern. It is now right at the freezing point. Sure enough, little spots of ice are forming right in the center of the windshield. That's not good. But just as they form, the light gets rapidly brighter. I'm reaching the tops of the clouds. The altimeter shows 3300', still climbing to my assigned altitude of 4000'. A few seconds later, the brightness is overwhelming and I put on my sunglasses. One of the common mistakes green IFR fliers make is to forget their sunglasses because it is gray and raining on the ground. But few things are as blinding as the inside of a cloud near its top.

Then, without warning, we are suddenly above the clouds. The altimeter shows now 3600'. About a minute later, I level the plane off at 4000' – as instructed in the clearance - and reduce power to 2500 RPM. The sight of racing low over a cloudscape is something I will never take for granted. Today, the clouds are a mixture of mostly smooth stratiform clouds and some cumulus hills rising above the white plane below. The ride through the clouds was quite smooth. Thus I must have been lucky, avoiding the areas of vertical air motions.

In the distance one can see, dark green, the real mountains which are surrounding Silicon Valley at altitudes of up to 4000'. To the right, barely sticking through the clouds, is the top of Black Mountain, which is near my home in the hills. To the left, in the distance, is the big mass of Mount Hamilton, with the distinctive cluster of white domes on its summit. Here the first of the big, privately funded telescopes of America were built at the end of the 19th century. They used mules to carry the telescope and dome parts to this summit…

My reverie about the privilege of being alone in such a magical place is broken by a call from ATC.

"Cessna 52U, a Skywest Boeing 737 11 o'clock, descending through 5000 for Oakland. Caution, wake turbulence.

"52U, looking," I reply. Wake turbulence is nothing to be trifled with. It can flip a light plane like mine on its back in seconds and I have hardly any aerobatic experience. Once, back in Rochester, I encountered the fringe of an airliner's wake turbulence. It was unlike any natural turbulence, more like being hit by a giant sledgehammer.

The cause of wake turbulence is closely related to the creation of lift itself. The pressure below an airplane's wing is higher than above it. At the tip of the plane's wings, the two pressure zones interact as air rushes from the underside of the wing to its upper side. This creates horizontal twin tornados of astonishing power. The bigger and slower the plane, the worse the tornados are. For some reason, the Boeing 757 is particularly bad, even though it is not a very big plane, compared to a 747 or an A380.

Back to the warning. I'm not good at spotting planes, but eventually I see it and do not like the situation. Our present courses will put me directly into the path of the slowly descending wingtip vortices.

"Cessna 52U, request course change 30 degrees right."

"Cessna 52U, approved as requested,"

ATC comes back immediately. I make a shallow right turn, away from the invisible monsters churning and twisting below the Boeing, which is now only about 2 miles away. This does the trick. Not even a bump of wake turbulence is felt.

"N52U, contact approach on 133.0,"

ATC instructs me. I confirm the transmission and call ATC on the new frequency, which is used for the western half of the Monterey basin. A new voice answers quickly and gives me the altimeter setting for the new sector.

To our right, remnants of the old cold-war radar station on Mount Umunum are passing by. The mountain is nearly level with my plane. What a great state park this summit would make - if only the poisonous fluids from the old transformers were cleaned up. A good friend, Robert Garner, is volunteering on making this state park happen.

It is time to get the current weather for Monterey. I look up the frequency for Monterey's automatic terminal weather forecast and dial it into the second communications radio.

"Information Kilo is current at Monterey, time is 20:14. Wind is 080 at 3, ceiling 300 overcast. Temperature 37, dew point 35. ILS One-Zero Right is in use. Caution for bird activity on and in the vicinity of the airport."

Good, I think. The low ceiling forces the use of runway 10, which is the only one which supports IFR approaches that low. At least I won't have to land with a tailwind. The narrow gap between temperature and dew point is a warning sign that sudden ground fog could spring up any moment. But as the day wears on, the temperature gap will widen and fog should become less likely. I'm not very worried about it as there is plenty of fuel in the tanks. I can always retreat to another airport, further from the coast.

By now I have passed the mountains of the coastal range. Even though I can't see anything but a sea of marine stratus below, I know that it would be safe to descend now. The next transmission instructs me to do just that.

"Cessna 52U, descend and maintain 3000. Turn right to 200,"
Norcal approach advises me. That makes sense. I acknowledge, reduce power and turn to a heading of 200 degrees. They are setting me up for the ILS. The simple GPS in the Skyhawk shows no ground features, but I know that I'm now out over the ocean. Darned, forgot to bring my life jacket and yellow marker dye – once again.

It was right here where John Denver died when his newly acquired experimental plane crashed into the cold waters of the Pacific. The builder of the kit plane wanted to be safe and modified the fuel system to prevent fuel lines from entering the cockpit. John Denver was unaware of the operational details of this modification and ran out of fuel right here, over Monterey bay. The water is very deep here and his plane was never found.

Damned, do not think about this. It is not important now, I admonish myself. Review the approach, that's what counts. The approach plate for the Monterey ILS Runway 10R is already clipped to my yoke. (page 215). I review the pertinent details – localizer frequency, final approach course, decision height, nearby obstacles, their height and location and set up the various radios for the approach. Last but not least, let's review and commit the missed approach procedures to memory. It is a definite possibility that we will need to do a missed approach today and there is no time to fumble when it happens. Seconds count then. I hate actual misses, but fortunately they are rare in the life of a chicken driver.

Now the instructions from ATC come fast.

"52U, descend and maintain 2000. Turn right to 290 degrees."

Aha, he is sending me parallel to the ILS, outbound. Years ago, flying the same approach with some breaks in the clouds, Karen had seen whales below us, leaving big, muddy footprints[39] in the water. I was too busy to look for them, but the memory makes me smile. Sounding mermaids make footprints, too, just smaller, about 4' across. I have a photo to prove that. Stop this, no more irrelevant thoughts now, I grumble to myself.

"52U, turn left to 140 degrees. Cleared for the ILS Runway 10R approach. Maintain 2000 till established. 6 miles from MUNSO. Contact tower at 118.4"

I repeat the sacred words of the approach clearance, not only because it is required, but also to get them on the slowly spinning audio tape down below - just in case there is ever any dispute after something went wrong. The controller is turning us onto an intercept course with the shallow electronic glide slope emanating from the runway. He told me to stay at 2000' until the needles of the glide

---

[39] A whale footprint is a large circle of very smooth water which forms over the site of a whale's sounding (dive).

slope receiver come alive and then follow their guidance down to runway 10R. I am very busy now, working on maintaining course and altitude while switching to the tower frequency.

"Monterey Tower, Cessna N1252U established on the ILS 10R. 11.7 miles out."

"Cessna 52U, good morning. Report MUNSO." a friendly female voice answers me from the tower somewhere below and ahead. I like getting instructions from female controllers. Their voices are easier to understand and often they are more friendly than their male counterparts.

The glide slope receiver is driving an instrument with two crossed needles. The vertical needle gives the pilot left/right guidance, and the horizontal needle up/down guidance. When you are exactly on the center of the glide slope, the needles are crossed. If you are not, you have to get them into the center. This, if done badly, is called a sword fight. No sword fight today, I promise myself. This will be a good one!

I check groundspeed – 90 knots. Good. That means I should need 450' per minute of vertical speed to follow a 3-degree ILS slope to the runway. That's just geometry. The left/right needle slowly centers and I turn the plane to a heading of 98°. This is the published approach course for the runway. Yet the wind may push me sideways and I will have to correct for its influence. A quick glance to the old-fashioned magnetic compass mounted on top of the dashboard tells me that the directional gyro hasn't drifted much, so 98° is a good first swag at the reference heading on the gyro. The wind is rarely strong in a marine layer, so I do not expect much in terms of wind correction.

It is very smooth today in this white cocoon. Now the up/down needle, which has been resting against the top of the instrument display – comes alive. This means that the electronic glide slope is not far above us. The plane flew for some time level at 2000' and sooner or later it was bound to intercept the gentle 3 degree slope of the ILS. We are entering it from below.

It is a big no-no to enter a glide slope from above because of antenna side lobes, which can confuse an IFR pilot. I watch intently as the up/down needle centers, while paying attention to the left/right guidance, airspeed, power setting and rehearsing the missed approach procedures.

Did I mention that single pilot IFR flying is not for the slow or lazy? Pilots have a saying about 'getting behind the plane'. During an IFR approach this can happen only too easily. But today, all the pieces fall into place. The vertical guidance needle centers and I reduce power to 2000 RPM. As usual, I have some difficulties to nail the 450'/minute descent rate, which will keep me on the glide slope.

The left/right needle has moved two dots to the right. That was either compass error, sloppy flying on my part or changing wind. I turn a few degrees right, to 102° and hold that course for a while. This is precision flying, where a couple of degrees on the heading matter. The needle stops its creep to the right. Good – that should do it. I turn to 106°, and the needle slowly creeps back towards the center of the instrument. When it is re-centered, I take out four degrees with the rudder pedals, reestablishing a 102° heading. At least for now, this seems to keep me on the localizer.

For a second the irrelevant thought about the general sloppiness with which sailors operate, compared to airplane pilots, crosses my mind. Focus on the approach, I admonish myself, again - absolutely nothing else matters now. The altimeter shows 930'. The Decision Height (DH) for Monterey ILS – where I have to absolutely, positively make a decision to continue the approach and land or abort it - is 480' above sea level. Since the elevation of the runway near the touchdown zone is 193', I would have only 287' of air above the runway at Decision Height. That is not much! Still, I'm not really nervous. Being engulfed in the apparent safety of the white cocoon, flying a smooth approach feels like playing some kind of video game. One exists for the sole tasks of positioning needles to where they belong. The thought that I'm sitting in a fragile aluminum cocoon, hurtling towards rocks, trees and concrete becomes an abstract concern. But there is no 'Game over – want to try again?' option here.

Now I am paying intense attention to the altimeter. "700', 220' to go," I mutter to myself. A few seconds later – 600', 120' to go. A quick look above the glare shield still shows only grey. This doesn't look good, I think, but I will fly to the DH (decision height) and only then make the decision about going missed. When the altimeter hits 480' I quickly look up – and there it is. In the mist ahead, the flashing strobes of the runway's optical guidance system are clearly visible. The strobes create the impression of a physical thing - usually called the rabbit- racing toward the touchdown point of the runway. And there is the runway itself - the big 10R painted at its beginning looks really good.

IFR pilots have been known to say that the feeling of breaking out of a low hanging cloud and seeing a runway straight ahead is the best feeling known to man. But they *never* say that when their wives are around. Otherwise they may end up sleeping in their hangar.

White Cocoon - IFR

Thunderstorms, Sharks and Pirates of the Caribbean

See also pages 212,213

After decades of diving and taking underwater photos and videos, I got sick and tired of not having taken a single good picture of a shark. I do not know what it is – perhaps the wrong choice of deodorant. Locals in many places have assured me that there are always sharks 'there'. Then I go diving 'there' and find none, except for a few harmless nurse sharks asleep under ledges or small sand or lemon sharks. A few times, in the distance, I have spotted the hazy shape of a real shark. But as soon as I head towards it, it invariably disappears into the blue mist. What is wrong with this picture? Some people may say – nothing, but I didn't like it.

After 33 years of this frustration, I finally decided to do something about it. Some internet research located a dive resort in the southern Bahamas, called Stella Maris, which sounded promising. It had a 20-year history of offering shark dives to visitors and a good reputation. Stella Maris had been created by a couple of Germans with Wanderlust. More about that later.

I packed my Scuba gear, including a Nikonos V underwater camera and 25 pounds of aeronautical charts and approach plates and a folding Dahon bicycle into my trusty Bonanza A36 and headed for Stella Maris, 3000 miles away. As I was single and flying solo, the sky was mine. Or so I thought.

This is still a significant flight for a single-engine propeller plane, from northern California to the southern Bahamas. In preparation for the flight, I had spent $20,000 to equip the plane with external tip tanks and a few other goodies. This, combined with a special mode of operating the engine called Lean of Peak (LOP) – which greatly reduces fuel consumption – increased the range of the Bonanza to nearly1300 nautical miles. That's a lot, considering that the great circle distance from San Francisco to Miami is only 2200 nautical miles. In other words, it was nearly possible to do this flight with only one stop!

But a Bonanza – even though it is fast for a propeller plane – is slow compared to a jet, flying at about 160 knots (nautical miles per hour) in this slow, fuel saving mode. It takes about 8.5 hours to cover this distance, and the plane would arrive at the destination with an hour worth of fuel left in the tank. That's an amazing endurance. The fact that I am male and alone in the plane, carrying a special red bottle made it physically possible to stay in the saddle for so long.

The first part of the trip was from the San Francisco Bay area to the vicinity of Dallas in Texas, with a stop in Las Vegas where I had to take care of some incidental business, not related to gambling. It was a beautiful and relaxing flight, helped along by a nice tailwind. It carried us over the southern Sierras, Las Vegas and the edge of the Grand Canyon, then past Flagstaff and the San Francisco mountains of Arizona, past my old hangouts of Los Alamos and Santa Fe into the flatlands of eastern New Mexico and Texas. As I was entering the Albuquerque airspace, I heard a memorable transmission.

"Eclipse 501, cleared to flight level 250."

At that time, I was already thinking about buying one of these new jets. The thought that a real Eclipse was somewhere in the airspace ahead and above was a big boost in believing that this jet could be in my future.

I landed near Dallas after a very long but uneventful IFR flight and had a serious Mai-Tai. Admittedly that's not the proper drink for Texas, but I like to check out Mai-Tais anywhere in the world. Then I went back to the motel and planned for the next day's flight, using a laptop computer, am internet link and a portable Canon i80 printer, which had spilled pink ink all over itself at high altitudes. What a mess it made! But it is good to have a paper copy of the flight plan in the cockpit. Paper doesn't crash and is readable in full sunlight. That's more than one can say about computers.

I got up very early next morning to fly the leg from Dallas to Vero Beach, FL. Thunderstorms were expected to become active later in the day. The flight plan showed a distance of 1000 nm, not a big deal from the Bonanza's range point of view. But there are thunderstorms to reckon with when flying in these parts. I took off into the early morning light, with a close eye on the IBM R50 laptop computer strapped into the copilot's seat. It was hooked to an XM weather satellite receiver, which gave me a nearly instantaneous view on the weather anywhere in the US.

Initially, everything was fine. But during the late morning, the computer's display started to show lightning strikes ahead. Soon it was possible to correlate the lighting shown on the screen with the ominous anvil shaped thunderstorm clouds towering over the featureless, flat cloudscape below. It was fascinating to correlate the real thunderstorms with the images on the screen.

As time wore on, more and more of these storms popped up. The direct flight towards the northern part of Florida was now out of the question. At first I contemplated to squeeze through a hole in the long line of thunderstorms forming over southern Alabama. When I discussed this strategy with ATC, the controller, in a fatherly voice, said essentially
"Son, you do not want to do that."
Being a chicken pilot at heart and knowing that the man deals with the weather here all the time, that advice sent me scurrying northward, towards Atlanta. As usual, ATC was cooperative and approved a major course revision to avoid

Thunderstorms, Sharks and Pirates

the big cluster of thunderstorms now building over northern Florida and southern Georgia. A long flight would get even longer…

But I did not care, because I was quite scared. As a California IFR pilot, I had little actual experience with thunderstorms, except circumnavigating them from a safe distance. But like any pilot, I knew that thunderstorms like to chew up airplanes big and small and spit them out as debris. It was a scary, but fascinating flight. Thunderstorms popped up like mushrooms. Once I flew under the wide overhanging anvil of one of these, well knowing that hail thrown from the anvil can damage a plane a long way out. The laptop screen showed a superposition of intense rain (dark green), lighting symbols and the grey patch of the anvil cloud. The latter was an image taken from space, superimposed on the radar returns. All this was visible on the screen as I was motoring along, under that anvil, at 11,000' altitude. It would have been good to go much higher, but I was afraid that the disk of my laptop would physically crash in the thin air. The read/write head of a disk literally flies over the disk's surface, relying on the availability of air. Disk's don't work at high attitudes, as I once found out the hard way.

Some more discussion with the helpful controllers of the Atlanta ATC center encouraged me to forego the direct route along the Florida west coast and head first for Atlanta, then fly down the eastern coasts of Georgia and Florida instead. By now I was cutting in and out of cumulus clouds. But they still showed no lighting activity on the onboard Sferics lightning detector. Still, they gave me a good scrubbing with strong turbulence. The thought of entering an actual thunderstorm was terrifying, after reading all the vivid description by pilots who had done it yet lived to tell the tale.

Finally, I was turning south again, heading for the Florida coast. Then came a moment I'll never forget.

Suddenly the Bonanza popped out of a towering wall of white clouds. It was like tunneling through the walls of a gleaming white castle, breaking out of prison and seeing green landscapes below. Ahead was a joyous sight – the coast of Florida stretched as far as the eye could see and nothing more than harmless scattered fair-weather clouds below and ahead, This view was one of the biggest reliefs of my life. There are few activities which can make (or break) your day like aviation. No wonder that one can become addicted to it. It makes much of ground bound life pale in comparison.

The weather got worse again as I flew southbound along the Florida east coast. But it was just rain, no thunderstorm activity. I could see the Kennedy space center, Merritt Island and Cocoa Beach. As a space buff since youth, these were holy names for me. Dipping in and out of the clouds, I was vectored for the approach to Vero Beach, 90 miles southeast of Orlando. After the wheels touched the ground, I sat in the cockpit for minutes, exhausted after this seemingly endless flight of 9 hours. It did not help that during half oft this flight I was very tense. The arrival of the helpful lineman shook me out of my reverie and I crawled out of the cockpit, completely drained of energy.

Karen's sister, Janet, and her mother, Genevieve, lived nearby, and I spent a couple of relaxing days with family. I took my nephew flying, and he took me kayaking. We played with dolphins in the Indian river and explored hidden coves and the wreck of a boat which had sunk in the river.

A few days later, time had come to head for the Bahamas. I flew to Ft Pierce, where the local FBO rents over water equipment such as inflatable rafts. The 6-man version which I rented – even though I was alone – was amazingly small, about the size of a seat cushion. Does this thing really work? It seemed like a toy. Recently I watched a show called Survivor Man, where they tested one of these rafts. It sank in minutes.

I prepared the international IFR flight plan with the help of the friendly folks at Fort Pierce and took off. Once again, thunderstorms were a consideration. ATC vectored me directly towards a major buildup. Yet the frequency got so busy that I couldn't get a word in edgewise. At the same time, I saw the red circle of a temporary flight restriction (TFR) pop up over Ft. Lauderdale. Finally, ATC explained to all aircrews that the reason for the congestion on the frequency and the sudden appearance of the TFR over Ft. Lauderdale was an unannounced Florida visit by Vice President Dick Cheney. Damned politicians, I thought, while still heading for that big cloud in the sky. Do they have any idea what a mess their arrivals create?

Finally, ATC vectored me away from the monster, towards Bimini Island. Soon I found myself in a wonderland of big towering clouds, deep blue and turquoise waters below and green islands in the distance. Fortunately, the strike finder showed no lighting activity anywhere. Soon thereafter, Nassau Center took over control of my flight. In a delightful thick British accent, Nassau Approach cleared me into Bahamian airspace and vectored me directly over the island of Nassau. Soon I could make out the international airport and cruise ships, 11,000' below. After passing Nassau, my course took a sharp right, down the long chain of islands angling towards Long Island and Stella Maris. On starboard, one could see the deep blue of the Tongue of the Ocean and big Andros Island. Ahead, a cloud street announced the long line of narrow islands guiding us towards Stella Maris. It was a relaxed flight. The only concern was an engine failure, something that is never entirely out of one's mind while flying over a lot of deep water behind a single engine. So many things have to work...

But the engine, as always, ran like a sewing machine.

Finally the Bahamian ATC cleared me for a descent at pilot's discretion. It was time to cancel IFR and head directly for Long Island. Clouds were building over all the islands, but there was never any concern about re-entering serious IFR conditions. Soon I spotted the little airstrip owned by the resort. Rather than landing directly, I circled the north of the island and took beautiful pictures out of the storm window of the trusty Bonanza. It had brought me that far without the smallest hiccup. Finally, I lined up with the runway and landed - steering with my left hand and shooting pictures with my right hand.

After a smooth landing on the airport of the resort, I taxied up to the little customs building, got out and did the simple formalities required when entering the Bahamas. Jimmy Buffett, in his entertaining book *"A Pirate Looks at 50"* mentions that it is much easier to deal with banana republic customs and immigration if one wears a dark tie and a short-sleeved white shirt with four striped shoulder bars. I have since tested his theory when driving boats and planes, and Buffett is absolutely right about that.

As I got out of the customs building, I saw a large ATR42 turboprop land. That is odd, I thought. To my knowledge, there was no scheduled traffic to this island, and the ATR was a rather big plane to land on this short strip. The mystery deepened as the passengers disembarked. They did not look like the typical tourist crowd with luggage, rather more like a bunch of Hollywood types. Boxes upon boxes of gear were taken off the plane, too. I got curious, wandered over and chatted with some of the gold chain wearing guys.

It turned out that they were the second unit for the movies *Pirates of the Caribbean II* and *III*. They were here to film outdoor scenes for the two sequels of *Pirates of the Caribbean*. That movie had been released recently and was a big hit. It turned out that they stayed at Stella Maris too.

Thunderstorms, Sharks and Pirates

That was no surprise, of course, as it was the only hotel on the northern end of the island.

It was fascinating to see movie scenes which were clearly taken in Hawaii and joined seamlessly to beach scenes shot right here in the Bahamas. The fight of Johnny Depp with his antagonist on the big rolling wheel – as they roll out of the jungle onto the beach – is the best example.

Unfortunately, two local technicians were killed this week when they climbed a rusty cell phone tower and it collapsed. As a result, just while the second unit was down there, the entire thin communications link of the southern Bahamas with the rest of the world was broken down for several days (except satellite phones, of course).

Stella Maris is am impressive resort, with its own airstrip, Scuba operation, marina and housing developments for sale. I chatted a lot with its German owners. As young men, they had felt that Germany was too crowded and emigrated in the late sixties to this island in the outer, southern Bahamas. They told me the story how they first opened a little bar and had their very first customers. These drank a few beers – but then left without paying. The founders of Stella Maris, at the time, did not even know how to yell at them, as their command of English was very limited. They sure have come a long way from these very modest beginnings!

I had a few relaxed days before the shark dive. With a rented scooter, I explored the island, including a visit to a deep ocean *blue hole* at its southern tip. It looked beautiful, but I carried no snorkeling gear on the scooter and therefore couldn't see it from underwater.

A main reason for this voyage was to go diving with sharks. Two days later, several dive instructors, a honeymoon couple and I headed for the spot where the shark dive would take place. The sharks, having been fed for years there, associate the rumble of a Diesel engine with

Thunderstorms, Sharks and Pirates

food. Our anchor was hardly down when several sharks were circling the boat. Their brownish, torpedo-shaped bodies looked serious. I slowly started to realize that sharks could be real, not just something you read and laugh about. By now, the couple decided that they would stay aboard. Good move for a honeymoon couple, I thought. That left the four professional dive guides and me to hit the water.

We suited up and the leader of our dive gave us a short briefing. We were anchored at 20' of water over a sandy bottom. The guides had shark sticks and one had a small camera. I carried my Nikonos V, which could make a good weapon, too, as it is machined from solid steel.

The dive master admonished us to hit the water together and immediately descend to the bottom, then form a defensive ring on the sand. We did that, and immediately the sharks showed a strong interest in us. They arrived to investigate, circling us closely. Up to now, I had not taken all this very seriously. But the view of a 6'/2m long blue shark heading directly towards you dispels any pretense that this was Disney land. I was ready to smack him fiercely on the nose when he (or she) finally veered away. A few times, the dive guides needed to physically push sharks away, using their blunt sticks.

Ten minutes later, the crew on the dive boat dropped a bucket with fish heads. It tumbled down slowly and the sharks, like a squadron of fighters, raced towards the bucket. It disappeared in a flurry of twisting, thrashing shark bodies, soon engulfed in dark clouds of fish blood. By the time the bucket hit the sandy bottom, the food fight was over and the bucket seemed empty. The sharks were still circling it, looking for more food.

Then we noticed that one fish head was still in the bucket. One of the dive guides had a long spear with him. It wasn't very useful as a shark stick, but came in handy now. He speared the lone fish head and offered it to the circling sharks. But it did not trigger a mad rush for this last piece.

Thunderstorms, Sharks and Pirates

Rather, the same sharks, which had been so ruthlessly aggressive a moment ago, were now circling the offered bait, but did not attack it.

This went on for some time and was more akin to the timid behavior I had seen before with sharks. Finally, another fish -a wrasse- shot forward, grabbed the fish head and quickly disappeared into the background. Sharks are just mysterious creatures – fearsome one moment, shy and timid the next. But I finally got good close-up pictures of real sharks to add to my underwater photo collection.

On the flight back home, I landed in Fort Pierce, Florida. Dealing with US customs was easy, contrary to the horror stories one hears about returning by private plane from the Bahamas. Then I spent a night in St. Augustine, which is a lovely city.

On the return flight, I overnighted in Tucumcari, New Mexico. As I was preparing to take off the next morning, an Osprey 22 VTOL aircraft arrived and was fooling around. In its helicopter mode, with its wing vertical, it looks like a huge black bat. Count Dracula would have wanted one. This view could scare any enemy to death - if he doesn't choke from the dust clouds the Osprey generates. We'll see how well it works in combat. It certainly is an impressive looking piece of hardware.

Hydrodynamics and more (ħ)

See also pages 161,166,190 216, 218, 204

This story talks about hydrodynamics, mermaids and dolphins. Fish and marine mammals have a single tailfin rather than two, because single fins are far more efficient. It has to do with the same wingtip vortices which are discussed in the story about Instrument Flying (page 329ff). Much of the following is based on a classical textbook[40].

As a wing of an airplane, or the fin of a diver moves through air or water, a high-pressure zone is created below the wing (corresponding to the down going side of a fin) and a low-pressure zone above it. This creates the wingtip (or fin-edge) vortices. These vortices contain so much energy that they can flip a trailing aircraft upside down.

Looked at it differently, this energy is all wasted from the point of view of the vortex generating plane, fish or diver. If a wing were infinitely long, air would have no opportunity to circle around from the bottom to the top surface and there could be no wingtip vortices. Infinitely long wings are kind of impractical, but that's the reason why modern sailplanes have such long wings, giving them their amazing soaring efficiency. In technical terms, the aspect ratio (length/width) of efficient wings is very high.

The two fins of a diver - from a wingtip vortex point of view – are especially inefficient. They present *four* edges where wingtip vortices will form. Even worse, fins must be narrow or they will collide with each other when a diver uses the normal or 'scissor' kick. This extremely low aspect ratio is the exact opposite of what makes for a good fin or wing.

---

[40] Ira Abbott and A.E. von Doenhoff , 'Theory of Wing Sections'

A single fin solves both problems. It can be made very wide and there are only two energy-robbing edges, not four. The result is a very big increase in efficiency. Check on *Youtube* for keywords Tanya Streeter BBC Teil 1 to see a beautiful video of her swimming with wales and among corals, wearing a monofin.

We saw plenty of evidence of that increased efficiency. Karen, wearing her mermaid suit and I were once diving at a place called Vanishing Point. As one can surmise from this name, rocks are close to the surface there. Currents must squeeze between the rocks and the surface and this greatly accelerates them. We were diving against such a strong current and I just couldn't make any headway. Karen saw my predicament and came to my rescue. She just dragged me along like a guppy. As athletic as Karen was, she could never have done this while wearing standard Scuba equipment. It was always a challenge for me to get in a good position for taking pictures or videos of her, because she was swimming so fast with her suit.

I mentioned elsewhere how the weaker vortices of a monofin make it easier to approach fish closely. For Karen, this was her reason to wear the mermaid suit. I certainly enjoyed it, as she made a stunning underwater model.

Anita observed the same calming effect on marine life. We once dove near the cove in Hawaii, where Captain Cook had been killed in 1798 and came across a group of nearly 20 dolphins. Anita wore her turquoise mermaid suit, and it allowed her to get close to the dolphins, who paid her some attention. Often they are quite aloof to divers, but Anita was lucky. By the way, some experts advise against diving with Scuba gear near dolphins, because the exhaling of bubbles is supposedly interpreted as an act of aggression. Anita and I did not see evidence of that.

Mermaid suits aren't available from wetsuit manufacturers, so how did Karen and Anita obtain their cool outfits? Karen's first suit was homemade. She was a very good tailor and quickly learned how to glue neoprene sheets. We acquired 3mm thick neoprene sheets, which were covered with yellow Lycra and black nylon to protect the material. Karen designed the pattern for the suit, and we cut and glued it. This first suit was only glued, not sewed, but held up to many dives in the open ocean just fine.

As for the fin, we did not buy a finished monofin, because it would be awkward to carry it onto an airliner. Rather, we got a pair of conventional Cressi racing bi-fins. I made a little stainless steel and fiberglass gizmo, which allowed to reversibly combine the two fins into one wide monofin. The whole setup was hidden under the soft neoprene of the tail, which flared out to cover it.

The trailing edge of the fin cover was closed with a two-inch wide Velcro strip. We found out that this design - trailing edge of the fin not being watertight - had unexpected advantages. First, it allowed water to enter the suit and expel trapped air. For a wetsuit, this is important. Second, as a mermaid swims, the trailing edge of her fin moves quickly through the water. The Bernoulli effect creates a local zone of low pressure at the fin's edge, which draws water out of the suit. This creates an admirable fit, as can be seen from the various images of Karen and Anita diving. The weak water flow through the suit reduces its warmth, but in tropical waters that is not much of a concern. We should have patented this concept!

It took both of them only a very short time – one or two dives - to get used to the suit. They just needed to move like a dolphin, but this comes naturally with legs confined in a tail. The only drawback of a tail –at least while in the water- is that it is harder to maneuver precisely. It is sometimes helpful to hold onto something and therefore the wearing of protective gloves is a very good idea. But one should never touch living beings, especially corals.

Karen and Anita found it surprisingly easy to get in and out of the water, at least for boat dives. The key is to minimize wearing the heavy Scuba tank outside the water. The tank may be suspended from a line dangling from the boat and put on while in the water. Upon returning to the boat, they just used the boat's swim ladder to push themselves with their covered heels from rung to rung of the swim ladder while facing away from the stern.

Another return method is to jump into the dinghy, which usually floats behind a cruising boat. A tail provides so much thrust that this is can be done. Recently a sequel to the movie "Open Water" was released. It is the story of a group of friends who are out on a boat, forget to lower the swim ladder, jump into the water and can't get back out. Exactly that happened to us once in Vava'u. But for us, it was not a big deal. Like a dolphin, Karen leaped out of the water and solved the problem.

It is possible to dive from the beach in a mermaid suit, but one cannot recommend it. Karen tested this once and found the water entry possible, but not graceful.

As fast as human 'mermaids' are, they are no match for dolphins. Is not only that dolphins are stronger – they also have an unfair advantage hidden within their skin. Again, it has to do with vortices. Small vortices are triggered by imperfections in the surface of any ship or animal. These add to the drag. The skin of dolphins has tiny sensors, which detect vortex formation. Small muscles then change the local shape of the skin to suppress further growth of the vortex. This saves energy and contributes to the amazing speeds with which dolphins can swim.

Prof. Grzimek, the revered long-time director of the Frankfurt Zoo, reports an encounter between sharks and dolphins. A shark and a pod of dolphins were peacefully sharing one tank. Then a dolphin got pregnant. One morning, the crew found the shark– dead – in a neighboring tank. Its body showed deep impacts from dolphin noses. Apparently they decided that the shark would be a liability with a baby dolphin around and decided to throw him out of the tank - clear across into the adjacent tank. This is the way dolphins kill sharks. They ram them at high speed, and as the inner organs of sharks are lying loose inside their bowls, they are very vulnerable to sudden impacts. This is also the concept behind the very effective explosive shark sticks. Sharks fear dolphins and avoid them. The question is - does a diver in a mermaid suit look like a dolphin to a shark?

Back to making the suits…

Before the long-term sailing trip in the Caribbean, Karen brought her homemade mermaid suit to a custom wetsuit shop. They improved the pattern and made a beautiful, professional version, stitched and glued. Later, they did the same for Anita, creating her turquoise suit. They charged $600, which is $150 more than for a standard custom-made suit. Today, they are selling these mermaid suits – in very small numbers – to the diving public. But this underwater fashion is not catching on quickly. That is not a surprise, but it is a pity. Mermaids sure look good on videos and in underwater photos. Maybe some serious marketing effort is needed.

But let's at least be thankful that Scuba diving is no longer a male dominated sport. When I started diving, around 1970, that was still the case, with hardly any women participating (in Europe). It probably had to do with the military origin of Scuba diving in World War II and the onerous training requirements at the time. These were directly derived from Navy frogman training programs. Fortunately, the American Scuba community – unlike the

European one – soon realized that it was silly to impose this severe regimen on recreational divers and introduced a more practical and simpler curriculum. It was safer, too, because the traditional training killed students[41]. For decades, European divers (including the author) made fun of American 'Easy Divers', but we were behind the times. Today, men and women enter this fascinating sport in equal numbers.

---

[41] Whenever practicing for a particular emergency–like diver's out-of-air ascends or spinning aircraft – kills more students and instructors than the actual emergencies ever did, practicing should be stopped. That sounds like a pretty basic concept, but old-timers always invent dumb arguments why the continued killing of students is a good idea.

RMS RHONE

See also pages 170, 218

RMS RHONE is one of the most famous and beautiful wrecks in the world. It served as the underwater backdrop in the 1977 movie 'The Deep'. This visually stunning film, based on the best-selling novel by JAWS author Peter Benchley, stars Nick Nolte and Jacqueline Bissett as a couple on a romantic holiday in Bermuda. There they find drugs and treasure while diving on a wreck.

The real story of the Royal Mail Steamer RHONE is even more dramatic than the movie. The RHONE was the newest, high-tech ship of the British Royal Mail Steamer Packet Company. It is big, 310' long, 40' wide and was powered by sails and a steam engine. The ship was equipped with one of the new-fangled propellers, instead of paddle wheels. It wasn't lost on its maiden voyage, as the locals say, but two years later.

In late October of 1867, the RHONE and a smaller ship of the same company were anchored in Big Harbor on the north shore of Peter Island. This island is located in the British Virgin Islands, just across the Sir Francis Drake Channel from the main island of Tortola. Big Harbor is a large bight, where even big ships can anchor. It is very deep, and yachts have a hard time anchoring there, except extremely close to the beach.

The morning of October 29, 1867, dawned bright and clear, with no clouds in sight. As I described in the story about hurricanes, that – in the Caribbean – is a bad sign, because, the cloudless sky is mostly likely caused by a hurricane lurking over the horizon. Captain Robert Wooley of the RHONE and his colleague on the smaller ship knew that and conferred what to do. The nearest real hurricane hole was on St. John, but it was far too small for handling a ship of the size of the RHONE. The captain of the smaller vessel decided to head across the Sir Francis Drake channel and anchor in Road Town Harbor, Tortola.

Captain Wooley decided to ride out the coming storm right where he was, in Big Harbor of Peter Island. The decision of the Captain of the smaller ship should be viewed with skepticism. Tortola's main harbor is wide open towards the ocean and funnel shaped. It is anything but a safe hurricane hole. He must have had some doubts as to the wisdom of his action and his chances for survival, since the two Captains agreed to transfer all passengers from the smaller ship onto the big, 'safe' RHONE. This accomplished, the smaller ship departed and the RHONE was now alone in Big Harbor.

The indications of the clear sky had been correct – a hurricane was on the prowl. The sky darkened, the barometer fell and soon the hurricane unleashed its fury on the waters of Big Harbor and the RHONE, riding at anchor. The ship survived the onslaught of the hurricane's front side. However, Captain Wooley decided that he did not want to ride out the backside of the storm in the Bight and ordered to raise the anchor while the eye of the hurricane passed over them. His new plan was to seek the relative safety of the open sea, outside the Sir Francis Drake channel.

Things did not go well. The anchor chain got stuck and put the ship in a truly bad situation. He gave the command to chisel through the anchor chain, which took quite some time, but eventually the crew succeeded. The big ship left the harbor and steamed with everything she got towards the open sea. This meant that she had to round the northern point of Peter Island, pass in front of Dead Man's Chest and avoid treacherous Blonde Rock lurking in the middle of the channel. Then she turned starboard and sailed past a rocky point on Salt Island before she could reach the open sea.

RMS Rhone

But the RHONE never made it. As they were steaming past that point of Salt Island, the backside of the hurricane hit with full force. The steam engine was running at emergency power, but it was to no avail. The ship was driven by the hurricane winds against a rock, which punctured the ship's hull.

The rock is an evil looking black horn, and it shivers me timbers each time I sail past it. As cold water entered the breach in the hull and hit the boiler, which was operating at maximum pressure, the thermal shock blew the boiler up. The force of the explosion broke the keel of the ship and flung the boiler far away from the rest of the hull. The two halves of the ship sank independently. The bow section rests in about 90' of water, whereas the rudder and propeller of the stern section are close to the black rock, lying in only 13' of water. The stern is easily seen from the surface when snorkeling over it.

All passengers and most of the crew perished. Only five sailors made it to the nearby shore with the aid of the inhabitants of Salt Island.

Now, 150 years later, the RHONE is still where she sank. The wooden deck has disappeared and from above the stern section looks like the skeleton of a fish, with the big propeller shaft as the backbone and the ribs of the hull looking like the bones of a fish. The rudder broke off and is jammed vertically between some rocks, whereas the 15' ship's propeller is clearly visible. Or so one should think.

Anita and I were diving on the RHONE once. She wore her mermaid suit and this gave us the opportunity for shooting great photos. In a well-known picture, she sits in the carve-out for the lower hinge of the rudder blade. (see photo on page 218) After this dive, something funny happened. I mentioned casually that many people dive the RHONE and never see the 15' propeller, which is so clearly visible. Anita was swimming around it, touched it

and posed next to it. Her question was:" Which propeller?"
She had not seen it either.

Salt Island has an inland salt pond, where salt was
collected by the islanders. The British crown rewarded
them for their heroic rescue efforts by relieving them of all
taxes, except for one bag of salt per year. Queen Elizabeth
II visited the tiny island after her coronation, when she
toured the world. The first time Karen and I were there, the
two remaining islanders, elderly women dressed in their
Sunday finest, were still proudly telling the tale of the
rescue and the royal visit. But they were gone a few years
later. Now Salt Island is uninhabited again.

RMS Rhone

Buying Airplanes

See also pages 196,214,210,194, 217

  I currently own a Cessna Skyhawk, a Beechcraft Bonanza A36, share a German LS4 glider with a good friend, Dr. Wolf Weber and share a Cessna Skylane with several partners, including my old friend Ron Labby. The four planes are distributed over several airports in the San Francisco Bay area. In addition, I made a big down payment on an Eclipse 500 twin jet. This motley collection of five aircraft gives me an excuse to write about owning such toys.

  Buying an airplane in 2008 has an old-fashioned feel to it. One can imagine that the paperwork for getting a car in 1930 was as simple and straightforward as buying a plane today. No odometer statements, inspections and emission certificates are required. All one needs is a very simple Bill of Sale, which lists buyer and seller, address, price (which most people fill out as $1+ OC), registration and serial numbers of the plane. That's it. The buyer sends the original to the FAA's Mike Monroney Aeronautical Center in Oklahoma. A few weeks later, the registration for the plane arrives in the mail. The important airworthiness certificate stays with the plane upon a sale. Next time you board an airliner, look for it. It is a 5x6 card, always posted near the entrance of the plane.

  But the insurance companies aren't quite as relaxed as the FAA. They have strong opinions as to whom they deem worthy of insuring. It is easy to insure a simple plane, like a Skyhawk. Aircraft insurance is similar to car insurance. There are liability and comprehensive insurance components. The latter is called hull insurance, as in the maritime insurance business.

A typical, 1980 model Cessna Skyhawk costs about $1000 per year to insure. A Bonanza of similar age is about four times more. That is, if you are considered qualified in the eyes of the insurance company. Qualified means you have enough total flight time, flight time in this aircraft type, the proper ratings (IFR rating is needed for a complex and high performance aircraft like the Bonanza) and sufficient recent flight experience. Fortunately, there is no law stating that one needs to insure an aircraft and some operators go without this protection.

Unlike most cars, airplanes often keep their value or sometimes even appreciate. My first wife and I bought our second plane, a Skyhawk, in 1986 for $19,000 and I sold it in 1998 for $48,000! That beats many other investments. The Bonanza is currently worth about $200,000, the Skylane $90,000, the sailplane $29,000 and the jet will be around $1.8Million.

I also bought a two-seat Cessna 150 for $19,000 as a present to Anita, my second wife. But the Cessna had some landing gear problems and I sold it cheaply after her death. A hangar which I bought for $33,000 may be worth $50,000 now. Still, flying is not inexpensive. Other than the cost of purchasing and insuring, planes use special aviation gas and need careful maintenance. The costs go up exponentially with the complexity of the plane.

A simple Skyhawk is easy to maintain, often going an entire year requiring only routine maintenance like oil changes. However, by law, every certified plane must be inspected by a highly qualified IA (Inspector, Aircraft) once a year and, if used for hire, every 100 flight hours.

Quite a few fond memories are associated with these seven plane purchases.

Cessnas

In 1984, I was with IBM Research for a year and we felt optimistic, even though Karen and I had just bought a house in Yorktown Heights, which we could barely afford. But I was lusting for an airplane. After all, I had doubled my university salary by going to IBM and Karen had a good salary, too. Karen was fine with the idea and we went on a search, using the Trade-A-Plane newspaper. It is printed on trademark thin yellow paper and it is the bible of aircraft buyers and sellers since 1937. We found a 1974 Cessna Skyhawk for sale ($17,000) in North Carolina. The specs looked good. We took an airliner from NY to NC and met the seller, who was a professional aircraft broker. The plane looked fine to my untrained eye. I wrote a check and off we went. That was a mistake. One should always hire an experienced aircraft mechanic to look a prospective plane over.

The flight home dealt with some weather, and while flying - legally - over the Chesapeake Bay, we were 'strafed' by a flight of F16. The boys certainly had fun, but it was a miserable feeling sitting there in this slow plane, knowing that we'd be dead if the fighters had any bad intentions. We headed for Poughkeepsie airport, in Duchess County, New York. This was nearly an hour's drive north of our home in Westchester County, but I did not dare yet to land the plane on the tiny dirt strip near our home.

It took months before I mustered the confidence to land near Yorktown Heights. The name of the privately held strip was Mahopac airport and it was located in Putnam County, across the border to Westchester County. The field was only 1800' long, bordered by tall trees, a cemetery, and a hill beyond the departure end. Today I'd consider it a slam-dunk (literally) to land a Skyhawk in a strip of that length, but back then it was a blood-pressure raising challenge.

On our first landing in Mahopac, we had barely rolled to a stop on the grassy field when a pickup truck chased us down the runway. Out jumped a fellow in a leather jacket and started yelling at us for landing without permission. That was our introduction to the world of crusty Art Neeves, his sons and the private airport of Mahopac. Why is it that the word *crusty* comes up so often when talking about older fliers? Mahopac airport is now closed, because Art moved further upstate to build another airport. But we had a few interesting and fun years in Mahopac.

It is rumored that Art had been flying since the world was young. He drove ancient DC3 twins over the Great Lakes, in the winter, when the moist air over the lakes could turn any flight into an icing nightmare. He was the owner and FBO of Mahopac, which he ran as his private fiefdom. It was hard to get comfortable there. Even after having a plane there for years, the FBO and his wife invariably greeted us with "May I help you?" Well, flying attracts all kinds of characters. All kinds!

We had quite a few adventures in Mahopac. In the spring, the southern end of the runway turned into muck and only about 1300' were useable. 1300' is a short strip by any measure except for specialized bush planes, but over time we grew accustomed to it. Karen got her private pilot's license from Art and she became an excellent stick and rudder pilot. But since this was such a private field, she never became very comfortable with the microphone and the world of ATC. That's not uncommon for pilots learning in small fields with little traffic.

Dr. Scott Kirkpatrick – who hired me into IBM Research in 1983 and became a good friend and mentor – also learned to fly there. He has since gone on to get numerous aviation ratings, including becoming a flight instructor.

We lost our first plane in Mahopac. It was a icy, but beautiful winter morning in 1986. Karen and I took off from Mahopac, flew to Connecticut and had a great Sunday brunch. (No champagne for the pilot, though). The visibility was excellent, and the plane climbed like a homesick angel in the cold air. The temperature was around zero degrees Fahrenheit. Thus the normally muddy ground of the runway in Mahopac was frozen rock-hard, and the plane shook badly on the rough ground during the landing roll. As the plane slowed to a stop, the propeller stopped spinning. That was most unusual. I tried to restart the engine in a hurry – knowing that someone else was taxing onto the runway for takeoff. But the engine would not start. That was unusual, too, since I knew the engine in and out and it always started, even when it was very cold. Then Karen yelled

"There is smoke!"

She jumped out and ran in front of the plane. She looked under the cowling and confirmed – she could see the glow of flames. It is funny how time slows down in such moments. I remember storing the seatbelts carefully where they belong. That was stupid, of course, but I was so preoccupied - as in any emergency - to not let panic take over.

When I finally jumped out of the cockpit, the fire had grown much bigger. We had no fire extinguisher in the plane – many pilots do not carry one, because it is often useless for in-flight fires. I ran up to the FBO shack, where a big fire extinguisher was kept. But since it was still very early on a Sunday, nobody was there and the shack was locked.

I ran back down where the plane was now very visibly burning. Karen pointed out that her purse was still lying on the back seat of the cabin. I went to the burning plane, opened the door and started fishing for her purse in the dark, dense smoke. The was absolutely no visibility in the smoke. I caught a whiff of the smoke into my throat, and nearly choked on it. Now I understand why most fire victims die of smoke inhalation!

But there was a layer of clear air on the bottom of the cabin. That was quite a surprise, but remember that if you ever get into a fire situation. Ever since, when flying in an airliner, I carefully count the number of seat rows between the exit and my row. This would give me a better chance to find the exit while crawling low on the floor. Note that many airliners have guiding lights on the floor, with different colors to indicate exit rows. If one wanted to be more prepared, one could carry a folding smoke hoods aboard an airliner. I rarely bother, since airline flights are so safe.

Getting Karen's purse rescued was a good move for a husband and a dumb thing to do for a pilot! By the time the fire trucks arrived, alarmed by the column of smoke, the whole front of the plane was engulfed in flames. The engine got so hot that the big starter ring wrapped around the flywheel fell off. It was impossible, afterwards, to diagnose the reason for the engine fire. I talked with the FAA and NTSB, but they did not care, since it happened on the ground and no one got hurt.

"Maybe the fuel hose fell off from the shaking on the frozen rough ground,"
was the opinion of the NTSB technician whom I had called. It was classified neither as an incident nor as an accident – it never happened as far as the government was concerned. It was impressive to see how well the firewall protected the back of the plane. The insurance paid full hull value and the wreckage was stored for years behind the hangar. But eventually someone bought it and trucked it to the Midwest. There the plane was rebuilt and is flying around again. If only the student pilots flying it for the last few years knew the history of this plane – they might have second thoughts stepping aboard.

Buying Airplanes

We soon went searching for another plane. Since the first one had spent its youth in Florida and showed signs of corrosion, we were determined to find a plane, which had spent all its life far away from the ocean.

Kansas seemed like a good place to start. We flew to Kansas City on Eastern Airlines and began our search there. I believe that *really good* planes never make it to Trade-a-Plane (the aviation classifieds) because the locals grab it first. So I was determined to find a plane before the owner even had clearly announced his intent to sell it. We rented a car in Kansas and just drove around, with aviation chart, compass and roadmap, looking for the numerous small airfields surrounding Kansas City. It was surprisingly difficult to find the airfields. Today, with GPS, it would be simple. Back then the best strategy was to stop, climb on the car and look for landing planes.

Eventually we came to a small airfield where we heard rumors of a nice 1976 Cessna Skyhawk which the owner just might consider selling. We tracked down its owner. Slowly he allowed that he might consider a sale because of the poor health of his wife, Nadine. But he wasn't sure. We looked at the plane and really liked it. Simple avionics, but squeaky clean and only 600 total flight hours. But the owner couldn't be talked into selling it and we flew home again.

But we did not give up. Two weeks later, we were back in Kansas. Well, it took three trips from New York to Kansas to convince him to sell us the plane. I test flew it and it flew great. The owner watched me like a hawk during the test flight. If I had done anything, which he would have considered detrimental to his beloved bird, he would not have sold it. But we could eventually convince him that the plane would find a good home with us. It helped greatly that Karen and Nadine had become friends.

Karen was a natural in forming relations, even though she always thought of herself as shy. She wasn't.

The long flight home to New York has a few amusing incidents of its own, but I will skip them. This Skyhawk was a wonderful companion for decades. We flew it all over the eastern seaboard and eventually even flew it to California. Years later – after Karen had passed away- I sold it after buying a much bigger Bonanza. But when it flew away, with the new owner at the controls, I cried. They say about *boat ownership* that the two best days are when you buy it and when you sell it. The latter part is absolutely not true for any of the planes I owned!

So I could never forget that wonderful Skyhawk and a few years later, I tracked it down with the help of the FAA database. The buyer had sold "my" Skyhawk to a student pilot in Colorado when he upgraded to a much heavier Cessna. A phone call to Colorado revealed that the student pilot was willing to sell it, mostly because he found it difficult to learn to fly. A couple of friends and I flew to Colorado in our Skylane Cessna 182. The Cessna 182 is the bigger sister of the Cessna 172. Both have four seats, but whereas the C172 struggles with four adults, a 182 can carry four linebackers and their luggage. It has a 230HP engine, compared to the 150 or 160HP engine of the C172. A variable pitch propeller in the C182 efficiently converts the 230HP into thrust. The C182 is not fast, but rugged, reliable and nearly as safe as the C172.

I quickly negotiated the deal and we flew home in the two ships. It was a beautiful flight, over the Rocky Mountains of Colorado, the red rocks of Utah, Bryce and Zion National parks, Lake Powell and finally over the snow-covered Sierra Nevada. It was fun to fly as a group of two, being able to chat in flight. I finally understood the appeal of group flights. When it came home, I lavished money onto the long lost love with a new engine, new avionics, leather interior and so on. We will stay together as long as I can fly.

Bonanza

Currently a Bonanza A36 is the flagship of the little fleet. While Karen was already suffering from cancer, we had joined a 20 person club – the Seagulls of San Jose - which owns both a Skyhawk and an A36. This was a great opportunity to learn to fly a complex, high performance aircraft. These terms have very specific meanings in the lingo of the FAA and the insurance industry. For years I enjoyed my association with this group of colorful airmen. In particular, the crew chief for the Bonanza, Hal Beers, is a great guy who flew in the Navy and loves to hold forth on all things aeronautical. I always learn new things listening to him. Recently Hal had invited a fellow pilot, Bill Randolph to give a talk. Bill decided in 2004 to build a plane for the express purpose to fly around the world. So he did just that – built an RV8 in record time and flew it in 2005 solo from Watsonville to Watsonville, the long way around. His talk was hilarious and fascinating. By the way, Bill is 80 years old! Flying keeps you young.

The previous owner of my Bonanza was the Chief Engineer of an 85,000 ton German container ship. He spends a couple of months at sea, followed by a couple of months at home. He lives in an airpark north of Sacramento. An airpark is a special settlement, where the houses are located on taxiways and have hangars. Thus you can live with your plane.

A friend, Gene Rugroden, who is an experienced Aircraft Inspector (and entrepreneur) and I gave the Bonanza a rather cursory inspection. We figured that the Chief Engineer of a huge German ship would take good care of his personal plane. He sure did, but he also negotiated the price *up*! I'm not good at this negotiating game...

We shook hands and I flew off with my new pride and joy. It was one of the best buys of my life – and not only because I paid for it with Intel stock, which declined precipitously soon afterwards. In a sense, the purchase of the plane was free.

The Bonanza has already carried me well over hundred thousand miles all over the continent, in comfort and relative safety and with amazing reliability for a complex plane. The outstanding reputation of Beechcraft as the Mercedes of General Aviation is well deserved. (Older American pilots call Bonanzas the Cadillac of GA. But they mean well.)

Still, anything so complex has its shares of little issues. For example, just yesterday, I approached the home airport while being bounced around in a California winter storm. When I lowered the landing gear lever, only two of the three green gear lights came on. These lights show that the landing gear is down and locked. Usually it is a minor problem, like a burned out light bulb. That was the reason, but still, something like that always triggers a healthy Adrenalin flow. Nobody ever gets killed or seriously hurt in a gear-up landing, though.

Recently Dr. Wolf Weber, whom I worked with at HAL, suggested buying a high performance sailplane with him. It did not take much arm twisting – say 2° – before I agreed. He located a beautiful single-seat German Rolladen-Schneider LS4 glider. True to form, we bought it before it ever hit the market. This promises to be great fun. I had to get the formal FAA glider rating to fly this plane, which was a surprising amount of work, in spite of all my flying experience. The LS4 can glide 40 miles for each mile up – and that is without any help from thermals or other updrafts. In the coming spring, we'll move it to

Truckee in the Sierra Nevada, which is one of the best soaring areas in the world.

Jet – Eclipse 500

My -still mostly platonic- love affair with jets started when I was a little tyke. My father and I used to wash dishes after my mother had prepared the Sunday lunch. While doing so, he told me stories about nature and science and all kinds of technical things. His true avocation is art and music, but his wide-ranging interests made him knowledgeable about many subjects. I owe him a lot; he triggered my curiosity in many things. Once he explained how jets worked, and I was smitten by their simplicity and elegance, compared to piston engines which seem to be prone to pound themselves to death.

Fifty years ago I'd never dream that I'd ever own an airplane, let alone buy a jet (if I really can afford it, which remains to be seen.) But sometimes life exceeds one's dreams. It is important to maintain wishes and dreams as long as possible. People are old when they have no more dreams for their future.

The Eclipse is the result of a man's big dream…
Vern Raeburn was one of the earliest employees at Microsoft, but quit to start a chain of computer stores. This made him quite wealthy, even though not as wealthy as if he had simply stayed with Microsoft. As an avid pilot, he was dreaming building a light jet based on the promise of low cost jet engines from Williams International[42]. So he started a company to build the first of a new generation of jets.

---

[42] These engines turned out to be very problematic and Eclipse switched to Pratt&Whitney. It was a 'bet-your-company' decision. It was a good choice, the P&W engines work great.

Eclipse Aviation is now the grand daddy of the Very Light Jet (VLJ) industry. Some people think that an on-demand air taxi industry based on these relatively affordable (around $2Million) light jets may give the traditional airline industry serious competition. I'm a bit skeptical about the short-term economic realities of this concept, but there is no denying that Eclipse and nine other light jet vendors are revolutionizing the market for general aviation jets. So I flew to Albuquerque, NM, where Eclipse is located, looked at their sleek plane and fell instantly in love with it.

I had not planned to buy one yet, but there was this crumbled blank check in my wallet. It is there for emergencies. This clearly qualified as one! So I pulled it out and signed a six-digit figure down payment. Now, sometime in 2010, life will present a major new adventure. Learning to fly one of these babies will require another quantum jump in aeronautical proficiency and be a neat competency challenge.

The actual flying of the jet is not difficult. Today I spent my first 30 minutes in the left seat of an Eclipse, in the uncrowded airspace over the vineyards of Napa Valley and Lake Beryessa. The Eclipse is a delight to fly. It has a hefty side stick rather than an old-fashioned yoke. There is nothing to block your view of three large computer panels in front of you. It feels like a heavier version of the Bonanza, which is known for its great handling.

Jet engines are a lot easier to manage than big aviation piston engines, which are finicky beasts. This is particularly true for the Pratt&Whitney 610F jet engines in the Eclipse, which are highly automated and respond nearly instantaneously to throttle changes. Of course, one has to think faster in a jet. Fortunately, the universal speed limit of 250 knots below 10,000' puts a cap on how fast one has to think in a busy airport environment! Today was the first time I ever had to think about legal (rather than aeronautical) speed limits in an airplane. The biggest challenge in flying a jet is to understand its many systems and fly it with extreme precision. The test ride for the type rating of any yet is flown to ATP (Airline Transport Pilot) standards, which is as challenging as it gets. There is so much to learn – procedures, normal and abnormal, engine fires, V1-cuts, two and single engine aborts, overheats, asymmetrical flaps, pressurization failures and emergency descents, autopilot malfunctions, fuel management – the list goes on and on.

I can't wait.

Musings on Energy (ħ)

There is currently a lot of hand wringing about energy and global warming. Solving the former crisis is mostly a problem of political will, not of technology. No major technological innovations are needed to make the US energy independent by the middle of the 21st century and wean it completely off fossil energy by the end of the century.

This does *not* require major new scientific achievements like controlled fusion on an industrial scale. I still think that controlled fusion can be realized, given another fifty years of research and enough resources.

But solar energy alone is sufficient to achieve the goal of US energy independence. Solar energy is nuclear fusion energy, albeit with the reactor 150 Million kilometers away.

To give a sense of scale: Large industrial societies use energy on a scale of a Terawatt or two. A TW is equal to 10^{12} Watts or over a billion HP. The solar energy flux at the earth's orbit is somewhat over 1 kW/m^2. Therefore a square area with a length of $\sqrt{(10^{12-3})} = 31$ km perpendicular to the incoming rays of the sun receives an energy flux of 1 TW.

But many factors whittle this impressive number down. They include night, the low efficiency of solar cells (10%-30%), clouds, non-normal incidence of sunshine etc. Let's assume that the combination of all these factors reduces the overall efficiency to 5%. Then the required solar collection area becomes a lot bigger - an area with 140 km (90 miles) on a side.

But anyone who has flown over the deserts of Nevada or Arizona knows the vast amount of empty, unused space available there. 10,000 square miles is not a lot on the scale of these deserts. In other words, even with today's photovoltaic technologies, it is feasible to produce Terawatts of energy and do so at a price per kW-hour which, in 20 years, will approach those of fossil fuels.

The respected magazine Scientific American, in its January 2008 issue, has presented a bold plan, complete with financial analysis, how USA could become independent of foreign energy imports by 2050. Its three key components are

(1) Low cost photovoltaic power generation in the sunshine-rich western states.
(2) Distribution of the generated energy via a new network of 500,000 Volt DC power lines and
(3) Transient storage of energy – for night time use – in the form of compressed air (at 1100 psi / 80 bar) in vast underground caves.

The latter sounds far fetched, but it is not. The natural gas industry uses this storage technology on a large scale today. Still, all this can't be done without government subsidies for several decades. The Scientific American team, in collaboration with a wide range of experts, estimates that a total of $400 Billion government subsidies will be necessary to make this happen. That's less than the cost of the Iraq war, currently (Spring 2008) estimated to be 3 Trillion dollars.

The recent progress in battery technology and the emergence of useful pure electrical cars – such as the Tesla Motor Car – will make it possible to get largely rid of wasting precious oil for energy production. Fortunately, even today, no oil is used to produce electricity. It all goes to transportation and to the petrochemical industry to make plastics. The latter is an absolutely sensible use of oil.

Eventually, we should be able to make the hydrogen economy work. This complements, but does not replace the vision of large-scale solar energy production. After all, hydrogen needs to come from somewhere. Unless one wants to 'steal' it from natural gas, it is produced by the electrolysis of water, which requires electricity. Thus hydrogen is not an energy source per se. Rather, it is an energy storage and transportation medium.

It is not necessary to fully develop fuel cells for powering cars with hydrogen. Normal internal combustion engines, with minor changes, will happily run on hydrogen, emitting only water. BMW has converted some of its large 7-series sedans for hydrogen use. There are already a few high-tech hydrogen gas stations in Munich, Bavaria. But they are complex and expensive. There are also hydrogen busses in San Jose, Silicon Valley, CA.

Efficient and cheap hydrogen storage is the real problem, which must be solved. Simply compressing the light gas is not safe and efficient enough, nor is turning it into a cryogenic liquid. Some companies have been working on metal-hydrogen alloys, wherein hydrogen – which is a very small atom- is squeezed into the voids between large metal atoms.

It is like pouring sand (hydrogen) into a tin can already filled with marbles (Palladium atoms). Palladium absorbs hydrogen extremely well, but it is far too expensive for practical use. The challenge is to find a material which absorbs hydrogen as readily as Palladium, but is cheap. Mercedes and other companies have been working for decades on this problem, so it is hard. But when it is finally solved, the path to a hydrogen economy is reasonably clear.

An alternative is a compromise where one combines hydrogen with a little bit of carbon, forming a liquid substance like Methanol. This could be a good intermediate solution until pure hydrogen can be stored efficiently. One can only hope – and do whatever one can – to turn this 21st century peaceful Manhattan program into reality. It would do more to world stability than about anything else.

Intelligent Computers ? (ħ)

During the last forty years, computing has made little progress. In fact, by some important measures it is hitting a wall. This statement may surprise the casual observer, since computing is seen as the paradigm for rapid technological progress. It is true that for decades, computers got faster and faster at a high rate. Every year, computers increased performance by 60%. Over decades, this factor compounded into huge speed improvements. The rate has greatly slowed down now, because of power and energy limits of silicon chips.

But the more important issue is that there has been not much progress in the fundamentals of computing. The basic idea – the sequential von Neumann model of programming – is still underlying nearly all commercially relevant computing. The basic components of a computer – microprocessor (CPU), silicon-based memory, disks and tapes haven't changed architecturally for 30 years.

Interesting progress has come from new communication models – packet switching, which gave us the internet - and from combining many of these basic computers into monster machines by Google, IBM and others. This has enabled us to solve qualitatively new problems. It surely seems that the first systems which will *appear to a user* to be intelligent are the Google-like systems, which search and extract previously stored knowledge. These are not intelligent machines in the artificial intelligence sense of the word, but they sure are useful in real life. *It is better to wrap a modest amount of algorithmic cleverness around a lot of data than doing the opposite* [43].

---

[43] Barry Bakalor of *KnowWhere, Inc.*

The traditional artificial intelligence community tried to do the latter and failed, at least in the sense of producing something widely useful.

Nevertheless, breakthroughs in the understanding of the human brain and the construction of artificial neural networks seems to be near. The book[44] '*On Intelligence*', written by the inventor of the Palm Pilot, Jeff Hawkins, presents a remarkable working hypothesis of the neo-cortex. Best of all, it makes verifiable predictions which can be tested and it describes specific architectures for intelligent machines.

At the same time, new algorithms - for example, the ones developed by Dr. Dharmendra Mohda and his team at the IBM Research Lab in Almaden, California - help to solve the communications bottleneck which bedeviled previous attempts to build very large neuron networks.

I expect that it will be possible to build -by 2020- a neural network which equals the human brain in terms of raw capacity, measured in neuron update rate and communications capability. Key inventions, which will make this happen, are occurring now. Among these are algorithms for scalable inter-neuron communication and technologies, which can efficiently store synaptic weights.

It will take a long time to train this network – as it takes time to raise a child. But once this works, electronic technology will soon thereafter create artificial neural networks, which will leave the human brain in the dust. That is absolutely inevitable. Let's hope that our electronic offspring will get over its teenager stage quickly and be friendly to its parents.

I'm very much looking forward to 2038. It should be an interesting year.

---

[44] **ISBN** 0-8050-7456-2

Intelligent Computers

Dr. Anita Borg's Acceptance Speech, Heinz Award

See also page 219

"I would like to thank the Heinz Foundation for recognizing with this award that the development of the technology for the future must have positive social and human impacts. In the near future, technology will affect everything: our economic, political, social and personal lives. Will technology be used to help solve problems of energy, food, water and clean air? Control disease? Nurture our children? Care for our elderly and disability? Will technology be used to increase literacy, particularly among women? Will it enable a fair global economy? Will we live in peace? Will it be used to solve the problems or create the futures that women want? Thank you to Teresa and the Foundation for helping those who ask those questions.

Around the world, women are not full partners in driving the creation of the new technology that will define their lives. This is not good for women and not good for the world. The involvement of women can bring important perspectives and directions to the technology of the future. Women must have dramatically higher representation in technical fields. But bringing women into the existing system as technologists is not sufficient. All sorts of women—

technical and non-technical, rich and poor, from the developed, developing, and underdeveloped worlds, must define the technology of the future. The system that creates the technology of the future must change to include all of these women, as women, not just as faceless technologists.

And now a few thanks. Thank you Teresa. When you called me, I was completely flabbergasted. I am sure you remember that I cried and laughed at the same time. Thanks to the Heinz Family Foundation and thanks to the judges and nominators.

I have a few personal thanks. First, I'd like to thank my family of rebels. Dad showed us that we could choose our own paths and try wild things. I am sorry that he could not see this – he would have been very proud of his revolutionary daughter. Thanks to my Mother and my sister, Beverly and Lee Naffz who are here and share their own fantastic lives with me. Then to two dear friends who are here-- Gerald Belpaire, my rebellious thesis advisor, and Caroline Kearney who with me was part of a wonderful group in the 80's learning about politics and feminism. Telle Whitney has been my co-conspirator creating the Grace Hopper Celebration for Women in Computing and making sure that it has a disco!
Finally, there is my husband, Winfried Wilcke, a great scientist and friend, who, at the age of 50, completely swept me off my feet.

Dr. Anita Borg's Acceptance Speech

I want to take a few words to honor all of the women who are now working in computer science and technology as programmers or researchers or systems developers, building the future in the way that they think it should be built. It is often difficult to continue in spite of the fact that their environments may not be supportive. To any women who has stuck with her ideas, believing that there are different ways to do it, thank you for sticking with it!

Finally, thank you to the people, women and men, who share and support the passion and vision at the Institute for Women and Technology. We can change the world!"

Acronyms / Glossary

2-WD	Two wheel drive
4-WD	Four wheel drive
AA	Battery size
ABQ	Albuquerque Airport
AC	Alternating current
ADF	Automatic Direction Finder
ALU	Arithmetic Logic Unit (inside a computer)
AM	Amplitude Modulation (radio technology)
AT6	World War II advanced fighter trainer
ATC	Air Traffic Control
ATP	Airline Transport Pilot (top pilot level)
AWD	All wheel drive
A/I	Attitude Indicator (Artificial Horizon)
B17, B52	Bomber types (World War II)
BBC	British Broadcasting Corp
BC	Buoyancy Compensator (for divers)
Beneteau	French sail boat manufacturer
Binnacle	Housing for ship's compass, with magnets
BMW	Bavarian Motor Works
Bonanza A36	High performance single engine piston aircraft
BVI	British Virgin Islands
C&C	Canadian sail boat manufacturer
CAT	Computer Aided Tomography
CAT	Clear Air Turbulence
C-CARD	Certification card (for Scuba divers)
CEO	Chief Executive Officer
Cessna 172	Single Engine Piston Plane (Skyhawk)
Cessna 182	Similar, but larger as above (Skylane)
Cf ^{252}	Californium 252 – extremely radioactive material
cm	centimeter (0.01 meter)
CMAS	Worldwide federation for Scuba diving
CO	Carbon Monoxide gas
CPU	Central Processing Unit (in a computer)
CRESSI	Respected Italian maker of dive equipment
CTO	Chief Technical Officer

DNA	Deoxyribonucleic acid (stores genetic info)
DC	Direct Current (opposite of AC)
DC 3	Twin propeller airliner
DC 9	Twin jet airliner
DH	Decision Height (used in instrument flying)
DM	Deutsche Mark
Dr.h.c	Doctor honoris causa
DVD	Digital Video Disk
eV	electron Volt (unit of energy)
F16	Modern jet fighter
FAA	Federal Aviation Administration
FBO	Fixed Base Operator (in aviation)
FEM	Field Emission Microscope
ffx	Page number x and following
F104	Jet fighter (also called Starfighter)
G3	Gewehr Typ 3 of the German Bundeswehr
GA	General Aviation (all except airlines and military)
GEMZAR	Drug to fight pancreatic cancer
GHz	Gigahertz (frequency unit)
GPS	Global Positioning System
GSI	Gesellschaft für Schwerionen Forschung
H_2S	Poisonous gas, smelling like rotten eggs
HAL	Heuristic Algorithmic Computer (Movie 2001)
HaL	Computer Company in Silicon Valley
HILAC	Heavy Ion Linear Accelerator (Berkeley, CA)
HMS	Her Majesty Ship (British Warship)
HP	Horse Power (736 Watt)
HQ	Headquarter
I/O	Input/Output
IBM	International Business Machines
ICE	Inter City Express (Fast European Train)
IFR	Instrument Flying Rules (Cloud flying)
ILS	Instrument Landing System
IMC	Instrument Meteorological Conditions
ISA	Instruction Set Architecture
Ka4	Sailplane trainer, made by Schleicher
kg	kilogram (unit of mass, about 2.2 pounds)
km	kilometer (unit of length, about 0.6 miles)

km/h	kilometer/hour (unit of speed)
knot	Nautical mile per hour (speed of 1.852 km/h)
kp	kilopond (unit of force)
kW	kilowatt (electrical power unit, about 1.3 HP)
Lubber line	Line on a compass, aligned with ship's bow
LAMPF	Los Alamos Meson Physics Facility
LOP	Lean of Peak (operation mode, aircraft engine)
LS4	German single seat, high performance sailplane
m	Meter (unit of length, about 3 feet)
M&S	Mud and Snow tires
mA	milliAmpere (unit of electrical current)
M&A	Merger and Acquisition
Mach	Speed of sound
MD	Medical Doctor
MFN	Milford Sound Airport (New Zealand South Island)
MHz	Megahertz (frequency unit)
mm	millimeter (1/1000 meter or 1/25.4 inch)
mph	(Land) miles per hour
MRI	Magnetic resonance Imaging
MUNSO	A final approach fix for landing in Monterey, CA
muon	'heavy' electron, 207x mass of electron
MV	Megavolt (Million Volt)
MW	Megawatt (Million Watt)
NOAA	National Oceanic & Atmospheric Administration
NTSB	National Transportation Safety Board
Nucleon	Proton or Neutron (the constituents of a nucleus)
OC	Other Considerations (in Bill of Sale)
PARC	Palo Alto Research Center (Xerox)
PC	Personal Computer
PC	Printed Circuit Board
PDP	Minicomputers made by DEC
PHD	Scientific Doctorate
PIC	Pilot in Command – FAA term for captain
PS	Pferde Staerke (European horse power)
psi	Pounds per square inch (US unit of pressure)
REM	Unit of radioactive dose. (1000 REM is deadly)
RMS	Royal Mail Steamer
ROP	Rich of Peak (see LOP)

RP3	Research Parallel Processor
RPM	Revolutions per minute
RS 6000	Fast IBM computer (Workstation)
RUNWAY 22	A runway of 220 degrees magnetic bearing
SCUBA	Self Contained Underwater Breathing Apparatus
SCSI	A disk interface, popular in the nineties
SF6	A gas good at quenching electric discharges
Sferics	Lightning detection devices (for aircraft use)
SLR	Single lens reflex (camera)
SOA	Service oriented architecture
SP	IBM supercomputer
SPARC	Computer architecture invented by SUN
SPARK	Parallel computer built in IBM Almaden
STERN	German magazine (similar to TIME Magazine)
Sloop	Single masted sail boat rigged with two sails
S/V	Sailing Vessel
TF1	Teraflop 1 aka Vulcan (early IBM supercomputer)
TFR	Temporary Flight Restriction
TGV	Train Grand Vitesse (French high speed train)
TVD & DTV	Television, digital
TW	Tera Watt (a thousand Billion Watts)
UC	University of California
UCB	UC, Berkeley
UCSF	UC, San Francisco
USSR	Russia
UW	Underwater
V2	German rocket of World War 2
VFR	Visual Flight Rules (flying in visual conditions)
VHF	Very High Frequency (radio term)
Victor V256	IBM Research supercomputer, 256+16 nodes
VLJ	Very Light Jet
VOR	Very High Frequency Omni Range Nav Station
VTOL	Vertical Take Off and Landing
VW	Volkswagen
WGS84	A geographical reference system used by GPS
XM RADIO	A satellite radio and weather system
ZULU	Greenwich (London) time, also called UTC

The fictional chapter begins on page number 100000. It is not the story about soaring.